Co-evolution Strategy Canvas

"*Co-evolution Strategy Canvas* is inclusive and dynamic, profound and focused. It provides a very practical methodology for entrepreneurs and managers to build end-game thinking."

—Ming-Jer Chen, *a world-famous expert in Strategy*

"*Co-evolution Strategy Canvas* provides a great strategic thinking framework for entrepreneurs, as well as a channel for enterprises to operate amidst the fog of uncertainties."

—Chunhua Chen, *Chair Professor, National School of Development of Peking University*

"In such an amorphous mashup, if managers can rethink their own firms' strategy based on *Co-evolution Strategy Canvas*, they may take a tumble and get relieved from anxiety of strategic decision-making."

—Shanyou Li, *Founder of Hundun University*

"The dynamic and systematic strategic thinking framework of *Co-evolution Strategy Canvas* provides a set of framework and guidance of action for managers who are in urgent need of improving their strategic critical thinking capability."

—Jianwen Liao, *Senior Vice President and Chief Strategy Officer of Jing Dong*

"*Co-evolution Strategy Canvas* introduces the logic of evolution from start-ups to excellence through picture telling. Picture tells the truth. Congratulations! You find one greater book."

—Zhenyu Luo, *Producer of Luogic Talkshow*

"The most attractive thing of *Co-evolution Strategy Canvas* is that the framework of this book is built on the theory of complexity. Nowadays, a deep understanding of complexity and chaos is a necessity of an effective corporate strategy."

—Deng Fan, *Founder of Spiritual Wealth Club*

"*Co-evolution Strategy Canvas* is an operating system for Chinese firms, of which the theoretical thinking is palpable and the collective wisdom is interactive. It is a valuable book for firms to make strategic plans."

—Shi Xu, *Chairman of Beijing Seeyon Software*

"*Co-evolution Strategy Canvas* presents a framework for corporate strategy systematically and dynamically. it provides a set of practical tools for the implementation of co-evolution strategy."

—De Liu, *Co-Founder and Senior Vice President of Xiaomi*

"*Co-evolution Strategy Canvas* not only provides an example for scholars to develop original thoughts of management, but also offers a set of navigation charts for firm innovation to practitioners."

—Weiru Chen, *Chief Strategy Officer of Alibaba Group, Cainiao Network*

"*Co-evolution Strategy Canvas* is one of the best books on start-up' strategy I've read in recent years. It clearly explains how start-ups should develop their strategies."

—Lixin Nan, *Producer of Cyzone*

"*Co-evolution Strategy Canvas* offers a systematic and dynamic strategic framework, which allows you to keep the whole picture in mind but start with the daily route."

—Zhaofeng Xue, *Keynote Speaker for Xue Zhaofeng's Economics Class*

"*Co-evolution Strategy Canvas* is a 'unified theory' of firms' evolution from start-ups to excellence. It suggests that the most brilliant management happens to coincide with how species evolve."

—Weigang Wan, *Author of Elite Daily Class in Iget*

Jiang Yong Lu

Co-evolution Strategy Canvas

HZ BOOKS
机械工业出版社
华 章 公 司

Springer

Jiang Yong Lu
Department of Organization
and Strategic Management
Peking University
Beijing, China

ISBN 978-981-15-5987-7 ISBN 978-981-15-5988-4 (eBook)
https://doi.org/10.1007/978-981-15-5988-4

Jointly published with Beijing Huazhang Graphics & Information Co., Ltd, China Machine Press
The print edition is not for sale in China (Mainland). Customers from China (Mainland) please order the print book from: Beijing Huazhang Graphics & Information Co., Ltd, China Machine Press.

This Springer imprint is published by the registered company Springer Nature Singapore Pte Ltd.
The registered company address is: 152 Beach Road, #21-01/04 Gateway East, Singapore 189721, Singapore

Preface

Since the reform and opening up, China's economy has experienced remarkable development. Nevertheless, there still exists a big gap between Chinese companies and their leading counterparts in the world regarding the R&D capability.

Take the mobile phone industry as an example. Chinese companies have advanced a lot in producing mobile terminals, but are still weak at producing chips. As for the software of mobile phones, while many app developers are Chinese companies, the global operating systems are still controlled by two US companies, Apple and Google.

Therefore, although the number of Chinese companies listed among the Fortune Global 500 may catch up with that of the USA within a few years, the fundamental "operating systems" of major industries are still in the hand of European and US companies, with Chinese companies focusing mostly on developing "apps."

The situation is neither optimistic in the field of business management. Among the 2017 Global "Management Thinkers 50," the top 25 are all Western. Ruimin Zhang, CEO of Haier, is the only one from China who is short-listed, ranked 26th.

If you take a look at books related to corporate management in China's domestic market, you will find that most of the best-selling books are "imported goods." A few books written by Chinese that enter the best-selling list are mostly cases or entrepreneurs' personal biographies, whereas books introduced of Western countries are associated with rules or principles of management.

If we regard companies as "apps" developed based on entrepreneurs' management insights, the "operating systems" of Chinese companies are almost all imported. Despite the fact that "knowledge has no borders," it is hard to imagine that Chinese companies developed based on the "management operating systems" of Europe and USA can outperform European and US companies.

To this end, it is a need of developing Chinese companies' own "management operating system," based on their external environment, values, and management experiences.

A complete "management operating system" should cover four levels of philosophy, theory, tools, and experience. Philosophy is the value of management, theory is the mind-set of management, tools are the methodology of management, and experience is the accumulation of management practices.

Co-evolution Strategy Canvas is a "management operating system."

Philosophy: Understanding the "people," "issue," and "time" of companies from the perspective of "human, earth, sky"; understanding the "thesis–antithesis–synthesis" of decision-making from the perspective of systematicness and dynamics.

Theory: Developing a theoretical framework that addresses 5W1H, that is Why, Who, What, Where, When, and How, fundamental strategic issues of companies from the perspective of the four elements, four stages, and four paths of strategy.

Tools: Providing more than 50 practical tools that help to analyze the elements of people and issues, internal and external aspects of business strategy, and to understand the strategic points of different stages in firms' life cycle.

Experience: Summarizing a set of strategic mind-sets from more than 200 companies' cases, which has been verified by many outstanding entrepreneurs and managers.

No matter you are an entrepreneur, a manager, or a talent in companies, *Co-evolution Strategy Canvas* can help you to understand the current position, undertake the whole picture, predict the ending, and cope with changes.

At last, I appreciate the financial support provided by National Science Foundation of China (# 71525004, # 72072003).

Beijing, China Jiang Yong Lu

Contents

Chapter 1
Co-evolution

> In an era of chaos, from start to great, a make-or-break factor for firms is the systematic and dynamic **co-evolution** of strategic elements.

1.1 The Meaning of "Co-evolution" (共演)

Traditional Chinese

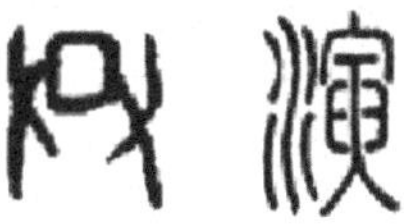

Simplified Chinese

共 演

"Co-evolution (共演)(gongyan)" is originated from ecology, which refers to the mutual adaptation of two interactive species in the process of evolution.

Drawn from the study of species' co-evolution in ecology and the law of firm development, "Co-evolution strategy" refines four elements of firm strategy (user, organization, product, market) and summarizes the pattern of co-evolution of the four elements across the four stages (start-up, growing-up, expansion, transformation), which provides a set of strategy analysis tools.

Cultural origin: "共(gong)" first appeared in inscriptions on oracle bones. The character looks like holding a urn in hands, and the urn in old Chinese evolves into a "口(kou)" in simplified Chinese.

Managerial implication: 共(gong): 共同(gong tong). "共(gong)" means staying together; "同(tong)" means synergy. "共同(gong tong)" indicates that elements are organized in a systematic way to achieve synergies. Everything mutually reinforces and counteracts each other, making the great world.

J. Y. Lu, *Co-evolution Strategy Canvas*,
https://doi.org/10.1007/978-981-15-5988-4_1

Cultural origin: “演(yan)” first appeared in seal script. The character looks like 「水(shui)」 (water), indicating that it is related to water.

Managerial implication: 演(yan): 演化(yan hua). “演(yan)” means flowing like water, “化(hua)” means keeping changing. “演化(yan hua)” reflects that elements are dynamic and change over time. As a person can’ t step twice into the same river, everything is evolving over time.

共演 **Co-evolution = systematicness × dynamism**

Co-evolution is a mindset of evaluating the environment from the perspective of systematicness and dynamics.

Co-evolution strategy emphasizes “graphic thinking”, which demonstrates the systematicness and dynamics of strategy with a 2 x 2 Matrix and Double S-Curve. A 2 x 2 Matrix represents a systematic mindset, whereas A Double S-Curve curves represent a dynamic mindset.

1.1.1 Formula: Co-evolution = Systematicness × Dynamism

1.1.1.1 Tool: 2 X 2 Matrix

Systematicness

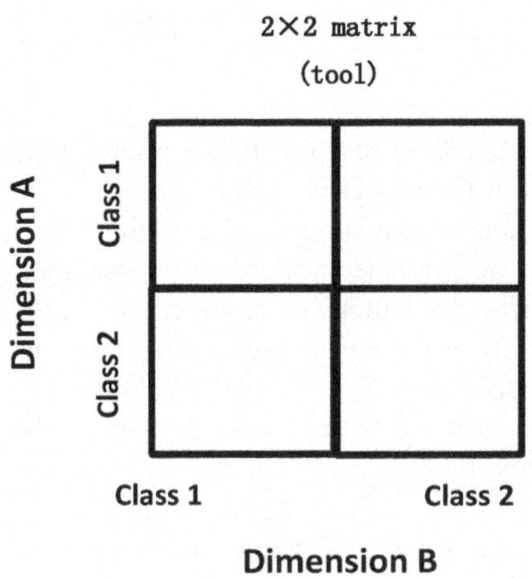

Features

2 × 2 matrix is the simplest and the most practical tools for systematic thinking.

The key feature of 2 x 2 matrix is "Mutual Exclusive, Collective Exhaustive (MECE)".

2 x 2 matrix classifies things without overlaps or missing items. It meanwhile captures the core of the problem and addresses it effectively.

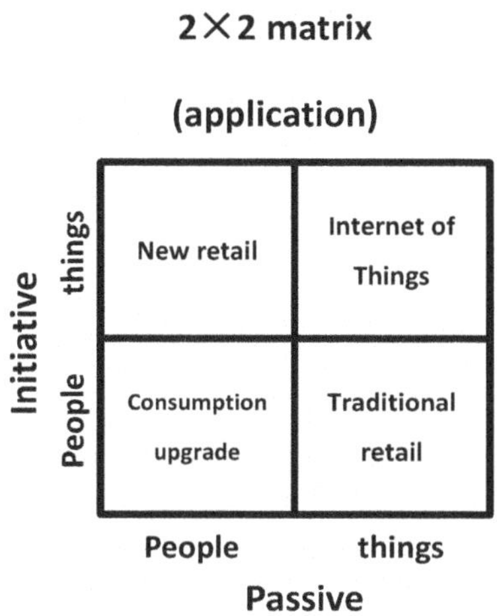

Examples

The three strategic directions of Xiaomi (the Internet of Things, new retail, and consumption upgrade) can be analyzed following three steps.

Step 1: Find dimensions and classes for analysis. Xiaomi is doing business, which is nothing but the business of people or the business of things. Xiaomi is making transactions, the two side of which can be either initiative or passive.

Step 2: Analyze four quadrants. Traditional retail is "people searching for things", new retail is "things searching for people", the Internet of Things is "things initiatively find things", upgrade consumption is based on the "people-to-people interaction".

Step 3: Conclusion: In the future business, things becomes intelligent and are conferred the initiative capability. At the same time, the interaction between people becomes particularly important. Giants should make up the "people-to-people interaction" quadrant.

1.1.1.2 Tool: Double-S Curves

Dynamism

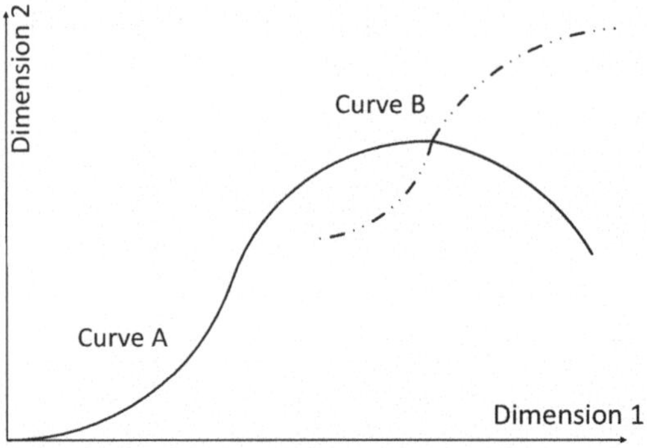

2S Curves

(tool)

Features:

Double S-Curves are the simplest and the most practical tools for dynamic thinking.

The key feature of a Double S-Curve is "mutually related and intertwined".

The dynamic pattern of 2S curves is reflected in figure above. In practice, there might be more than one A curves (A1, A2…) and B curves (B1, B2…), the pattern of which can be either steeper or flatter. The main idea of the Double S-Curve is that before reaching the peak of curve A (A1, A2…), another (set of) curve(s) B appears.

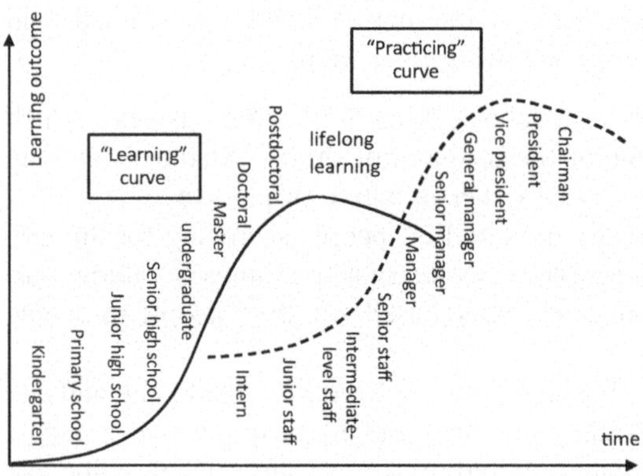

2S Curves

(application)

Examples

Everyone needs to learn. In a saying that "to learn something and put it into practice at due time (学而时习之)(xue er shi xi zhi)", "学(xue) " means "consciousness (觉悟)(jue wu)" rather than "learning (学习)(xue xi)according to Shuowenjiezi 《说文解字》; "习 (xi) "means repeating practice. "学 (xue)" is about knowledge, "习

(xi)" is about action, "学习(xue xi)" is "the unity of knowledge and action (知行合一)(zhi xing he yi)".

1. Under the current education system, "learning and practicing", "knowledge and action" are largely separated from each other. The whole process from kindergarten to senior high school and from undergraduate to doctoral study is about "learning", which relies largely on memorizing, but not consciousness.
2. After graduating from the high school or the undergraduate school, many people enter "practicing curve. Some of them start from working as an intern and finally climb up to the position of chairman, while some of them go back to schools to learn or learn by themselves.
3. Ideally, learning curve and practicing curve should have a greater degree of coincidence, which allows us to integrate learning and practice, knowledge and action, to band them into a "lifelong learning" rope, and to draw new S curves that extend the depth, width, and dimension of "learning".

1.1.1.3 Tool: 2 × 2 Matrix

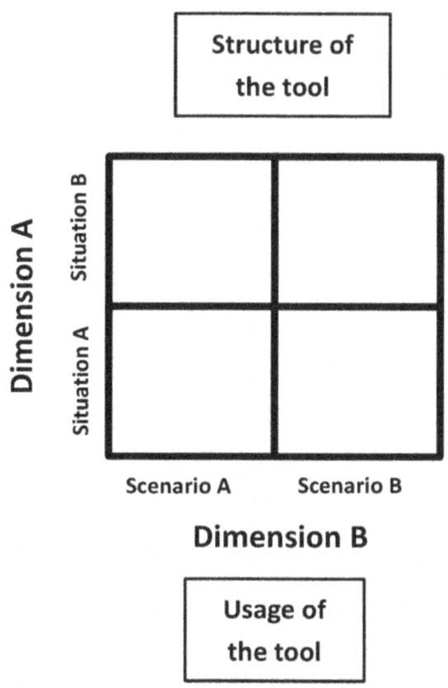

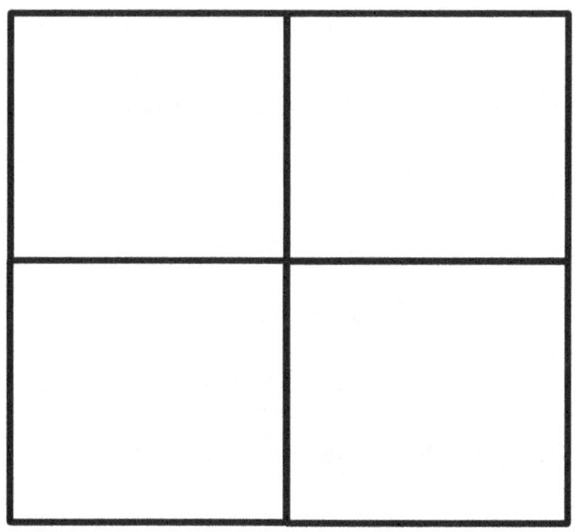

Write down the two dimensions for analysis on the left and the underneath of the 2 × 2 matric, as well as the two basic scenarios for each dimension.

Write down detailed explanations for each quadrant.

1.1.1.4 Tool: Double-S Curves

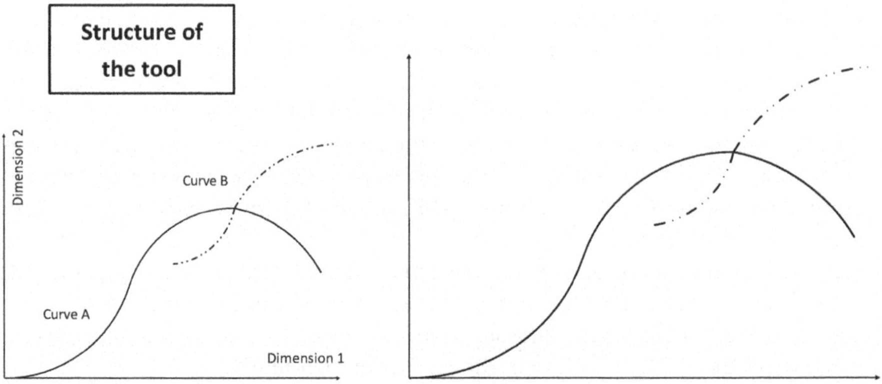

Usage of the tool

Write down the two dimensions for analysis on the horizontal axis and vertical axis.

Write down the name of the two curves.

Write down detailed explanations in the blank.

1.2 The Definition of "Strategy" (战略)

Traditional Chinese

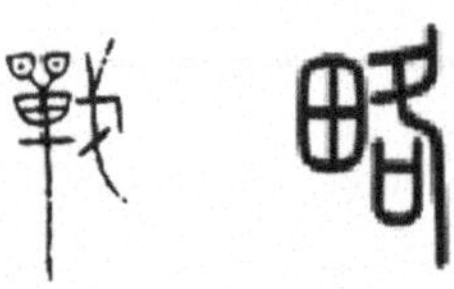

Simplified Chinese

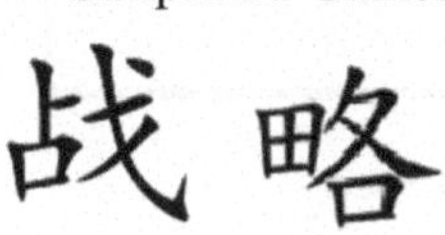

What is strategy (战略)(zhan lve)?Different people have different views.

The common view recognizes strategy as a comprehensive consideration of the overall objective, whereas tactics is the means to realize certain strategy.

Getting back to the origin of the culture, we can find that“战 (zhan)focuses on the outside, 略(lue) focuses on the inside”. Strategy is an integration of both internal and external aspects, and an art of both insights and visions.

Cultural origin: “战(zhan)” first appeared in Chinese bronze inscriptions, which looks like “戈(ge)、单(dan) “. Originally, 「单(dan)」 denoted an armament; 「戈(ge)」 is typical arm.

Managerial implications: 战(zhan): 征战(zheng zhan). The original meaning of“战(zhan)”is a military occupation, suggesting looking outside. Going on an expedition outward needs insights, and great insights lead to good strategy.

Cultural origin: “略(lve)” is originated from seal script. The character in seal script looks like 「田(tian)」 and 「各(ge). “田(tian) “ means it is related to the land.

Managerial implication: 略(lue); 谋略(mou lue). The original meaning of “略(lue)” is planning, suggesting looking inside. Planning inward needs visions – not only seeing far ahead, but also thinking in depth.

Managerial implication: Therefore, strategy can be understood as

战 略

Strategy = Expedition × Planning

Or,

Strategy = Insight × Vision

1.2.1 Formula: Strategy = Insight × Vision

“Insight” reflects systematicness,

“Vision” reflects dynamism.

Having great insights means taking a bird’s-eye view of the systematicness of the whole.

Having long-term visions means recognizing the dynamism between the present and the future.

Therefore, developing the mindset of co-evolution strategy requires insights and visions with systematicness and dynamism.

Two dimensions:

Insights represent the spatial dimension of strategy, while visions represent the time dimension of strategy.

Four types:

In terms of the space, there are the part and the whole.
In terms of the time, there are the present and the future.

Four quadrants:

"Understand the current position": focus on the present and the part.
"Undertake the whole picture": look at the earth from the moon.
"Foresee the ending": look at the present from the future.
"Cope with changes ": grasp the situation and adjust to it.

1.2.1.1 4 Chinese Characters Explanation

Traditional Chinese

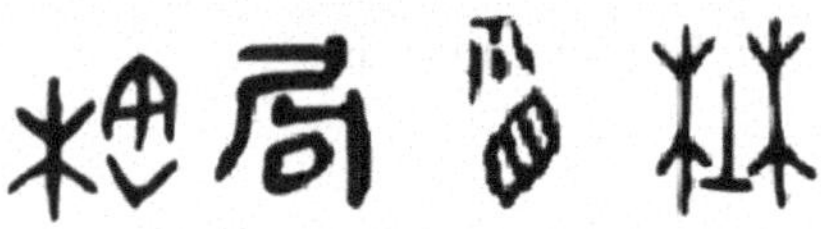

Simplified Chinese

格局视野

"格(ge)" first appeared in Chinese bronze inscriptions. The left part of it is "木(mu) ", which represents appliances. The right part of it is "各(ge) ", extended as the land acquired by the attack.

"局(ju)" first appeared in the Qin slips of the Period of Warring States. The upper part "尺(chi)" and the lower part "口(kou)" indicate the area under control. "格局(ge ju)", in together, indicate the size of the space.

"视(shi)" first appeared in the Oracle. The upper part "礻" means sacrifice and the lower part "目(mu)" means catching sights of something. Put together, "视(shi)" indicates that when offering sacrifices, we should look carefully for the signs.

"野(ye)" first appeared in seal script. The left and the right parts of it are two "木(mu)", which together become "林(lin)" of the forest (山林shan lin). Between the two "木(mu)" is "土(tu)", indicating the countryside. The left, middle and right parts together represent the transition between pastoral land and untamed forests.

1.2.1.2 2 × 2 Matrix Explanation

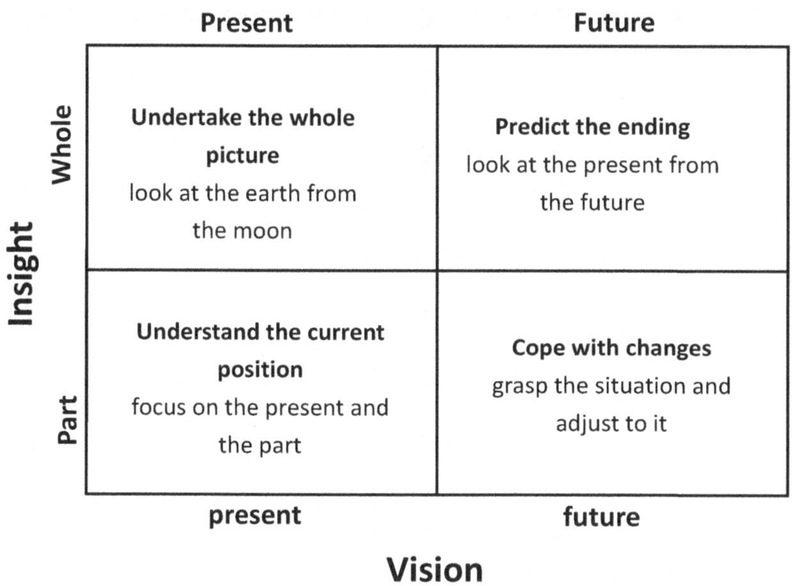

For example, the four steps of strategic planning in Alibaba is "ending, arrangement, positioning, and tactics":

Predicting the ending to have the direction;
Undertake the whole picture to make better arrangement;
Understand the current position to position accurately;
Cope with changes to realize the value of tactics.

1.2.1.3 SWOT Analysis and 2 × 2 Matrix

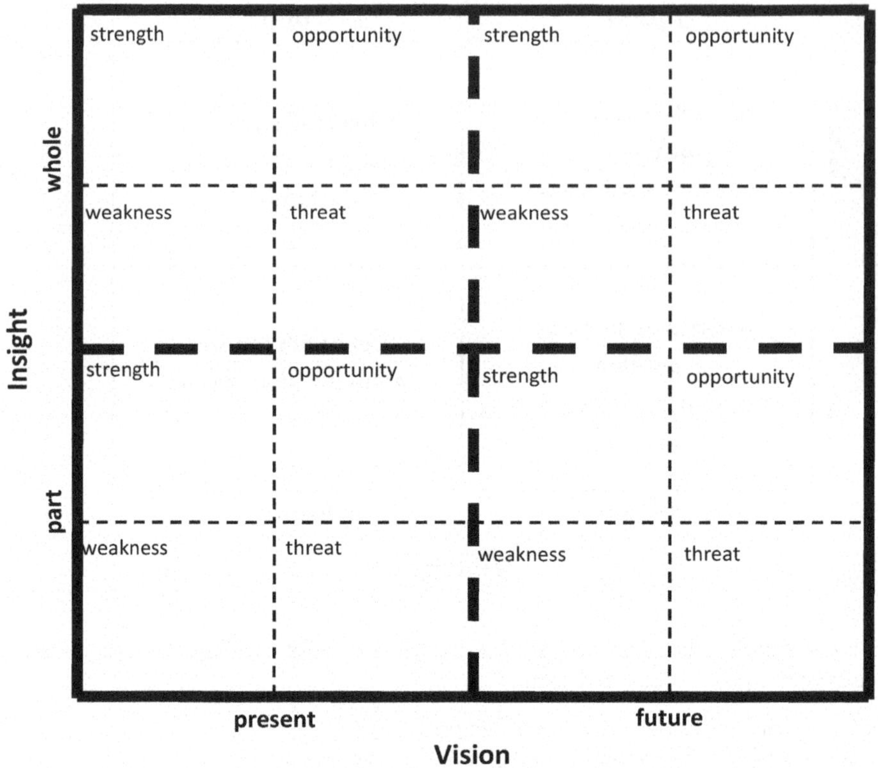

Tool instruction

1. Traditional SWOT analysis focuses on the present to analyze the strengths and weaknesses, opportunities and threats one possesses.
2. SWOT analysis for co-evolution extends the insight to "the part and the whole", and extends the vision to "the present and the future".

Usage of the tool

1. Write down the strengths and weaknesses, opportunities and threats a firm faces or possesses in the part and the whole, in the present and the future.
2. Analyze how the strengths and weaknesses, opportunities and threats transform across four quadrants.

For example, whether the strength of the present and the part becomes the weakness of the present and the whole; or, whether the threat of the present and the part becomes the opportunity of the future and the whole.

1.2.1.4 SWOT Analysis an Example: Iget App

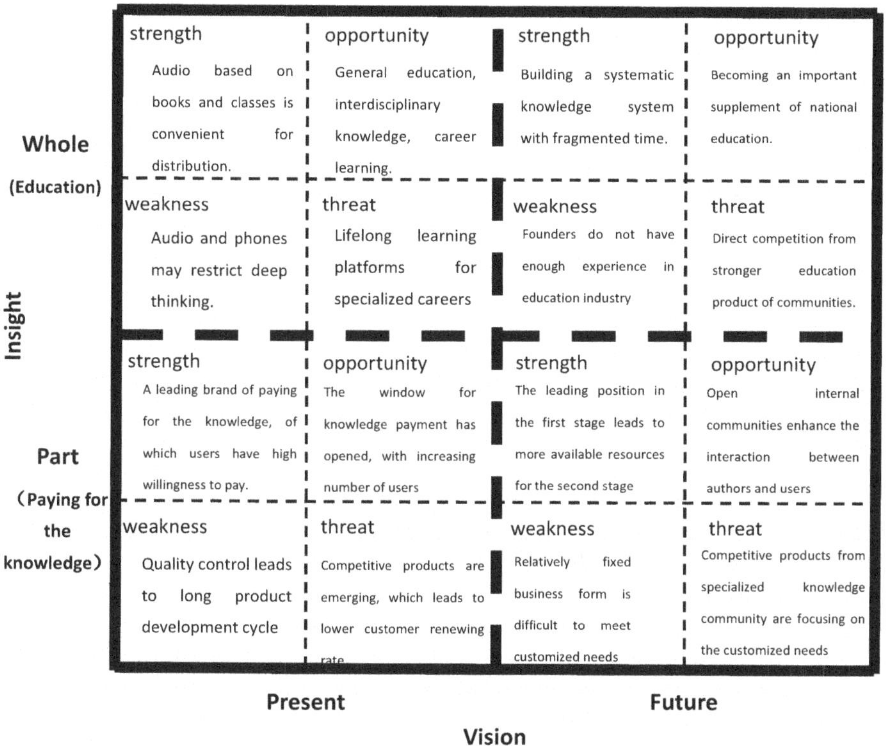

Example

Take Iget App as an example. For Iget, paying for the knowledge is a "part" while the education industry is the "whole".

Take the beginning of 2018 as the "present" to predict the strength, weakness, opportunity and threat of the "future".

Note: The example doesn't represent the author's assessment of the firm. It only serves as an example for analysis.

1.3 The World of “Complexity”(复杂)

Archaic Charaters

Simplified Chinese

复 杂

“复(fu)” is first seen in inscriptions on oracle bones, which is a pictographic character. In Oracle, it looks like a city with exits at both ends, plus a character “止(zhi)” that represents a stop during walk. In together it means going back and forth after leaving the city.

“杂(za)” is first seen in Warring States characters, which is an associative compound. The simplified character “杂(za)” is composed of “九(jiu)” and “木(mu)”. “九(jiu)” indicates the number is large,together with “木(mi)” it means many kinds of trees are mixed together.

“复(fu)” and “杂(za)” both represent a large number or types of things. According to the Modern Chinese Dictionary, “复杂 (fu za)(complexity)” means that the variety of things is numerous and miscellaneous.

“复杂 (fu za) (complexity)” has actually become a scientific system named complex systems. Based on the definition from the book Complexity, “a complex system is a network composed of a large number of components that operate without central control. It generates complex collective behavior and processes complex information following simple operation rules, and generates adaptability via learning and evolution.”

Complexity is often used to describe the real world. Things are complex; people are more complex. However, what exactly is complexity supposed to mean? In fact, complexity can be understood with a very simple formula:

1.3.1 Complexity = Uncertainty × Discontinuity

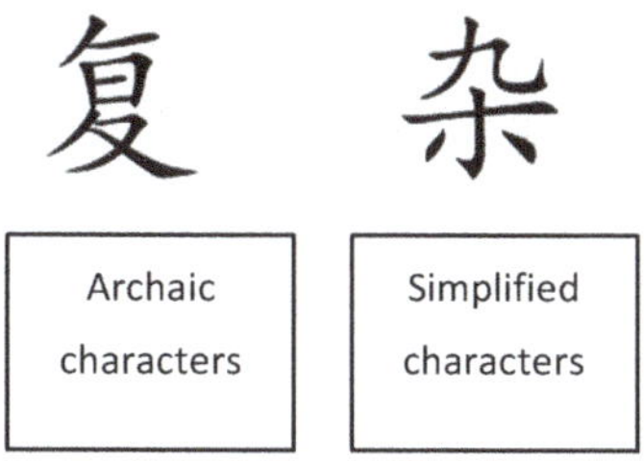

1.3.1.1 Uncertainty

Since ancient times, the evolution of human society and the development of science, to a large extent, are to reduce uncertainty. For example, the transition from the hunter-gatherer age to the slash-and-burn farming age was not due to the fact that farming was more efficient than hunting for energy, but rather to the certainty that it would be. For example, the purpose of human development science is to grasp certain laws of the world, and then use these laws to help human obtain certain results.

In **Aristotle's day**, people believed that the motion of objects on the ground was different from that of objects in the sky, and that objects made up of different materials on the ground moved in different ways.

Scientists such as Copernicus, Kepler and **Galileo** discovered that laws of motion based on objects on the ground could explain the motion of objects in the sky.

Astronomy, based on **Newtonian** mechanics, paints a picture of a "clockwork universe" that operates based on Newton's three laws.

1. Under all circumstances, all bodies are always at rest or continue at a constant velocity when they are not acted upon by an external unbalanced force.
2. The acceleration of a body is inversely proportional to its mass.
3. The action and reaction between two bodies are equal and opposite in the same line.

The main features of Newton's three laws are linearity and certainty. The mathematician Laplace once claimed that Newton's three laws made it possible in principle to predict what would happen at any given moment, by knowing the current position and the velocity of all the particles in the universe. Newton's classical mechanics was once regarded as the pinnacle of human's understanding of the world's certainty.

In 1927, **Heisenberg** proposed the "Uncertainty Principle" of quantum mechanics, proving that it was impossible to measure a particle's momentum as well as its position. Heisenberg's uncertainty principle was once thought to work only in the microscopic world.

The popularity of the science fiction, The Three-Body Problem, makes the uncertainty of the macro world a hot topic.

The Three-Body Problem refers to the motion rules of three celestial bodies whose masses, initial positions and initial velocities are all arbitrary and can be regarded as particle points under the action of universal gravitation among each other, which cannot be precisely solved. This is the science behind the tri-body stars described in The Three-Body Problem, which are blown hot and cold.

1.3.1.2 Discontinuity

Achilles paradox:

Once upon a time, Achilles, a legendary warrior in Greece, met a turtle. The turtle laughed at Achilles and said, "Others say you are strong, but I don't think you can catch up with me if you run against me."

Achilles laughed: "How can this be? Even if I run slowly, the speed is 10 times as fast as you, why can't I catch up with you?"

The turtle says, “Well, let’s make an assumption. You’re 100 m from me, and you’re going 10 times faster than me. Now you’re running after me, but when you get to where I was, you run 100 m and I run ten meters further. When you catch up with me, I run one meter forward. You run one meter, I run a tenth of a meter… In short, you can only approach me infinitely, but you can never catch up with me.”

What the turtle said sounds reasonable. Achilles thought, as if I could not run as fast as the turtle…

Understanding the Achilles paradox requires two kinds of knowledge, the first of which is infinite series. An infinite series can be easily understood as the sum of an infinite number of smaller and smaller Numbers, but the sum of an infinite series that converges is a finite number. For example 1 + 1/2 + 1/4 + 1/8 + 1/16 + 1/32….. equals 2, not infinity.

As a traditional Chinese saying goes, “one foot of the whip is eternally inexhaustible.” It means a foot can be infinitely long. But if you add an infinite number of Numbers, you’re going to get 1 foot. Applied to the Achilles paradox, Achilles will catch up with the turtle within a limited amount of time.

The only sentence on Planck’s tombstone: $h = 6.63 \times 10^{-34}$ J·S

The second piece of knowledge is Planck constant. In 1900, the physicist Max Planck found that the emission and absorption of energy in nature must be transmitted by at least a certain amount at a time, or by an integer multiple of that amount, but not by a half of that amount, let alone by an infinite number of subdivisions. The value, known as Planck’s constant, is tiny, about 6.63 times 10^{-34} joules per second (j.s.). However, the discovery laid the foundations of quantum mechanics and almost upended the architecture of classical physics.

Quantum mechanics tells us that the concept of “infinite partition” is ideal in mathematics, but the natural rules of the world are discontinuous.

The Planck length based on the Planck constant is 1.6×10^{-35} m, with no smaller unit of length in space than it. The Planck time is the time it takes for light to travel a Planck length, which equals 5.4 times 10^{-44} s, and there’s no shorter time than it.

1.3.1.3 Redefine VUCA

Uncertainty and discontinuity are two important developments in science over the past 100 years. They are also two basic dimensions for us to understand the complex world. The formula that "Complexity = uncertainty x discontinuity" can help us understand complexity better.

Uncertainty and discontinuity deconstruct complexity from two dimensions of space and time respectively. The reason that why the world is complex is one hand because of uncertainty about the direction of future development, that is to say, there are many possibilities at the same time; on the other hand, it is because of the discontinuity of the path of future development, that is to say, many paths to the future do not work.

By dividing the uncertainty of future development direction and the discontinuity of future development path into "high" and "low" conditions, we can get a diagram to deconstruct the complexity.

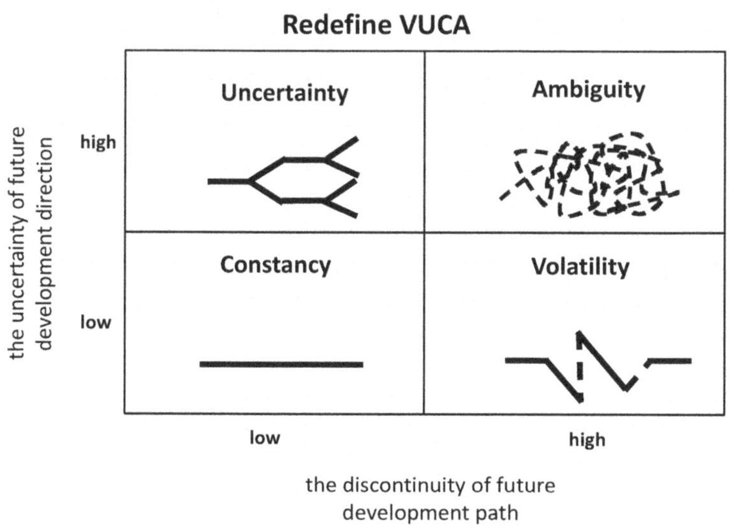

1.3.1.4 VUCA

"Uncertainty": Uncertainty refers to the situation of high uncertainty of future development direction and low discontinuity of development path. The development of things is like a branch of branches that forks from a starting point, with different branches pointing in different directions. This branch is characterized by many branches, but each branch is connected. In other words, although the direction of development is uncertain, the path to each direction is passable.

"Constancy": Constancy refers to the situation where the uncertainty of future development direction and the discontinuity of future development path are both low. The development of things follows a straight and solid line, without uncertainty of the direction or discontinuity of the path. In a constant state, the development of things can be predetermined.

"Volatility": Volatility refers to the situation in which the direction of future development is low and the path of development is highly discontinuous. The development of things is like a fixed line at both ends. Although the starting and end points are almost determined, the path between is not smooth and has many gap. In other words, it is discontinuous and cannot be crossed. In a state of "turbulence", the development direction of things can be determined in advance, but whether it can overcome the discontinuity on the path and reach the predetermined goal is unknown.

"Ambiguity": Ambiguity refers to the situation of high uncertainty of future development direction and discontinuity of development path. Graphically, it is like a broken ball of thread, or a maze with many traps. The direction to get out of the maze is uncertain and needs to be explored bit by bit. The path to get out of the maze is full of traps. In a state of ambiguity, the direction of things is uncertain, and whether or not the goal can be achieved is also unknown in advance.

Redefine VUCA: VUCA is a latest military term borrowed by Robert McDonald, the Chief Operating Officer of Procter & Gamble, to describe the changing landscape in the business world. The original introduction and use of VUCA, however, doesn't clarify the logical relationship among the four letters "V, U, C, A" and the four conditions (volatility, uncertainty, complexity, ambiguity).

The formula "**complexity = uncertainty** × **discontinuity**" clearly illustrates the relationship among "V, U, C, A" and redefines VUCA.

1.3.1.5 Tools for Uncertainty and Discontinuity Analysis

Tool instruction

1. Individual analysis: Mark the degree of uncertainty of development direction and the degree of uncertainty of development path for an object within a certain period in the future (1–10, 1 is the lowest, 10 is the highest).
2. Comparative analysis: Mark the degree of uncertainty of development direction and the degree of uncertainty of development path for several objects within a certain period in the future.

Example: the uncertainty and discontinuity of technology trend.

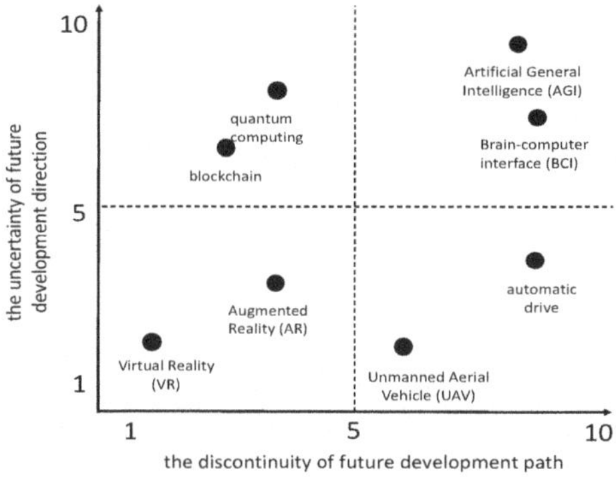

Usage of the tool

The future development of technology is influenced by two main factors: one is the maturity of technology itself (which affects the certainty of technology direction), and the other is the acceptance of technology by society (which affects the continuity of application path). For example, VR has high technical maturity and social acceptability. AGI, on the other hand, is far from mature and society is concerned about the negative impact of technology.

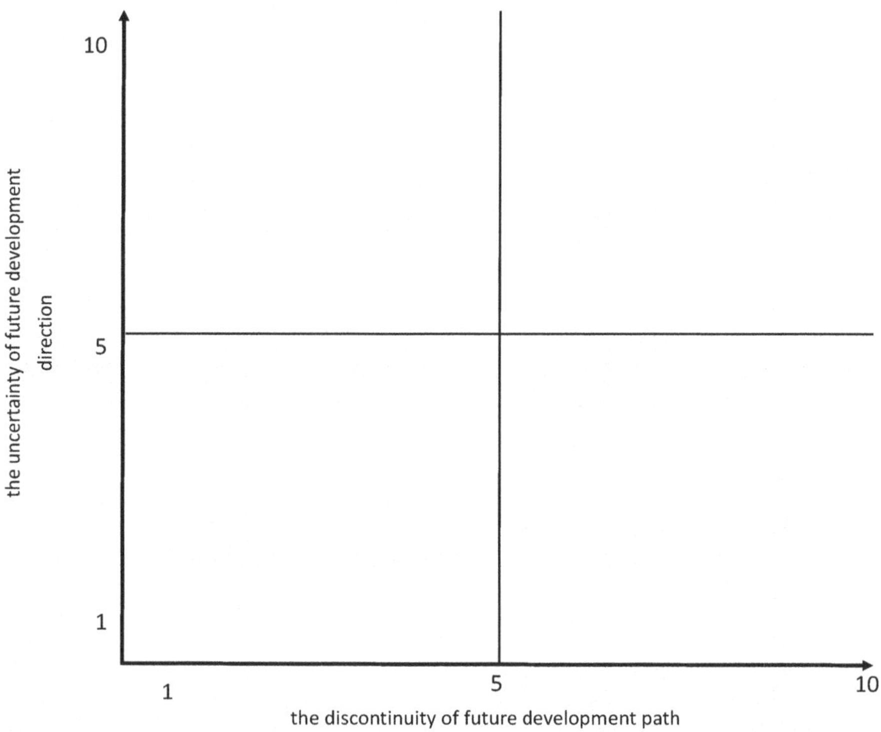

1.3.2 Complexity and Life

1.3.2.1 Life Four Stages

From childhood I heard a lot of truth, is still not good in this life.

There is a line in the movie "The Continent", which has touched many people: "From childhood I heard a lot of truth, but it still not good in this life". To understand this line, we need to understand life from a "complex" perspective.

One's life can be divided into four stages: childhood, youth, middle age and old age. People face different uncertainties and discontinuities in these four stages.

Childhood: It is the most imaginative period in one's life, and the future development direction of children has "unlimited" possibilities. At the same time, childhood is also a vulnerable period, ***as*** children are in lack of life experience and their physical development is not complete. Therefore, the future development direction of childhood is highly uncertain, and the future development path is also highly discontinuous, leading to an ambiguous childhood (Ambiguity).

Youth: Entering the youth period, the uncertainty of future development people face is still high, but the discontinuity of future development path is reduced. Young people have strong bodies and learning capability. Faced with various possibilities, once they make a choice, as long as they are willing to work hard, they can usually overcome the discontinuity in the development path. Young people can "sit up and take notice" if they work hard (Uncertainty).

Middle age: After middle age, the uncertainty about the direction of future development decreases rapidly due to sunk costs in life and work. We rarely see people in their 50 s constantly exploring the possibilities of life's direction. At the same time, middle-aged people have the greatest pressure, and may encounter a bottleneck in their career rise. Family responsibilities come from all aspects, and health problems may also occur. The future development path of middle-aged people may be discontinuous. Therefore, middle age is a period of low uncertainty of future development direction and high discontinuity of future development path (Volatility).

Old age: Entering the stage of old age, the uncertainty of people's future development direction will be further reduced, and the same as the discontinuity of future development path. Because older people often stop taking risks, the level of personal risk decreases rapidly, and the body's metabolism slows, older people generally live a smooth and peaceful life (Constancy).

1.3.2.2 Life Complexity VUCA

Attitudes in different life stages

Childhood: Experiment with possibilities and verify likability
Youth: Pursue growth and keep focused
Middle stage: Focus on gain and control risk

Old stage: Emphasize sustainability and avoid recession

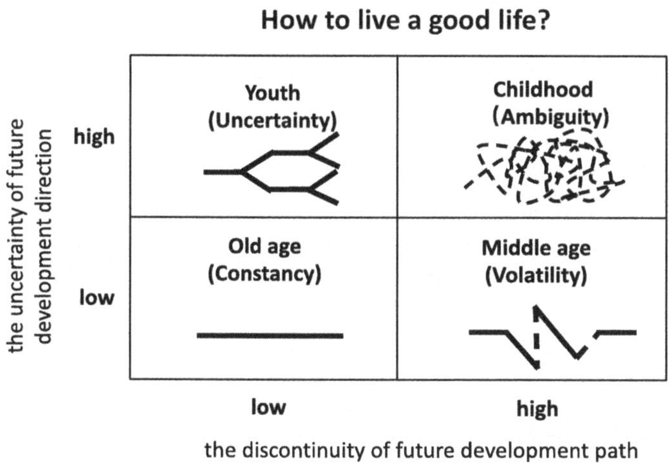

1.3.3 *Tools for Four Life Stage Analysis*

1.3.3.1 Tool Instruction

Role model analysis: Study a role model and list what they did in childhood, youth, middle age and old age to deal with uncertainty about direction and discontinuity of path. Think about what you can learn from your role models.

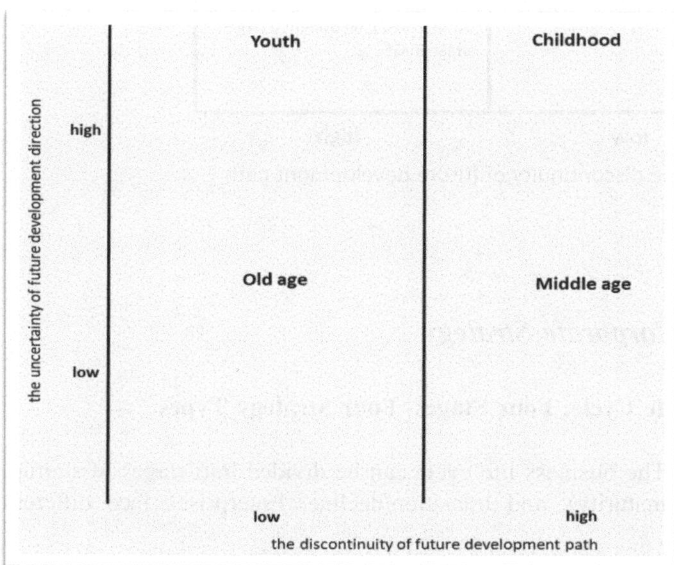

Personal analysis: Mark where you are in your life right now. Reflect on how you have dealt with the uncertainty of your development direction and the discontinuity of your development path. Think about what you should do in the present and future stages.

1.3.3.2 Example

Investor Warren Buffett has tried all kinds of businesses in his childhood and found his genius for business. In the youth stage, he focused on the study of finance and economics, got into business field without hesitation and grew rapidly. In his Middle age, he experienced the turbulence in the us stock market, but controlled investment risk by focusing on value investing. In his old age, he also experienced many financial crises, but by sticking to long-term value investment and attaching importance to fundamentals, he was able to maintain sustained growth.

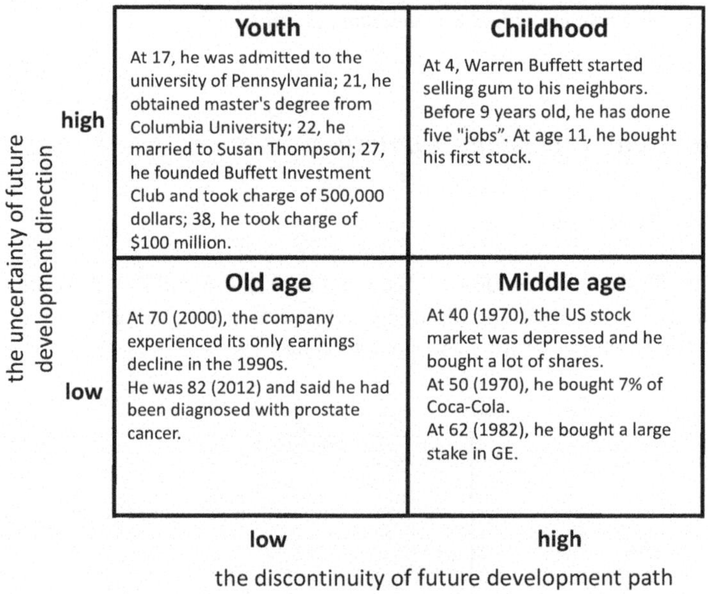

1.3.4 *Types of Corporate Strategy*

1.3.4.1 Business Life Cycle: Four Stages- Four Strategy Types

Business is like life. The business life cycle can be divided into stages of startup, growth, expansion (maturity), and transition/decline. Enterprises face different uncertainties and discontinuities in these stages, resulting in different applicable strategies.

1. The first type of strategy is the **"planning strategy"**, which applies to the expansion/maturity stage of the enterprise. At this stage, the "uncertainty of future development direction" and "discontinuity of future development path" of the enterprise are both low, and the enterprise can develop step by step according to the expected development direction. For example, in the era of planned economy, many enterprises adopted a planned strategy. They made their strategic plan 3–5 years in advance, or even 10 years in advance, and then implemented it by decomposition.
2. The second type of strategy is **"visionary strategy"**, which is suitable for enterprises in growth stage. At this stage, the "uncertainty of future development direction" is low, but the "discontinuity of future development path" is high. To put it simply, visionary strategy is to make a big wish, determine the development direction of the enterprise, and then forge ahead regardless of difficulties and obstacles and never give up. For example, Jack Ma, who founded Alibaba in 1999, was sure that e-commerce was the direction of the future, and he played the spirit of being able to "fool" people by talking about his vision and eventually achieved great success.
3. The third type of strategy is **"emergent strategy"**, which is suitable for enterprises in transition stage. At this stage, the "uncertainty of future development direction" is high, but the "discontinuity of future development path" is low. "Emergence" refers to the process that when individuals in a system follow simple rules to form a whole through interactions, some new properties or rules will emerge at the system level. Enterprises that adopt "emergent strategy" will give power to front-line employees, so that they who are closest to the market can continuously obtain new information. Through information exchange and collaboration, a large number of possible strategic alternatives can be formed. Then, enterprises can select from them through a certain mechanism. Faced with high uncertainty and looking for new development direction, Huawei, Haier, Tencent, Alibaba and etc. all adopt emergence strategy.
4. The fourth type of strategy is **"adaptive strategy"**, which is applicable to enterprises in startup stage. At this stage, the "uncertainty of future development direction" and "discontinuity of future development path" of enterprises are both high. In startup stage, enterprises can neither going without looking nor look without going, nor standing in the original place doing nothing. The key is to adjust the direction when you are walking, and adjust your pace according to what you see.

1.3.4.2 Life Complexity VUCA

Based on the two dimensions, uncertainty and discontinuity, "co-evolution strategy" points out four basic types of strategy applicable to enterprises at different stages, including adaptive, visionary, planning and emergent strategy. The category is concise, clear and instructive.

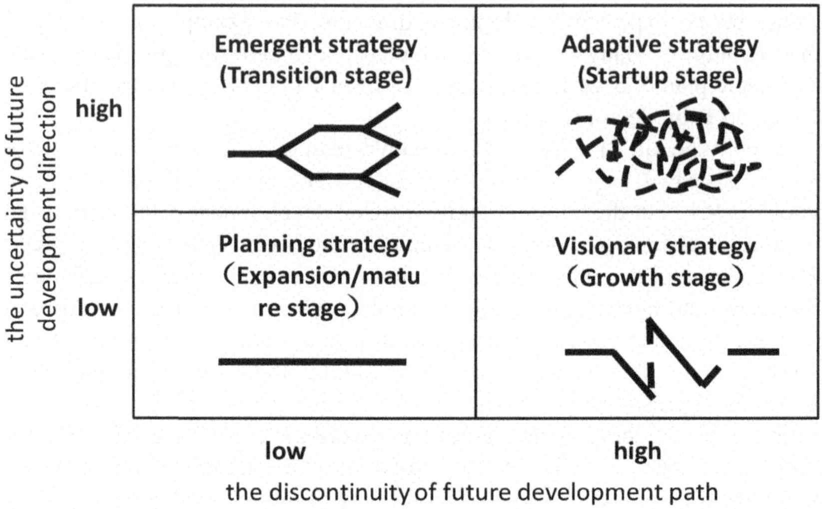

1.3.5 *Tools for Four Basis Strategy Analysis*

1.3.5.1 Tool Instruction

1. Longitudinal analysis: List the strategic changes of a representative firm at different life stages, and consider the uncertainties and discontinuities underlying these changes.
2. Horizontal comparison: List the names of enterprises using four different strategies in the same industry in the figure, and consider the differences in strategic attitudes of these enterprises when facing similar uncertainties and discontinuities.

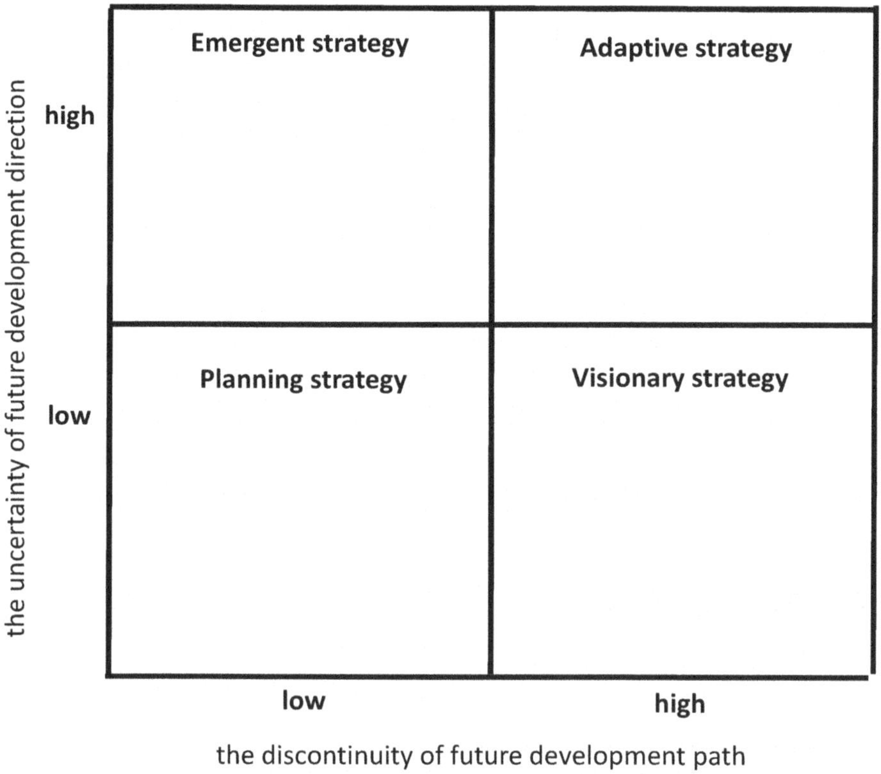

1.3.5.2 Example of Case

Huawei's history can be divided into four stages. From 1987 to 1994, faced with the environment of high uncertainty and discontinuity, Huawei put forward pragmatic slogans such as "spirit of confusion", which belonged to the "adaptive strategy". During the period from 1995 to 2004, faced with a low uncertainty but high discontinuity environment, Huawei put forward such visions as "in 20 years, huawei will possess one out of the three parts of the world", which belonged to the "visionary strategy". During the period from 2005 to 2010, faced with a stable environment with low uncertainty and discontinuity, the slogan that "The depth washes the beach, makes the batardeau lowly" was put forward, which was a planning strategy. After 2011, the environment Huawei faced became uncertain. Therefore, Huawei proposed the strategy of "Cloud, Channel, Device" integration, and new development directions emerged from the market.

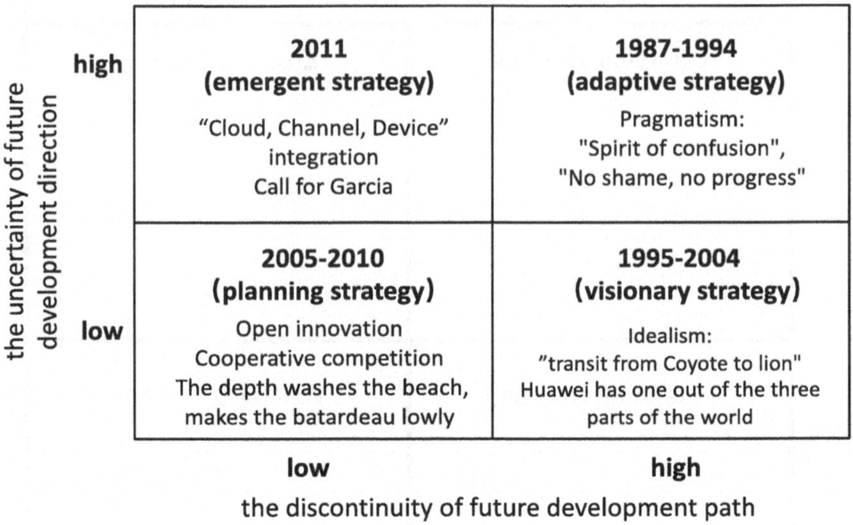

1.4 Knowledge System

1.4.1 Introduction

A knowledge system of human beings

To cope with the huge uncertainties and discontinuities, human beings have constructed a huge knowledge system, which can be divided into four levels: experience, tools, theory and philosophy.

First, people gain experience from their daily life. Second, people draw rules from experience and form tools and processes. Third, people abstract theory and scientific system from concrete laws. Fourth, people form culture and philosophy through long-term practice and thinking.

East-west difference

Chinese culture has a long history and has maintained its basic characteristics and deep structure through thousands of years. However, cultural continuity also leads to cultural uniformity. China has not had the opportunity to reflect on its culture and philosophy and to form the critical spirit, so as systematic theories and tools. Chinese society has always been a state that "Half the Analects of Confucius can administer a country", using culture and philosophy to direct practice. In other words, China's indigenous knowledge system lacks a "middle tier" of theories and tools.

The western society represented by Europe did not form a unified situation in history. The geographical division, coupled with the social and economic structure of half farming, half grazing and the emphasis on trade, led to a large number of philosophical schools in western society. In addition, after the dark time of the middle ages, the traditional culture and philosophy of the west broke off, but it was reflected and developed during the Renaissance and the enlightenment, which formed the basis of modern science and engineering. In other words, in the original knowledge system of the west, there is a complete knowledge system including cultural philosophy, scientific theories, engineering tools and empirical cases.

For more than 100 years, China has been learning science and engineering, which are the "middle tiers". However, for social sciences such as the management discipline, the applicability of western theories and tools in China is relatively low, which requires us to build a management knowledge system based on Chinese management practices, integrating experience, tools, theories and philosophy.

Co-evolution Strategy: Redefining Corporate Life Stages **and** ***Co-evolution Strategy Canvas*** **are such attempts**.

Example of case: Hundun University

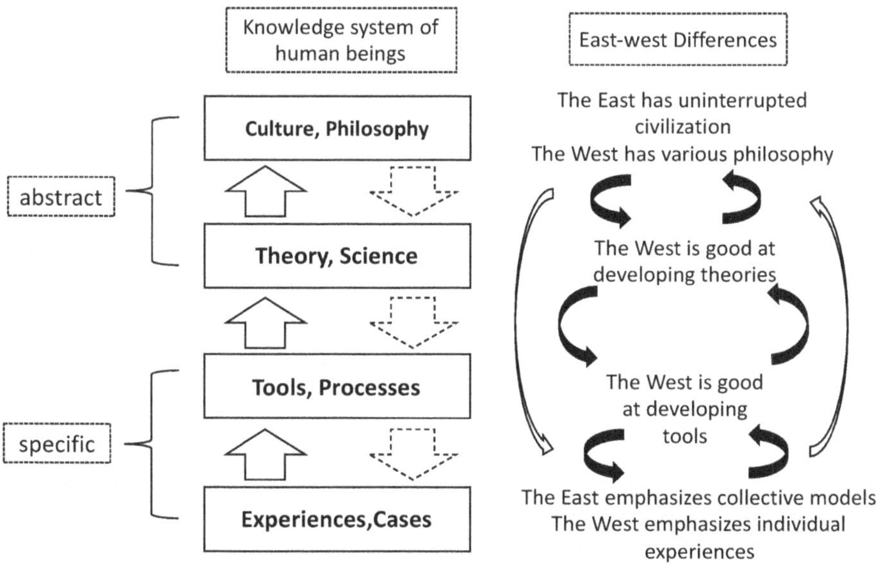

As influential learning communities for innovation and entrepreneurship in China, Hundun university and Hupan university have made some attempts. Taking Hundun university as an example, when Shanyou Li founded the predecessor of Hundun University, the research club of disruptive innovation, the main content was "disruptive innovation", which belongs to the theoretical level. At the beginning of founding the entrepreneurship camp of Hundun, Shanyou Li mainly talked about the "first principle", which was essentially philosophical (derived from Aristotle's "first cause"). Subsequently, Hundun university was established, which covers the first principle, multiple thinking models and innovation methodology. These contents, to some extent, cover three levels of philosophy, theory and tools, combined with the rich experience of students, can result in good results.

However, the construction of management knowledge system based on Chinese practice needs much more people's participation and efforts.

1.4.2 Two Examples of Knowledge System

1.4.2.1 The Knowledge System of Steve Jobs

Case Analysis: the knowledge system of Steve Jobs

Jobs's success is the result of a combination of philosophy, theory, tools and experience in his knowledge system.

Philosophy: Steve Jobs possesses a mixture of western rationalism and irrationalism. Rationalism is the time background that created jobs, and irrationalism is his personal characteristics. He found a balance between the most fundamental philosophical rationality and irrationality.

Theory: Jobs taught himself information theory, computer science, life science, complex systems and social science.

Tools: Jobs combines scientific rigor with aesthetic approaches to the arts and humanities, and attaches great importance to user experience, design thinking and other methodologies.

Experience: Jobs was adopted as a child. He was influenced by his adoptive father and cultivated an interest in electronics since his childhood. After entering college, he dropped out of it and worked on computers with Wozniak. In 1976, he found Apple, and left Apple to start Pixar in 1985. He returned to Apple in 1996 and died in 2011. His life is full of experience.

1.4.2.2 The Knowledge System of Co-evolution Strategy

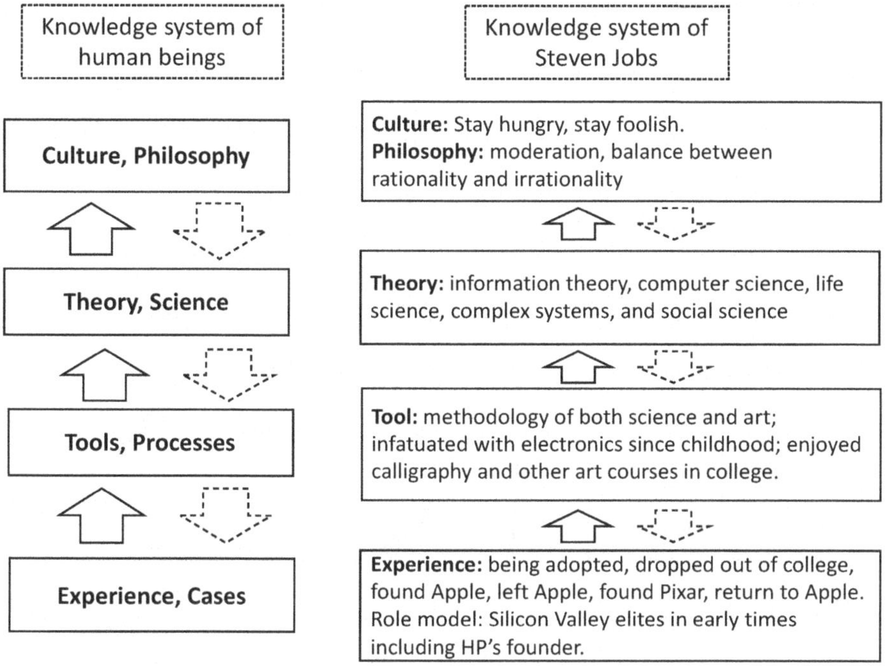

Case Analysis: the knowledge system of co-evolution strategy

Co-evolution strategy attempts to build a knowledge system that covers philosophy, theory, tools and experience.

Philosophy: Human, Earth, Sky; thesis-antithesis-synthesis. Human, Earth, Sky reflect the people, issues and timing in strategy. Thesis-antithesis-synthesis reflect the best, the worst and the most possible situations of strategy.

Theory: 4 elements, 4 phases and 4 paths. 4 elements are user, organization, product and market; 4 stages are startup, growth, expansion and transition; 4 paths are user strategy, organization strategy, product strategy and market strategy.

Tool: 2 × 2 Matrix; Double-S Curves. The two tools evolve into various analytic tools such as a four-stage co-evolution strategy canvas.

Experience: Co-evolution strategy is a knowledge system developed based on many cases of startups in China and through long-time and deep communication with those entrepreneurs.

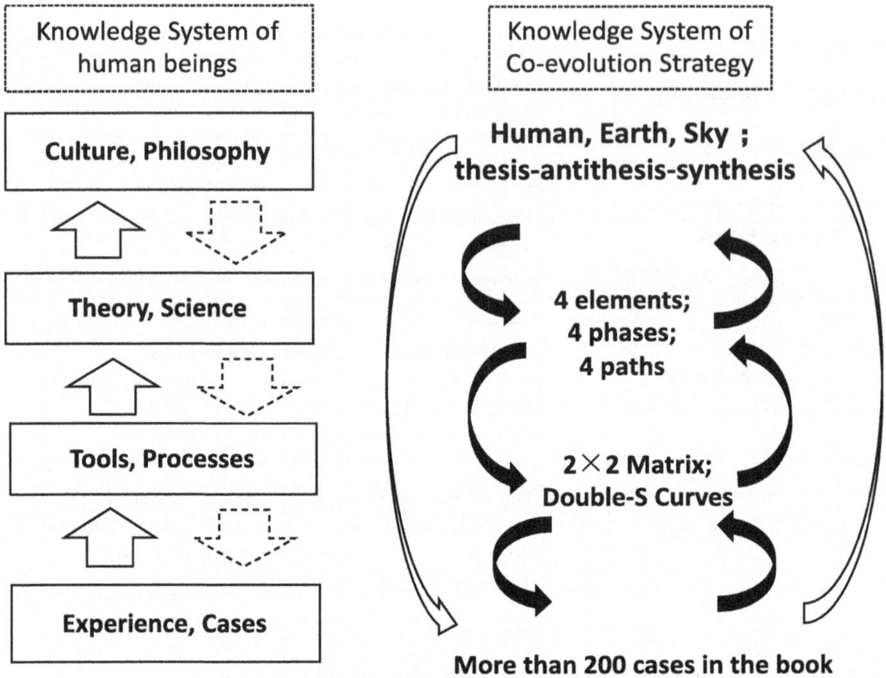

1.4.3 Tools for Knowledge System Analysis

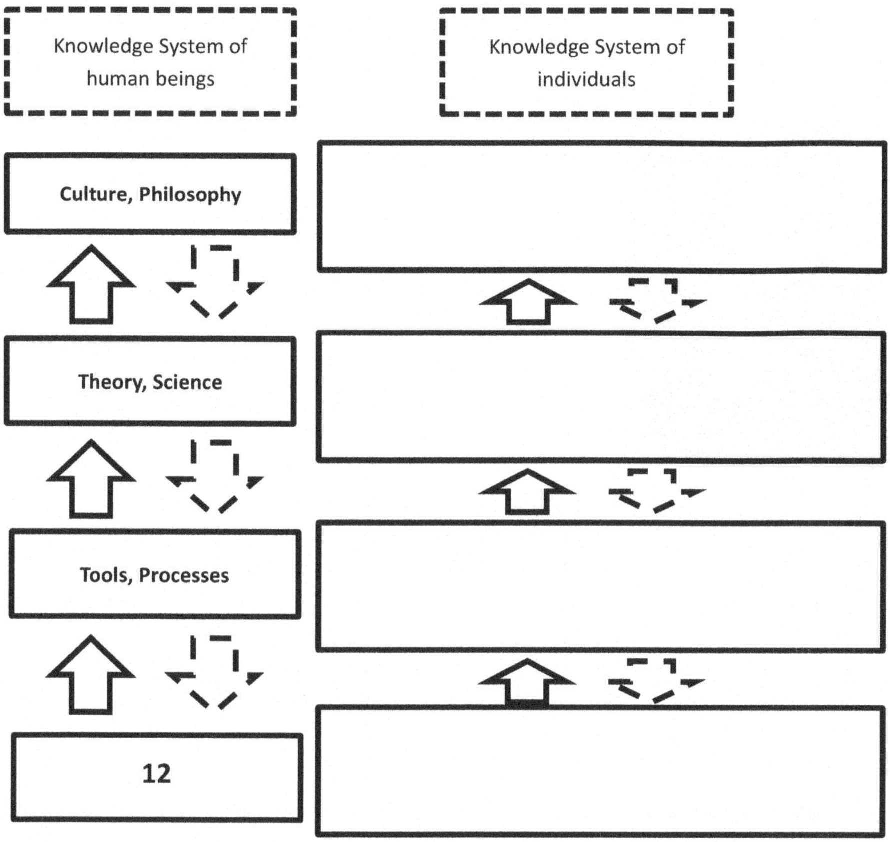

1.4.3.1 Tool Instruction

1. Role model analysis: Study one of your role models and write down his/her knowledge system, including his/her experience, tools and skills, theory and scientific knowledge, culture and philosophy.
2. Personal analysis: Reflect your own knowledge basis and write down your knowledge system including your experience, tools and skills, theory and scientific knowledge, culture and philosophy.

1.4.3.2 "Complexity" and "Simplicity" Cartesian Method

Rene Descartes, one of the founders of modern science thought, put forward the research method that is crucial to scientific research: "cartesian method". If a problem is too complex to solve all at once, break it down into problems small enough to solve separately.

The cartesian method has four propositions:

1. Never admit anything to be true unless you know it is true.
2. Break down each complex problem into many parts, and treat them as the key to properly solve the problem.
3. Guide our thoughts in sequence, starting from the simplest and easiest objects, and progressing step by step to the most complex one.
4. Do thorough and accurate accounting and general inspection to ensure that nothing is missing.

The cartesian method assumes that when all the partition problems are solved, the sum of the solutions gives the answer to the whole problem. It provides a guidance for us to solve problems for complex systems.

In the story of An Elephant and Blind Men, six blind men touched different parts of an elephant and say that the elephant is like a rope, a pillar, a fan, and so on. There is no one in the story who can synthesize the opinions of the six blind people into a whole concept. Faced with the complex system such as the elephant, blind people need to not only divide the elephant into several parts for research, but also integrate them to study the relationship and mechanism of action among the various parts of the complex system.

It is an important characteristic of complex systems that the total is greater than the sum of its parts. In the case of a living organism, when the system is broken down, something (including life itself) is irrevocably lost.

Of course, these limitations do not mean that we should not use cartesian methods, because there is no way to directly study a complex system. Humans have not yet understood all the properties of complex things in a single study, so they can only understand the world by breaking things down and then integrating them.

However, we must be aware of the limitations of cartesian methods, and we must understand that many systems, including living organisms, as truly complex systems. We should also understand the enterprise and its environment as a complex system.

Firstly, the strategic behavior of an enterprise is a complex behavior with uncertainty and discontinuity. Secondly, there is no global communication within the complex system composed of enterprise and environment, that is, no "invisible hand" can make a clear plan for this complex system in advance. Thirdly, this complex system is made up of parts whose interactions (rather than the simple sum of parts) form the whole enterprise strategy.

To understand enterprise, a complex system, requires a systematic and dynamic approach. In this regard, we begin our discussion of the basic elements that make up an enterprise in the next chapter. Before that, use four sentences to summarize the different stages of business and life, and how to deal with complexity.

Four "to dos" in response to complexity

Four stages of enterprise	Four stages of life	Four "to dos" in response to complexity
Startup	Childhood	To do complex things simply
Growth	Youth	To do simple things repeatedly
Expansion	Middle age	To do repeated things seriously
Transition/decline	Old age	To do serious things creatively

Chapter 2
Elements

> Just as genes are to life, four elements of strategy support the basic structure of an enterprise.
>
> Starting from the four elements of strategy, and then drilling down is the first principle to understand co-evolution strategy.

2.1 The First Principle

The first principle is a hot topic among entrepreneurs and senior managers.

More than two thousand years ago, Aristotle put it this way: "In every systematic inquiry there exists the first principle, the most fundamental proposition or hypothesis, which cannot be omitted, deleted, or violated."

The reason why the first principle goes back in vogue is largely because Elon Musk, Tesla's founder, claims that he likes to think in terms of the first principle. When he is confronted with a difficult problem, he usually thinks in the way of the first principle, which is to peel off the surface of things one by one, see the essence inside, and then go up from the essence gradually.

Musk said two things: one is to see the essence beyond the surface, and the other is to solve the problem from the essence. In reality, many people claim to have found their first principles, but cannot solve the problem with the first principle, or cannot "from the essence of the layer after layer".

The first principle is important because the world is full of uncertainty and discontinuity. Since everything has a unique, deterministic origin, it has a deterministic basis if it can be found. From this origin, it is possible to overcome uncertainty and discontinuity by "going up" step by step.

2.1.1 The First Principle of Firms

Thinking about the first principle of firms is thinking about the nature of them.

If you ask entrepreneurs the question that what is the most fundamental issue in management? The answer is usually about the objects and the boundaries of

J. Y. Lu, *Co-evolution Strategy Canvas*,
https://doi.org/10.1007/978-981-15-5988-4_2

management. The object of management is "people and issues", and the boundary of management is "internal and external".

Similarly, economists may tell you that Ronald Coase, the founder of firm theory, believes that a firm is essentially a mechanism for allocating resources, including both "people and issues", and the scope of allocation constitutes the "internal and external" of a firm.

Management scholars will tell you that there are ten schools of strategic management. If you read through them carefully, you'll find that five of them are about people, and the other five are about issues. Management scholars may also tell you that since its inception in the 1950s, strategic management theory has evolved from a focus on the internal, to the external, to the internal, and more recently back to the external.

Ask around and you may come to the conclusion that the nature of firm is about "people and issues", "inside and outside".

Congratulations, you have realized the first principle of firms = people x issues x internal x external.

Ten schools of strategic management

Schools	focus
The design school	issues
The planning school	
The positioning school	
The configuration school	
The environmental school	
The entrepreneurial school	people
The cognitive school	
The learning school	
The power school	
The cultural school	

The evolution of focus in strategic management

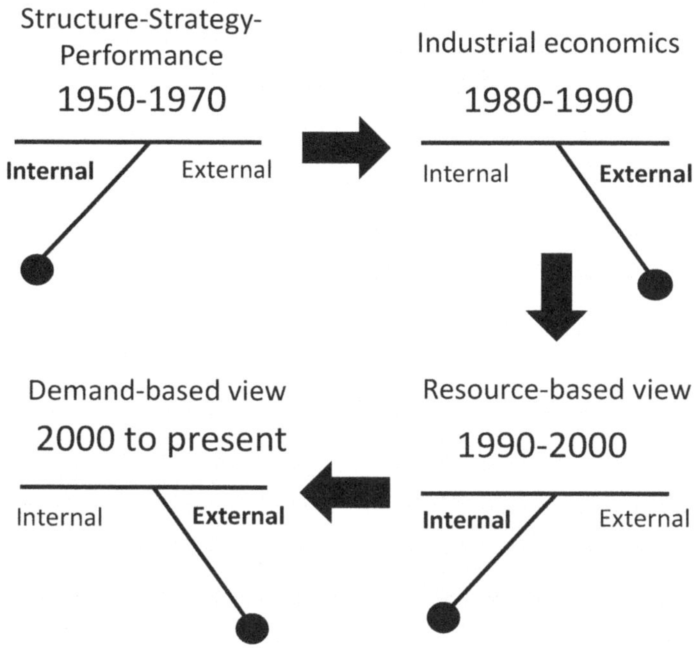

The first principle of firms = people x issues x internal x external

The first principle of firms that "firm = people x issues x internal x external" leads to the basic structure of firm strategy: four-element model of co-evolution strategy.

The picture is very simple, including two dimensions "people and issues", "internal and external". The two dimensions constitute four quadrants, the external people, the internal people, the external issues, and the internal issues. The next thing is to find the elements that represent the four quadrants respectively.

For firms, the most important external people are the user, the most important internal people are the organization, the most important internal issues are the product, and the most important external issues are the market. User, Organization, Product, Market are the four elements of co-evolution strategy.

The four elements of co-evolution strategy appear to be quite simple, but are actually very important. The world is complex, but every complex system follows simple rules.

Firm = people x issues x internal x external

	People	Issues
External	User	Market
Internal	Organization	Product

Einstein's mass energy formula, $\boldsymbol{E = mc^2}$ (E for energy, m for quality, c for the speed of light), is great because it uses extremely concise way to express the relationship between mass and energy.

Simplicity is an important strategic principle. In terms of the element "user", a firm should "keep the complexity to yourself and make the user experience simple." In terms of the element "organization", it is necessary to "use simple organizational rules to deal with complex management situations". In terms of the element "product", a firm should be able to "make complex products simply, make simple products repeatedly, make repeated products seriously, and make serious products creatively". In terms of the element "market", it is necessary to "take the overall trend and simplify the route to deal with the complex market environment".

$$E = mc^2$$

The complexity and simplicity of four elements

	People	Issues
External	User keep the complexity to yourself and make the user experience simple	Market take the overall trend and simplify the route to deal with the complex market environment
Internal	Organization deal with complex management situations with simple organizational rules	Products make complex products simply, make simple products repeatedly, make repeated products seriously, and make serious products creatively

2.2 Six Key Strategic Questions

"5W1H" in narratives

As a child, you must have learned how to write a narrative. Your teacher will tell you that a narrative has six elements: time, place, person, cause, process and result. These six elements together are called "5W1H". Time is "when", place is "where", character is "who", cause is "why", process is "how" and result is "what".

"5W1H" of co-evolution strategy

Corporate strategy, in essence, is to record the past and present of a firm, and describe the future of the it. Therefore, we should also consider the key issues in corporate strategy from the perspective of "5W1H".

Why

Why does the firm exist? Peter Drucker said, "the sole purpose of firm is to create customers." "Customers are the only reason we survive," Mr. Zhengfei Ren said. So the answer to the question that "Why does the firm exist?" is the "user".

Who

Who are the firm consist of? A firm is naturally made up of entrepreneurs, teams, and employees, but the key is whether the right people are be organized in the right way. So the answer to the question of "Who are the firm consist of" is the "organization".

What

What does the firm provide? Products or services are the means for firms to achieve the goal of creating and capturing user value. So the answer to the question "What does the firm provide is the "product".

Where

Where does the firm operate in? Market environment is an important factor affecting the development of firms. The history of firm development is often a history of discovering opportunities from the market environment and adapting to the changes of the market environment. So the answer to the question "where does the firm operate in?" is the "market".

When

When do important changes happen? The business life cycle consists of four stages: start-up, growth, expansion and recession/transition. So the answer to the question "When do important changes happen?" is the "four stages".

How

How do elements co-evolve together? The change of four elements in four stages is the answer to how. The answer to the question" How do elements co-evolve together?" is "four paths", including strategic paths of the user, the organization, the product and the market.

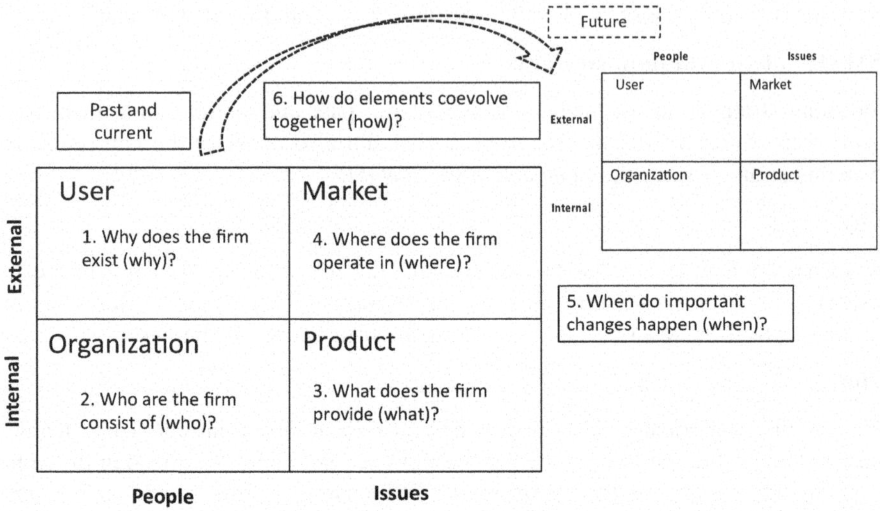

2.2.1 *Tools for Six Key Strategic Questions*

Tool instruction

Write down the answers to the six key strategic questions (Q1 Why, Q2 Who, Q3 What, Q4 Where, Q5 When, Q6 How):

Q1 Why (Why does the firm exist?)
Q2 Who (Who are the firm consist of ?)
Q3 What (What does the firm provide?)
Q4 Where (Where does the firm operate in?)
Q5 When (When do important changes happen?)
Q6 How (How do elements coevolve?)

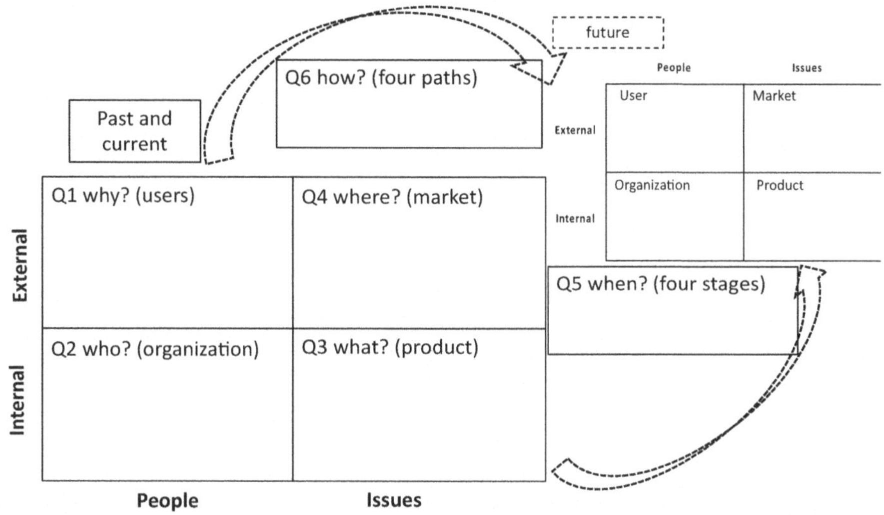

The figure below represents the six key strategic questions in Tencent's development. From this analysis, we can understand the basic characteristics of Tencent's users, organization, product and market during its development, when these elements changed and how they changed.

Why (users): From "building one-stop online living experience" to "connecting everything"

Who (organization): Organization development: From "Tencent five tigers" to "Mr. Ma" + professional managers

What (product): From imitation to innovation, from OICQ to QQ and WeChat

Where (market): From internet to mobile internet, from closed to open, from domestic to international

When (four stages): Tencent has four key milestones, including: in 1998, it was founded; in 2001, it received critical funding; in 2004, it went public in HK; in 2011, it developed WeChat and started to build its ecosystem.

How (four paths): Tencent keeps innovation in all areas: users, organization, product and market.

2.2.2 Golden Circle Principles

2.2.2.1 Traditional Golden Circle Principle

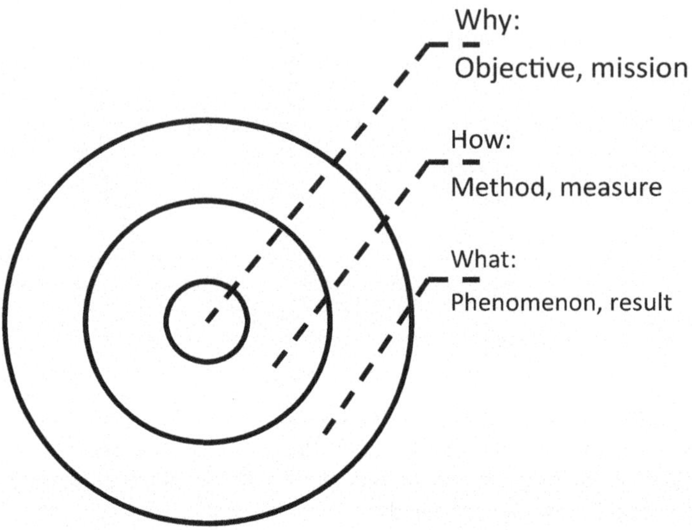

Before doing a thing, ask why should I do it.

Golden circle principle suggests that everyone knows "what" he/she is doing, among whom only a part of people know "how" he/she is going to do it and a few of them know "why" he/she should do it.

However, only those who know why he/she should do it can be the real leaders.

2.2.2.2 Golden Circle Principle of Co-Evolution Strategy

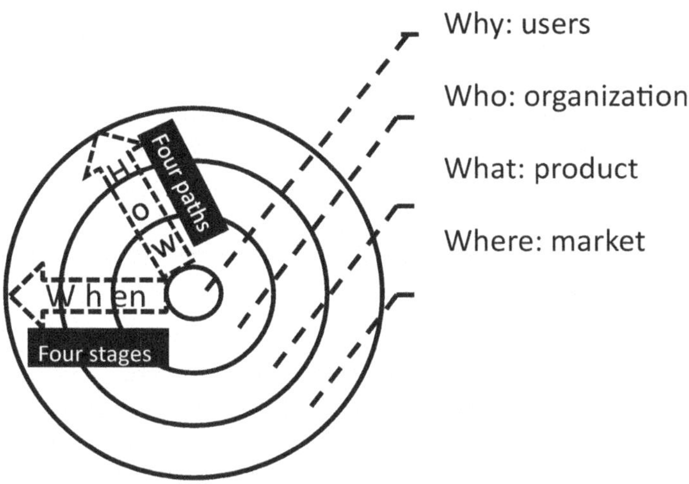

The first element, Why: firms must start from creating value for users.

The second element, Who: firms must be founded by appropriate founders and managed by qualified people.

The third element, What: firm must provided highly-qualified products.

The fourth element, Where: only in the appropriate market environment can firms realize constant development.

The fifth element, When: firms must be alert to the entry to the next stage of development.

The sixth element, How: firms must overcome discontinuities on their way to a new stage of development.

2.3 Users: Reason for Being

Users

Overall, we can understand users from three aspects: user characteristics, user demand, and user choice.

User characteristics: who are the users? What are their characteristics?

User demand: why are the users willing to pay?

User choice: what the process for the users to choose and use the product/ service?

User characteristics

User characteristics include their physical, psychological and social characteristics.

Physical characteristics: age, gender, height and etc.

Psychological characteristics: temperament, ability, personality and etc.

Social characteristics: job, salary, behavior, value and etc.

User demand

User demand includes the depth, breadth and frequency of the demand.

Demand depth refers to the potential of user demand that can be tapped.

Demand breadth refers to the scope of user demand.

Demand frequency refers to the number of times the demand occurs during a unit of time.

User choice

User choice includes the willingness, process and barrier of user choice.

Choice willingness refers to the price users are willing to pay for a certain product/service provided by firms.

Choice process refers to the steps and procedures for users to make choices.

Choice barrier refers to the barriers that users may encounter during the process of making choices.

2.3.1 *Case Analysis: The Application of AARRR*

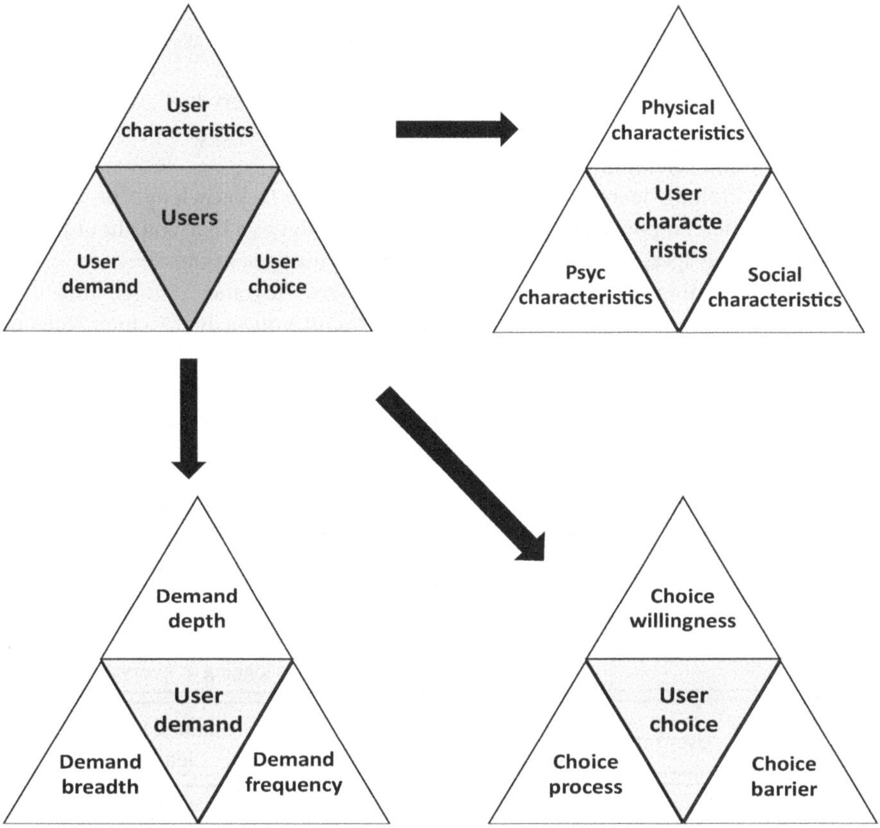

AARRR

AARRR is a model for user selection analysis. AARRR has five steps including acquisition,activation, retention, revenue and refer.

From the first to the fifth step, along with the increasing number of steps, remaining users become less and less. Therefore, AARRR can be regarded as a user funnel, in which the number of users decrease during the process of selection and overcoming barriers.

AARRR also reflects that along with firms' development, their understandings of users become deeper and deeper.

Case Analysis: Iget App

From the time of its launch to 2018, Iget App has used five versions of opening slogans. The first version is "learning more, talking less"; the second version is "studying hard and logging in everyday"; the third version is "saluting lifelong learners"; the fourth version is "lifelong learning together with you"; the fifth version is "building a lifelong university together". The five versions of slogans imply an evolutionary process.

(1) "Learning more, talking less" is very explicit, even sounds simple and crude. It emphasizes "talking less" rather than "learning more", as it focuses on acquiring users and letting them to download the App first.
(2) "Studying hard and logging in everyday" emphasizes "everyday", which means that you should use the App everyday. The slogan reflect Iget's pursuit of user activation and retention.
(3) "Saluting lifelong learners" is proposed in Iget's 001 knowledge press conference, which emphasizes "lifelong learning". It suggests that you should keep learning using Iget, which reflects its pursuit of user retention.
(4) "Lifelong learning together with you" emphasizes "together", suggesting that you can have many friends learning together with you in Iget, which reflects user revenue.
(5) "Building a lifelong university together" emphasizes "university", suggesting that in Iget you can learn what is to be learnt in university. The slogan pursues uniqueness and self-referral among users.

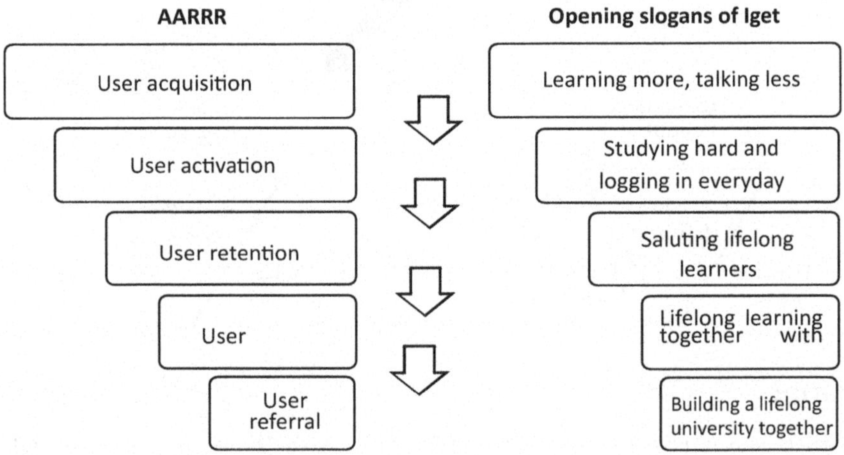

2.4 Organization: Source of Capability

Organization

To accomplish the mission of creating value for users, firms must organize the right people in the right way.

Leaders are concerned with who can lead the organization and what are their characteristics?

Team member are concerned about who the team and employees are, what are their characteristics?

Organizational management is about how to organize people effectively in the organization?

Leader

The insights and vision of a firm's leader determine the success or failure of the firm.

Leader experience refers to whether a leader has relevant experience in running a business.

Leader resources refer to what resources a leader can bring to the firm.

Leader potential is the ability of a leader to learn and to be a better leader.

Team member

The best way for teams and leaders to work together is to complement each other in skills and values. Companies also need employees to do fundamental work.

Team size refers to the number of team members and employees. Team quality refers to the quality of the team and employees.

Team growth refers to the growth potential of the team and employees.

Organizational management

"If you do not organize people in the right way, then the people will not work for you." Organizing people starts from organizational structure, organizational system and organizational culture.

Organizational structure is the skeleton of an organization that determines its scale potential.

Organizational institution is the muscle of the organization that determines the growth capability of the organization.

Organizational culture is the blood of an organization that determines its health.

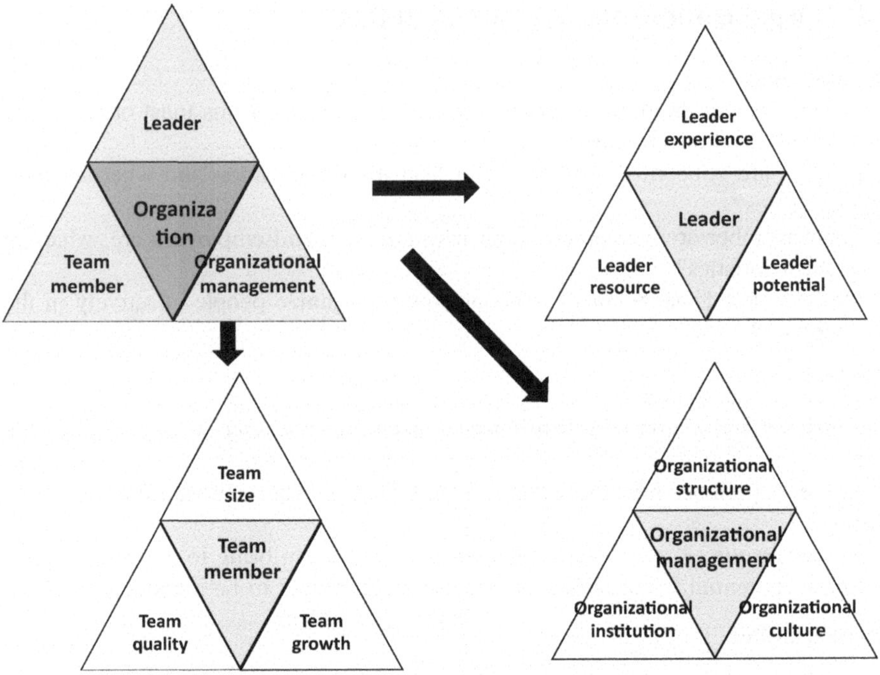

2.4.1 Case Analysis: The Organization of Alibaba

Leader

A leader should focus on the past, the present and the future.

Focusing on the past, Jack Ma once said, "Alibaba has been reborn at least 18 times in the past 18 years. I can't sleep well every night. Every night, I worry that my company will be eliminated by others if it doesn't run fast enough."

Focusing on the present, Jack Ma once said, "People who earn one or two million yuan a month are very happy, but those who earn 0ne or two billion yuan are very struggle because of the huge responsibility!"

Focusing on the future, Jack Ma once said, "It is a time which destroys you but has nothing to do with you; it is a time in which people cross borders to rob you, but you can't fight back; it is a time in which if you wake up too slowly, you don't need to wake up at all; it is a time in which it is not that your opponent is better than you, but is that you don't even know who your opponent is. In this era of great crossover, I tell you that only by continuous learning can you remain invincible!"

Team member

Alibaba's organizational development has several key milestones.

(1) The founding "eighteen Arhats": among whom seven became Alibaba's shareholding partners later.
(2) During the SARS in 2003, Alibaba separated a small team of seven people to develop Taobao, which entered a period of rapid development then.
(3) In November 2007, after listed on the Hong Kong stock exchange, Alibaba rapidly grew into a giant employing more than 20,000 people.
(4) After the delisting and privatization in 2012, Alibaba experienced a period of slow growth in terms of its scale, during which many structural adjustments and institutional changes were made.
(5) In recent years, through a series of buyouts, as well as listing on the New York stock exchange, Alibaba has built a huge ecosystem that covers e-commerce, logistics, cloud computing and finance. The organization has entered a stage of rapid growth.

Organizational management

Alibaba has put forward its management principle of "customers come first, employees come second, shareholders come third", and the value system of "Six Meridian Swords", including "customer first, teamwork, embracing change, integrity, passion and dedication".

The value system of "Six Meridian Swords" can be categorized into three layers.

The first layer is "customer first".

The second layer is "teamwork and embracing change", which emphasizes sharing, through which ordinary people do extraordinary things.

The third layer is "passion, integrity and dedication", which requires employees to be optimistic and honest, and to enjoy their work.

2.5 Product: Basis of Value

Product

Product answers the following strategic questions: what does a firm offers, and how? It can be analyzed from three aspects: product development, marketing promotion and business model.

Product development is how to make products.

Market promotion is how to sell products.

Business model is how to earn money back.

(1) **Product development**

Product development includes three aspects: product innovation, process innovation and innovation commercialization.

Product innovation focuses on the innovation of product function.

Process innovation focuses on the innovation of production process.

Innovation commercialization concerns innovation in product delivery.

(2) **Marketing promotion**

There is a famous 4P theory in marketing, which describes the four basic concepts of marketing: product, price, channel and promotion. The product has been discussed in product development part, with three Ps that are remained undiscussed.

Marketing positioning is related to the price of product, using attractive price to occupy the mind of the user.

Marketing channels related to product channels.

Marketing efforts related to product promotion.

(3) **Business Model**

Business model reflects the transaction relationship between a firm and various internal and external stakeholders.

Operation model is about the value creation process of a firm, which reflects the flow of goods.

Profit model is about the value capture process of a firm, which reflects the flow of value.

Cash flow model is about the value delivery process of a firm, which reflects the flow of cash.

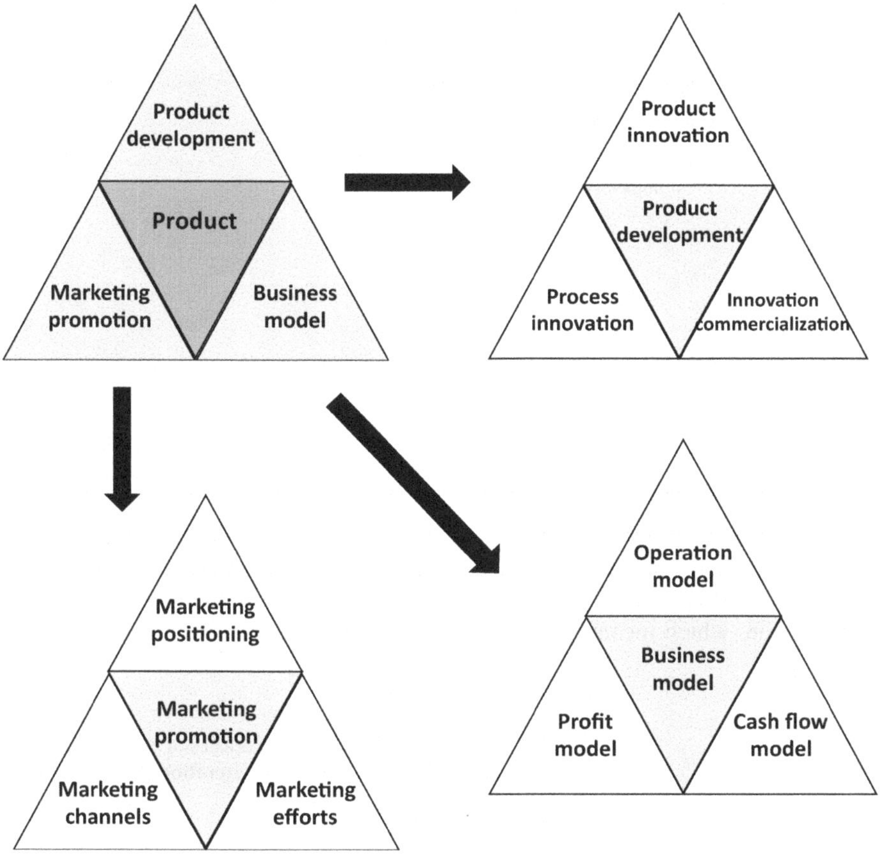

2.5.1 Case Analysis: Product Development

Waterfall product development

Traditional waterfall product development model strictly follows the pre-planned requirements analysis, product design, development and implementation, product validation, product maintenance and other steps.

Waterfall product development process assumes that both the problems users face and the characteristics of the product are known. However, such a strict processes can also lead to reduced degrees of freedom. In the later stages of product development, it is difficult to adjust to changes in demand. The failure of product development is costly.

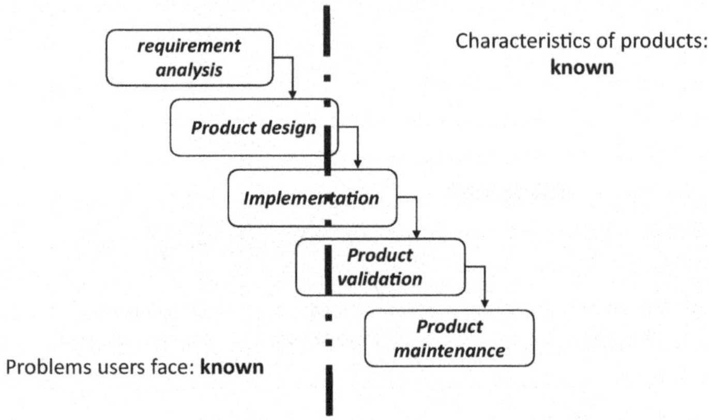

Agile product development

Unlike waterfall product development, agile product development emphasizes first developing the basic functions of the product and then adding additional functions in the process of constantly improving the basic functions. This process is called rapid iteration, which means quick updates based on user feedback.

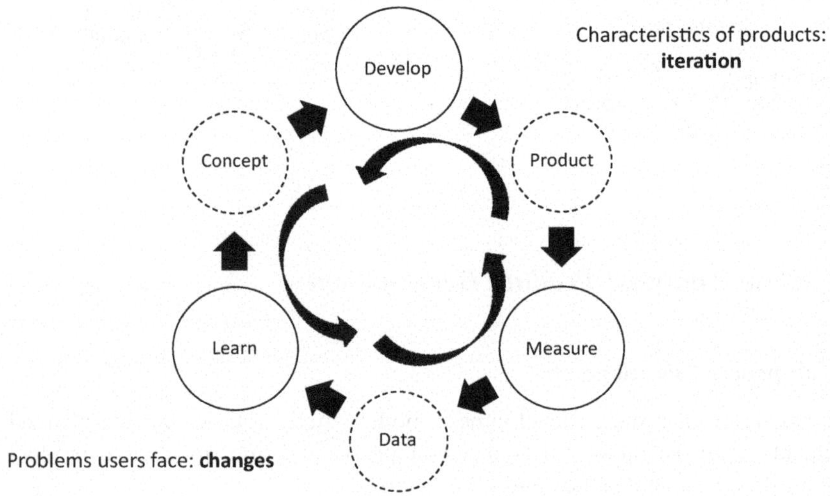

Agile development is to develop a Minimum Viable Product (MVP) with given resources and time, and then continuous learning and improving it in product iterations.

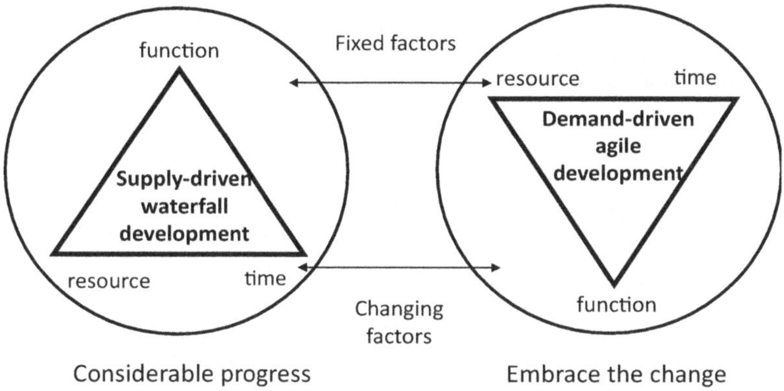

Waterfall development approach is to change the resources and time input under the premise of determining the product function, so as to achieve the functional goal of the product.

2.6 Market

Strategic question that market addresses are what is the environment for a firm? Is it conducive to the development of the firm? Market can be analyzed from three aspects: technology trend, capital resources and market competition.

Technology trend suggests that a firm need to keep up with the market trend.

Capital resources refers to a firm's continuous access to capital and resources from the market.

Market coopetition means that a firm should deal with the competition and cooperation with stakeholders well.

(1) **Technology trend**

Most technologies follow an S-shaped maturity curve.

Technical breakthrough is most obvious in the embryonic stage. As a technology grows and matures, technical breakthrough decreases continuously.

Technical stability increases gradually from the embryonic stage and becomes completely stable at the mature stage.

Technical economy develops synchronously with the stability of technology. The technology with higher stability usually has higher economic value.

(2) **Capital resources**

Firm strategy needs to pay attention to the dynamics of capital and resources, as well as the interaction between firms and external capital and resources.

Financial capital is still an important form of resources on which firms depend for survival and development.

Tangible resources such as land, plants and machinery are still vital for firms.

Intangible resources such as intellectual property rights and goodwill are becoming more and more valuable.

(3) **Market competition-cooperation**

Firms need to consider competitors and complements at the same time.

Market competition mainly considers the relationship with direct and indirect competitors.

Market cooperation mainly considers the relationship with direct and indirect partners.

Market ecology comprehensively considers the competitive and cooperative relations among users, suppliers, competitors and compliers drawing on the perspective of value network.

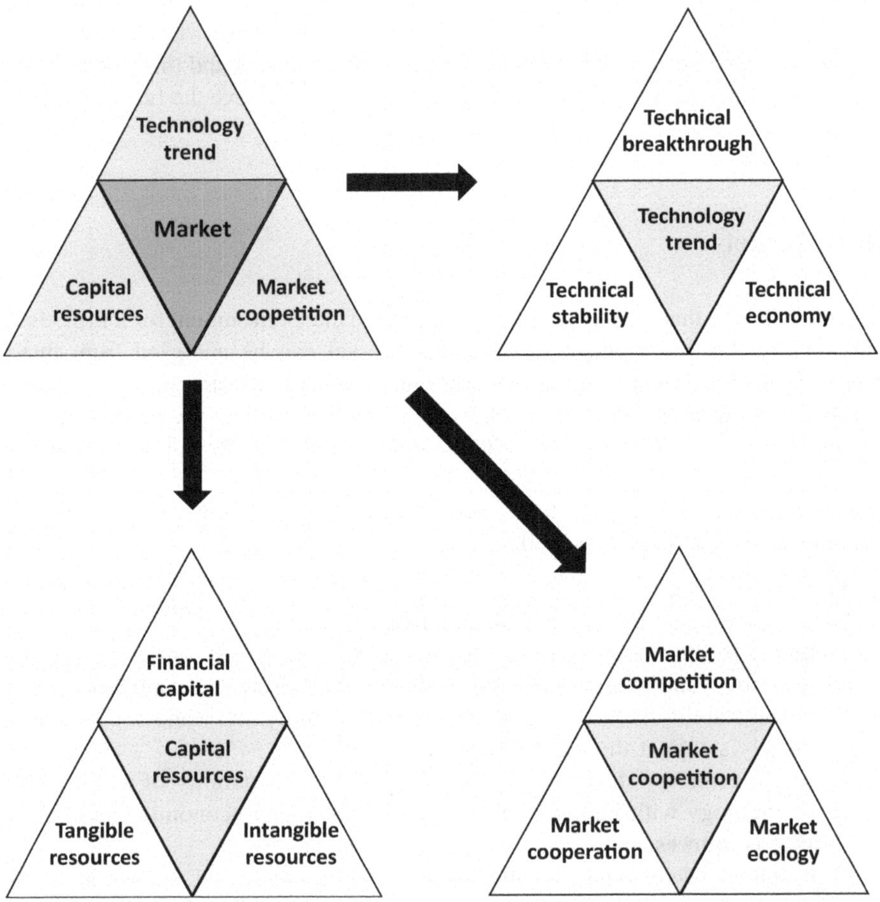

2.6.1 *Case Analysis: Value Network in the Market*

Value network

In recent years, platform business model has been widely used, especially in the Internet field. One important characteristic of platform business model is to consider the role of complements and design business model from the perspective of value network.

Value network includes suppliers, users, competitors and complements outside firms. Firms obtain raw materials from suppliers and provide them for users after production and processing. In addition to the competition from competitors, firms also need to consider the role of complements. In a platform business model, complements provide products or services on the platform for users to choose from. The more complements there are and the higher the quality of the products they offered, the more attractive a firm's platform will be to users.

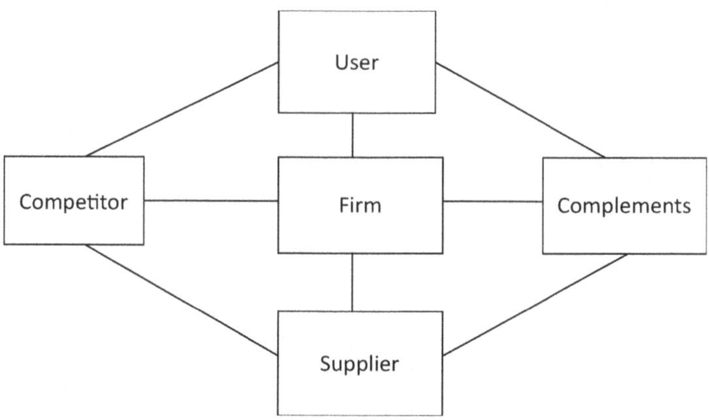

Value network of Microsoft and Intel

In business history, Microsoft and Intel had a classic coopetition relationship.

Intel provides the Central Processing Units (CPUs) that computers need, and Microsoft provides the operating systems and major applications that run on them. People buy computers for the purpose of using operating systems and applications to work or entertain, and CPU is the guarantee of high efficiency. Thus, the products of Microsoft and Intel are complementary to each other.

Driven by Moore's law, Intel continues to roll out faster CPUs to meet the challenge of its competitor AMD. Thus, Intel wants Microsoft to keep up with its pace of development, launching operating systems and applications that need faster CPUs. Because of this complementarity, Microsoft's software has become increasingly complex.

Challenges from value network transformation

When the mobile Internet era came, Microsoft and Intel were unable to adapt to the mobile Internet's requirement for convenience, the fundamental reason of which is the two companies are embedded in their value network.

Each side wants the other side to follow the original value curve, offering faster CPUs or bigger software. However, their competitors, such as ARM and apps based on android or apple, have trounced traditional software and hardware developers like Microsoft and Intel in the value network of the mobile Internet.

2.7 Co-Evolution Strategy Canvas

Why 4 $\times$ 3?

In order to make the 12-point framework of co-evolution strategy a practical tool, I designed the co-evolution strategy canvas and put the 12 points on a piece of paper.

The structure of the co-evolution strategy canvas is 4 by 3, 4 columns times 3 rows. Four columns represents four basic elements of co-evolution strategy. Three rows represents three strategic points of each strategic element.

4 times 3 is a very common ratio. Most laptop screens, the book in front of you and A4 paper, are all 4 by 3. The co-evolution strategy canvas provides you with a very convenient, very low-cost analytical tool. You can print this canvas on paper and write down your observations and thoughts without worrying about mistakes.

Several features of co-evolution strategy canvas

(1) Put the 12 aspects of firm strategy on a piece of paper to extract the essence of the strategy
(2) Through the iteration of different versions of the canvas, a firm can form and perfect its strategy gradually.
(3) Use the canvas of the four stages of co-evolution strategy to analyze the strategic direction of the enterprise in different stages of future development
(4) Leverage the synergy among elements of co-evolution strategy canvas to achieve coordination.

Usage of co-evolution strategy canvas

(1) Finish the canvas in a short time. Write down the first thought that comes to your mind. Don't be afraid of making mistakes or being careless. The canvas is just a tool to help you think.
(2) Try to use concise expressions. The purpose of the canvas is to help you think, not to write beautifully or logically. Use as few words as possible. One trick is to write words larger.
(3) After finishing the canvas, put it aside for a while and then go back to think about it.
(4) The canvas is a tool for a team to achieve the same frequency. Each member completes a group of canvases independently, and then several members discuss about them together. It's better to use a large piece of paper, or a white board, using post-it notes to write down key points and then stick them on the canvas.

Differences between co-evolution strategy canvas and the lean startup canvas

(1) Lean startup canvas only covers the lean startup stage, whereas co-evolution canvas covers four stages including startup, growth, expansion and transformation stages. Co-evolution canvas will help you keep systematic and dynamic thinking at different stages of development.
(2) The components of lean startup canvas don't show very clear logic, whereas the components of co-evolution strategy canvas comes from the two basic dimensions: people and issues, internal and external. It's important to know where something comes from, because only then can you know where it's going. This is why human are interested in the origin of the universe.

2.7.1 Co-Evolution Strategy Canvas (12 Strategic Points)

User characteristics	Leader	Product development	Technology trends
			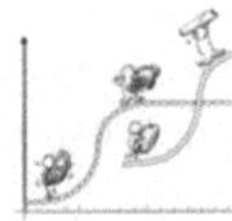
User demand	Team member	Marketing promotion	Capital resources
	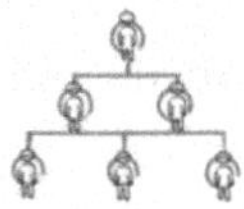		
User choice	Organizational management	Business model	Market coopetition

2.7.2 *Co-Evolution Strategy Canvas (36 Strategic Items)*

User characteristics	Leader	Product development	Technology trends
(1) Physical characteristics (2) Psychological characteristics (3) Social characteristics	(1) Leader experience (2) Leader resources (3) Leader potential	(1) Product innovation (2) Process innovation (3) Innovation commercialization	(1) Technical breakthrough (2) Technical stability (3) Technical economy
User demand	Team member	Marketing promotion	Capital resources
(1) Demand breadth (2) Demand depth (3) Demand frequency	(1) Team size (2) Team quality (3) Team growth	(1) Marketing positioning (2) Marketing channels (3) Marketing efforts	(1) Financial capital (2) Tangible resources (3) Intangible resources
User choice	Organizational management	Business model	Market coopetition
(1) Choice willingness (2) Choice process (3) Choice barrier	(1) Organizational structure (2) Organizational institution (3) Organizational culture	(1) Operation model (2) Profit model (3) Cash flow model	(1) Market competition (2) Market cooperation (3) Market ecology

Chapter 3
Phases

Just like all living organisms,
firms have their own lifecycle.
From start-up to growing-up, expansion
and transformation/decline,
co-evolution strategy redefines firms' lifecycle

3.1 Lifecycle of User Elements

3.1.1 Lifecycle for User Elements

3.1.1.1 Distribution Map of the Sequence in Which Users Accept New Products

The distribution map reflects the sequence in which different types of users enter the market and the stage of demand development before the market reaches saturation. According to the sequence in which users enter the market, they can be divided into five categories: innovators, early users, early followers, late followers and laggards.

Among them, innovators and early users enter the market in the embryonic period of demand development. Early followers enter the market in the growth stage of demand development, while late followers and laggards enter in the mature stage. When all the laggards enter the market, the market demand reaches saturation.

The characteristics of different types of users determine the sequence and proportion of their entry into the market.

J. Y. Lu, *Co-evolution Strategy Canvas*,
https://doi.org/10.1007/978-981-15-5988-4_3

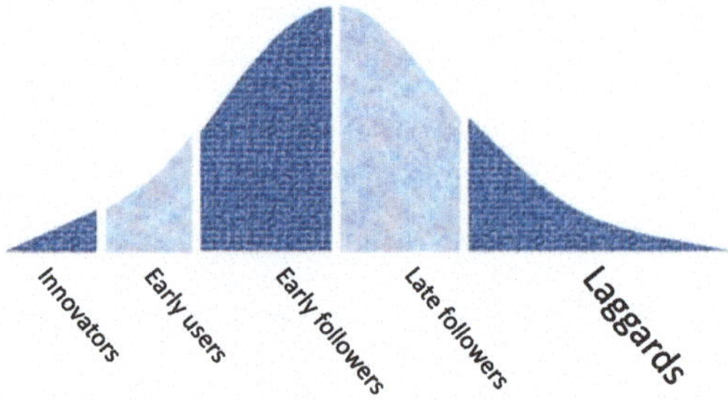

Innovators

Innovators are generally technical fans and enthusiasts. They have fun from being the first to experience new products. Even if the products are not perfect and the price is high, innovators are willing to try. Innovators account for roughly 2% of all users.

Early Users

Early users are the second to enter the market. They are generally followers of fashion, or they have seen the important application value of the products in the future. The forward-looking pursuit of technology or products prompts the innovators and early users to enter the market during the germination period of demand development. Early users accounted for roughly 13% of all users.

Early Followers

Early followers represent the trend-setting crowd in the mass market, whose participation marks the beginning of the growth phase of demand. Early followers are curious about new technologies and products, but they were also pragmatists who will assess the benefits and costs of using new technologies and products, and only if the products could bring them more than the cost benefits will they consider using. Early followers may reach 35% of all users when the market is saturated.

Late Followers

After the early followers have proved that the new products can meet their needs, the late followers will join the market. The channels for them to obtain information are usually traditional, the time to obtain information is relatively late, and their acceptance of new things is relatively low. Late followers may also reach 35% of all users when the market is saturated.

Laggards

Laggards are the last group to enter the market, accounting for roughly 15% of all users. They are usually conservative and don't like new things. These users usually accept the products only when they have to do that.

3.1.1.2 Double-S Curves of User Value

User value curve & User value innovation curve

From the perspective of user value, drawing the change of user value along with the phases of start-up, growing-up, expansion, and decline in the life cycle of the firm leads to the "user value curve" (A curve). In the start-up phase, the user value is realized; in the growing-up phase, the user value grows; in the expansion phase, the user value becomes stable; in the decline phase, the user value declines.

Based on the original user value curve, firms are constantly innovating. Usually, in the expansion phase, even early in the growing-up phase, firms begin to innovate the user value, and the resulting curve is called the "user value innovation curve" (B curve).

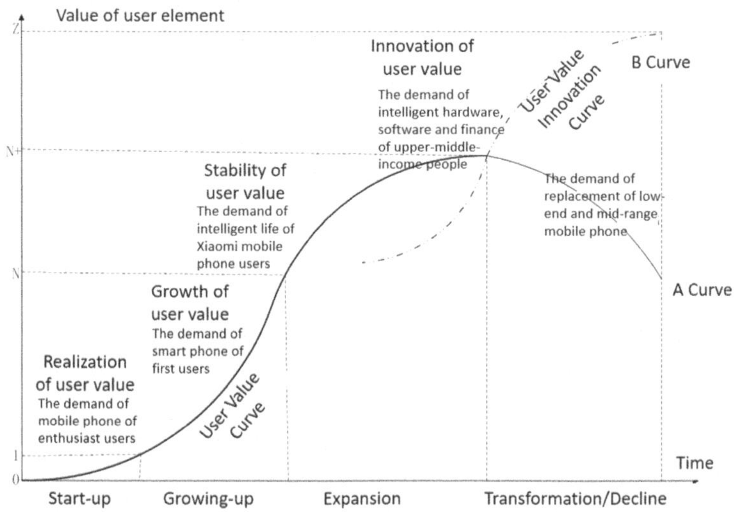

User value curve & User value innovation curve

(Case Analysis: Xiaomi)

In the start-up phase, Xiaomi developed the MIUI system which could better meet their individual needs in response to the needs of mobile phone technology enthusiasts.

In the growing-up phase, Xiaomi aimed at the characteristics of first-time smartphone users who are highly sensitive to the cost performance and satisfies their demands for mobile phone appearance, special performance and psychological aspects. As a result, Xiaomi has achieved rapid growth in user numbers and user value.

In the expansion phase, Xiaomi paid attention to the smart life needs of existing mobile phone users, and initially formed the ecological chain of Xiaomi intelligent life.

During 2015–2016, Xiaomi's mobile phone shipments experienced a serious decline. If it continued to target at young users' demand for low-end and mid-range mobile phones, Xiaomi would inevitably enter a recession.

Xiaomi began to develop products such as Xiaomi Note and Xiaomi Mix for a wider range of users during 2015–2016. The user group positioning has expanded from the original 17–35 years old to 17–45 years old. At the same time, it began to shift from hardware-based to creating comprehensive user value.

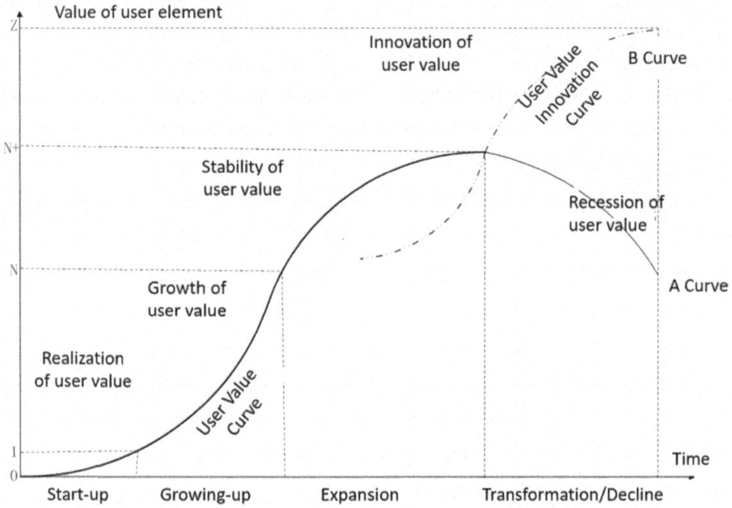

Realization of user value: The demand of mobile phone of enthusiast users.
Growth of user value: The demand of smart phone of first users.
Stability of user value: The demand of intelligent life of Xiaomi mobile phone users.
Innovation of user value: The demand of intelligent hardware, software and finance of upper-middle-income people.
Recession of user value: The demand of replacement of low-end and mid-range mobile phone.

Usage of the tool

1. Analysis of your own firm: In the blank space of the map, write down the characteristics of your firm's creation and innovation of user value in the phases of start-up, growing-up, expansion and transformation/decline.
2. Analysis of your business friends: In the blank space of the map, write down the characteristics of your business friends' creation and innovation of user value in the phases of start-up, growing-up, expansion and transformation/decline.

3. Comparative analysis: Briefly analyze and compare the similarities and differences of the characteristics of creation and innovation of user value in the phases of start-up, growing-up, expansion and transformation/decline between your firm and your business friends.

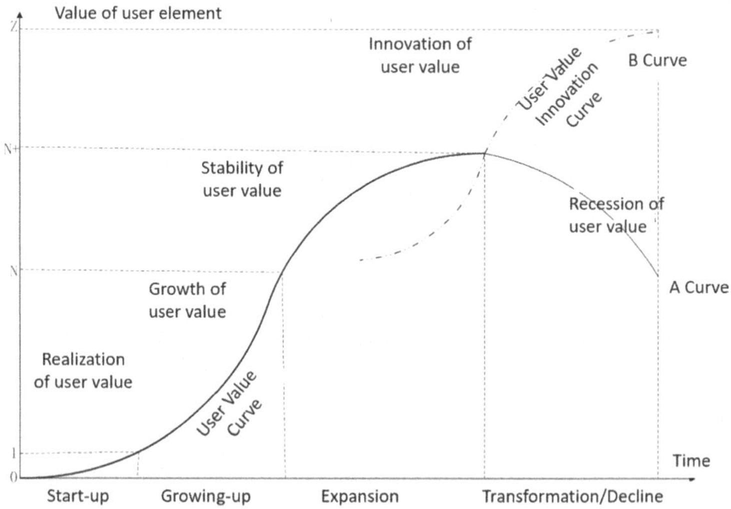

3.1.2 Lifecycle of Organization Elements

Characteristics and core propositions of organization in different phases

In the start-up phase, due to the very small scale of business, the development of the firm's organization mainly focuses on the start-up team with the entrepreneur as the core. As the scale of the business expands, the corresponding organizational functions will be added or adjusted.

In the growing-up phase, the core business of the company is basically determined and will develop rapidly. However, if the organizational capabilities of the company can not keep up with the development of the business and the expansion of the organization, it will lay troubles for the sustainable development of the firm.

During the maturity phase, the speed of business development is relatively stable. At this time, the relatively stable business determines the stability of the organizational structure of the firm, and to improve the efficiency of the organization has become the core proposition of organizational construction in the stable period.

If the firm can't break through the constraints of organizations' inertia, it will enter the decline phase. For a while, although the business of the firm may continue developing, it has lost the necessary organizational vitality.

In the transformation phase, firms that experience stable growth or face challenges of recession need to break through the constraints of organizations' inertia. Founders, executives and employees all need to change their way of thinking and promote organizational change.

Phases of organization development	Features of organization development	Core propositions of organization development
Start-up	The team is led by an entrepreneur. According to the needs of the business, its organizational function gradually complements or differentiates	Entrepreneurs and partners are more important than anything else. The core is to find the right one
Growing-up	The organizational capability develops with the rapid development of the business, and it is prone to the phenomenon that the organization lags behind the business	It is critical for the organization to quickly follow the business development and build a management system based on current and future business demands
Maturity	The relative stability of the business determines the relative stability of the organizational structure, and the importance of improving organizational efficiency is highlighted	In a relatively stable organizational structure, completing and improving organizational efficiency is the core
Decline	The organization is rigid, and the inertia of thinking and behavior has been hard to cast off	Reassess the organization's resources and capabilities, address historical issues, and find new opportunities
Transformation	The organization forms a path dependence based on past business logic, therefore it occurs big corporate illness and slow response to the market	Changing the way of thinking is the key, which promotes organizational change and drives firms to achieve new breakthroughs

3.1.2.1 Lifecycle of Organizational Function

In an article published in the 1974 Long Range Planning, the authors proposed differences in management functions among start-up, growing-up, maturity, decline and transformation phases.

In the start-up phase, R&D is very important; in the growing-up phase, production is very important; in the maturity phase, marketing is very important; in the recession phase, internal control is very important; in the transformation phase, R&D becomes very important once again.

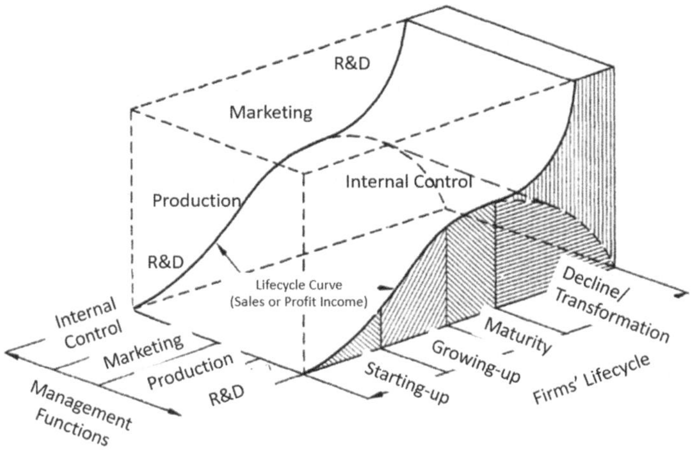

3.1.3 Double-S Curves of Organization Value

Organization value curve & Organization value innovation curve

During the start-up phase, the organizational structure can be compared to an "arrow". The founders are at the forefront of the business, working with founding teams and early-stage employees to break the barriers in entrepreneurship.

During the growing-up phase, the organizational structure can be compared to a "pyramid". The business leaders are at the top of the pyramid and the executive team is in the middle.

During the expansion phase, as the business line continues to increase in the process of diversification, the organizational structure evolves into a "rectangular organizational structure", and the business unit is organized according to different business lines.

During the recession phase, as the business continues to expand, organizational bureaucracy emerges and becomes more serious.

During the transformation phase, some firms can build new organization value curves at an early stage, and innovate organization value through adjustments in organizational structure, system and culture.

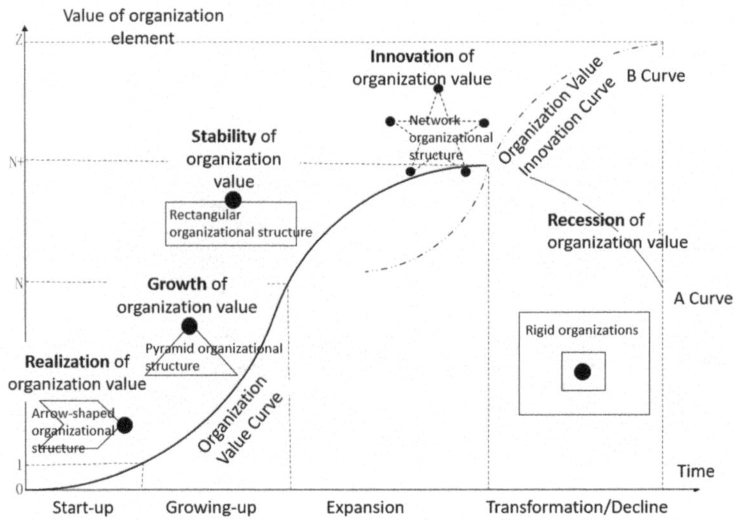

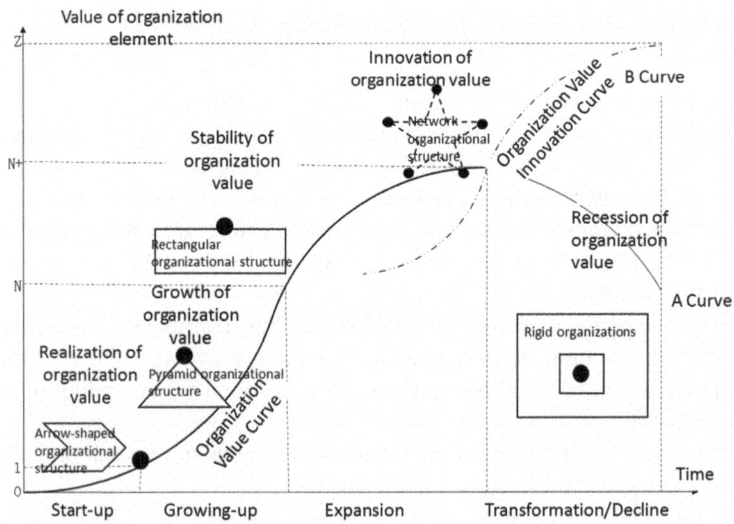

Organization value curve and Organization value innovation curve

3.1.3.1 Case Analysis: Xiaomi

During the start-up phase, Jun Lei and several co-founders, together with more than 40 early employees, adopted an arrow-shaped organizational structure to implement a horizontal management mode.

During the growing-up phase, Xiaomi adopted a three-tier organizational structure of founders, business leaders and employees to support the rapid growth of its mobile phone core business line.

During the expansion and transformation phase, Xiaomi combined the organizational structure of business unit and network. The main existence of the network-based organizational structure is the Xiaomi ecological chain business. Each Xiaomi eco-chain firm is independent. These firms and Xiaomi are brother-enterprise relationships. With Xiaomi as the core, a "matrix-type incubation" network structure has been formed, which produces a "bamboo forest effect".

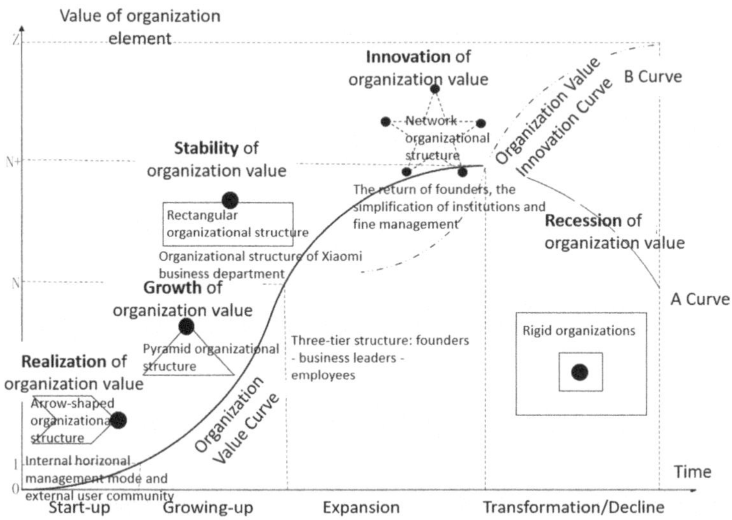

3.1.3.2 Tool

Usage of the tool

1. Analysis of your own firm: In the blank space of the map, write down the characteristics of your firm's creation and innovation of organization value in the phases of start-up, growing-up, expansion and transformation/decline.
2. Analysis of your business friends: In the blank space of the map, write down the characteristics of your business friends' creation and innovation of organization

value in the phases of start-up, growing-up, expansion and transformation/decline.

3. Comparative analysis: Briefly analyze and compare the similarities and differences of the characteristics of creation and innovation of organization value in the phases of start-up, growing-up, expansion and transformation/decline between your firm and your business friends.

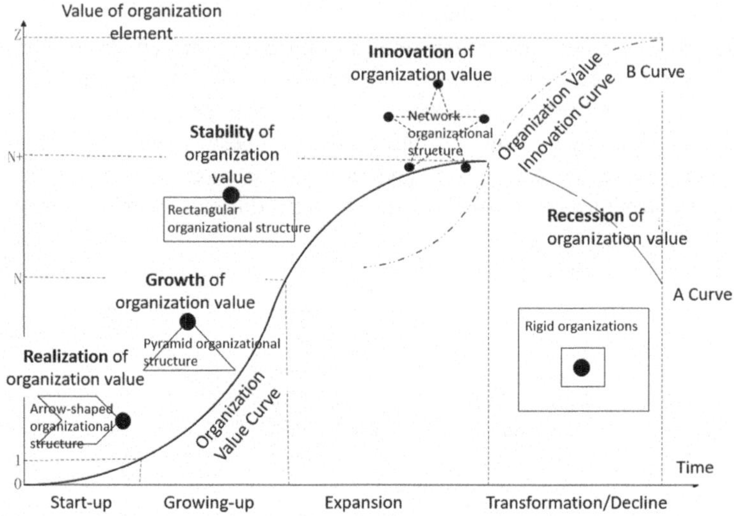

3.1.4 *Lifecycle of Product Elements*

3.1.4.1 Characteristics of Product Elements in Different Phases

During the development and lead-in phase, products are characterized by small volume and high cost, and those who focus on the products are mainly few innovators and early users.

During the growing-up phase, as early follower users begin to accept the products, product sales increase, costs fall, and price may also fall.

During the maturity phase, with the increase of the number of late follower users, the market demand tends to become saturated, the products are popularized and increasingly standardized, and the pressure and space of the fall of product price increase.

During the decline phase, due to the development of technology and changes in users' consumption habits, products cannot continue to adapt to the market demand, and the sales and possession volume of products tend to decline continuously.

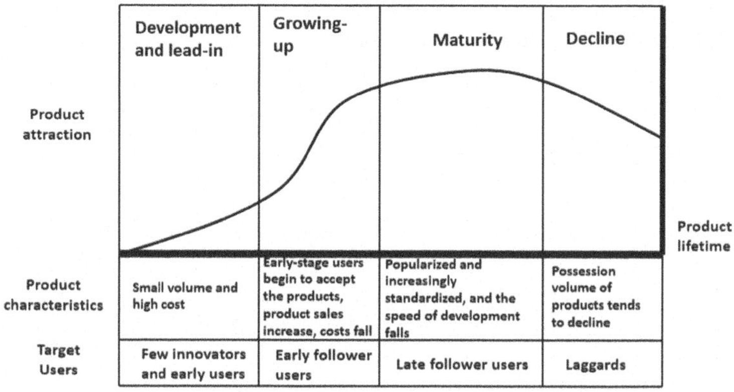

3.1.4.2 Product Lifecycle of iPhone

iPhone was released in January 2007 and sold only 1.36 million units that year. 2007 can be seen as its development and lead-in phase.

In 2008, iPhone sales increased to 11.6 million units, which is an increase of more than 8 times. During the four years from 2009 to 2012, sales of iPhone have grown almost twice as fast each year. In 2012, iPhone's annual sales have reached 125 million units. 2008–2012 can be seen as iPhone's growing-up phase.

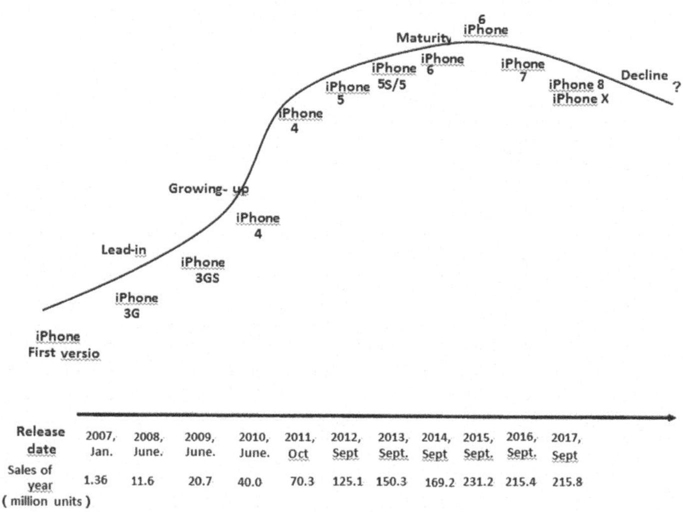

In 2013, sales increased only 20% from 2012. Sales growth in 2014 fell to 12%. In 2015, sales of iPhone hit an all-time high record of 230 million units. However, in 2016, sales fell for the first time in history, dropping to 215.4 million units. In 2016, sales increased slightly to 215.8 million units. Years after 2013 can be seen as the maturity phase of iPhone.

3.1.5 Double-S Curves of Product Value

During the start-up phase, generally regarding few products as the main products, and even use the slogan of "single point breakthrough" to find the combination of product and demand, organization and market, and realize product value.

During the growing-up phase, we will focus on the main products, deepen the market and dig deep into the needs of users, and strive to achieve "one centimeter wide and one kilometer deep" to achieve growth of product value.

During the expansion phase, the demand for the main products is slowing down. At this time, what the firm needs to do is to stabilize the demand for the main products and start to explore the relevant requirements around the main products.

During the transformation phase, the firm needs to innovate products on the new product value curve (B curve) and combine with the original curve (A curve) to avoid the decline of the firm's overall product value.

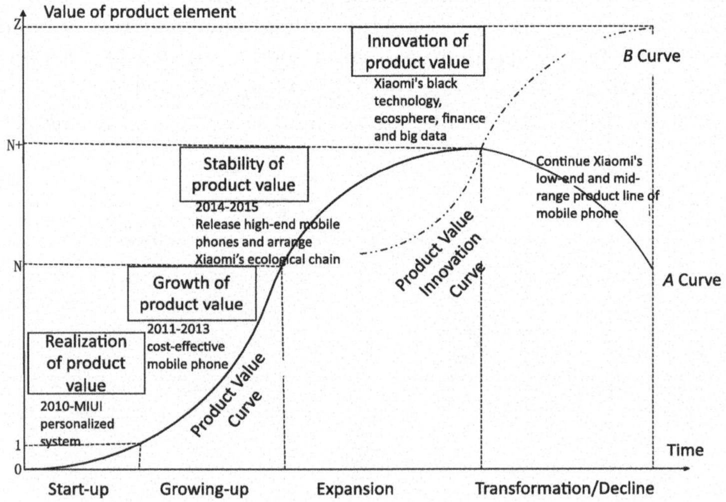

Product value curve & Product value innovation curve

3.1.5.1 Case Analysis: Xiaomi

During the start-up phase, Xiaomi used the MIUI system as the "hot product", starting from the needs of enthusiast users and creating an easy-to-use mobile phone interface.

During the growing-up phase, Xiaomi cut into software from the hardware, and focuses on the low-end and mid-range mobile phones, which has achieved explosive growth of sales in the short term.

In response to the challenge of the decline of production lifecycle curve, Xiaomi released Redmi Mobile Phone and Redmi Note mobile phone to extend to the low-end product line, and then released Xiaomi Note, Xiaomi Max and Xiaomi Mix to extend to the mid-to-high-end product line.

The year of 2010 is Xiaomi's realization period of its product value, 2011–2013 is its growth period of the product value, 2014–2015 is the stable period of Xiaomi's product value, and years after 2016 are the innovation period of its product value.

3.1.5.2 Usage of the Tool

1. Analysis of your own firm: In the blank space of the map, write down the characteristics of your firm's creation and innovation of product value in the phases of start-up, growing-up, expansion and transformation/decline.
2. Analysis of your business friends: In the blank space of the map, write down the characteristics of your business friends' creation and innovation of product value in the phases of start-up, growing-up, expansion and transformation/decline.
3. Comparative analysis: Briefly analyze and compare the similarities and differences of the characteristics of creation and innovation of product value in the phases of start-up, growing-up, expansion and transformation/decline between your firm and your business friends.

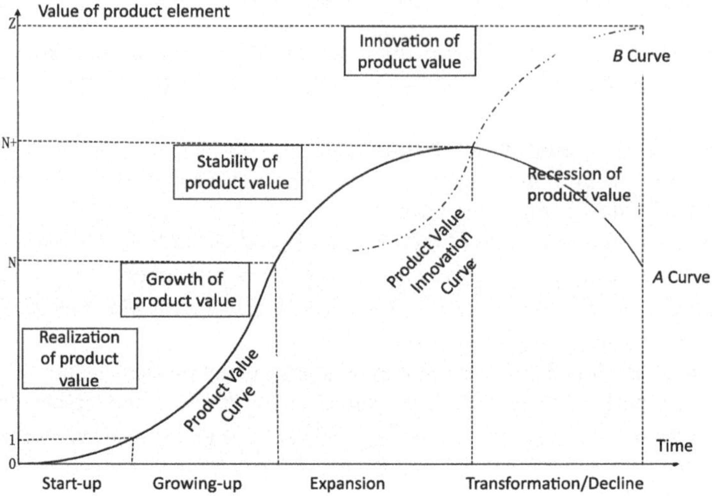

3.1.6 *Lifecycle of Market Elements*

3.1.6.1 Characteristics of Market Elements in Different Phases

In the burgeoning period, capital resources are scarce in the market, technology is just sprouting, and competition and cooperation are limited.

In the development period, capital resources are optimistic about the market prospects, therefore they pour in. Technology development is accelerating, and competition and cooperation are enhanced.

During the maturity phase, the capital resources attracted by the market reach a peak, and the technology reach a mature state with some capitals withdrew after the investors got profits, the competition intensified, and cooperation decreased.

During the decline phase, the efficiency of resource utilization in the industry declines, capital begins to flow to other industries, technology begins to fall behind, competition slows down, and enterprises jointly hold together for warmth.

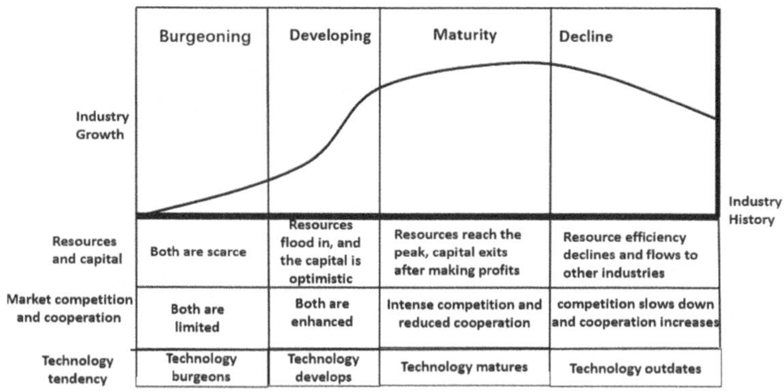

Lifecycle of Market Elements

3.1.6.2 Lifecycle of IT Industry

The IT industry is divided into three major aspects: communication, hardware and software.

The communications industry was the earliest. In 1876, Bell invented the telephone. Later, due to the failure of technology patents, wired communication experienced a period of rapid development. After that, wired communication experienced a mature period of seventy years and entered the decline phase under the double impact of wireless communication and the Internet.

The hardware and software industries are accompanied. The first wave of innovation in the hardware industry took place in the mainframe sector. Later, personal computers were able to meet the needs of information processing. They experienced a period of rapid development before the 1990s, and then gradually entered the maturity and decline phases under the impact of handheld network equipment.

In the IT software industry, the first to develop were mainframe-based enterprise solutions, followed by PC-based personal computer software, and most recently, mobile network-based apps.

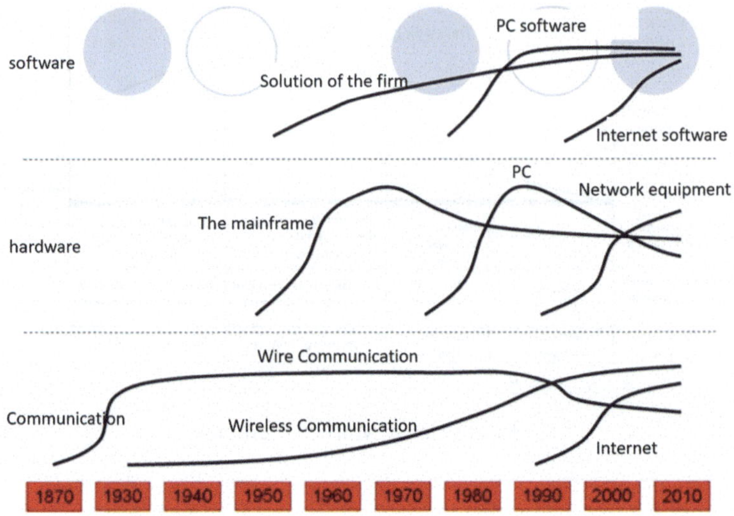

Market value curve & Market value innovation curve

3.1.7 *Double-S Curves of Market Value*

During the start-up phase, entrepreneurs seize the trend of new technology sprouting, use their available resources and capital, and also use the market space which competitors ignore to realize the market value of the firm.

During the growing-up phase, the firm follows the trend of technology development, seizes the market sectors with greatest investment potential, obtains the necessary resources and capital, and gains the opportunity of development before the market competition becomes fierce.

During the expansion phase, the firm uses the mature and stable leading design and relies on the resources and capital accumulated through their own development to achieve a strategic balance between market competition and cooperation and to maximize enterprise value.

During the transformation phase, the firm tends to lay out in advance, grasp new trends, utilize new opportunities, and make full use of resources and capital to create the market value innovation curve of the firm.

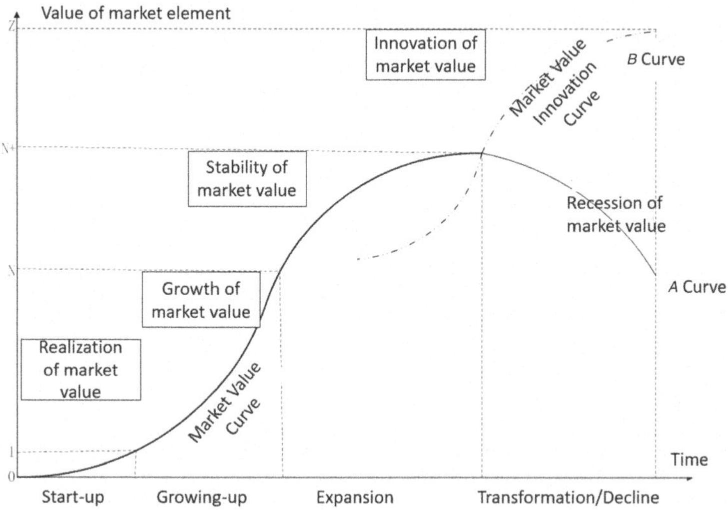

Market value curve & Market value innovation curve

3.1.7.1 Case Analysis: Xiaomi

During the start-up phase, Lei Jun and other co-founders seized the technological trends and market gaps in the outbreak of Android smartphones, inciting industrial resources and capital through their own capital investment and introduction of venture capital.

As the competition in the mobile phone market intensified, and a lot of resources and capital were invested in this industry, many competitors have appeared in the market. Xiaomi began to lay out the smart home eco-chain around core products such as mobile phones, and formed a differentiated competition with rivals to some extent.

In 2016, Xiaomi proposed a strategy for speed reduction adjustment. At the beginning of 2017, Xiaomi put forward a core strategy focusing on "new retail, the Internet of Things and consumption upgrade", and strived to create its new market value innovation curve. In May 2018, Xiaomi submitted a listing application.

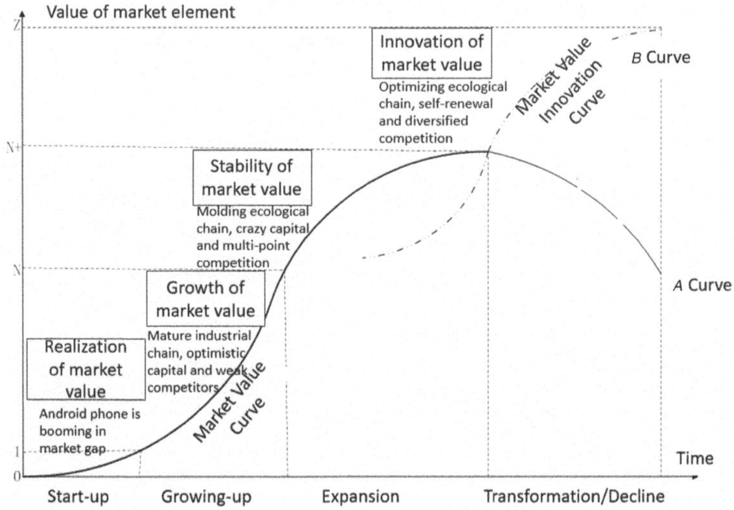

3.1.7.2 Usage of the Tool

1. Analysis of your own firm: In the blank space of the map, write down the characteristics of your firm's creation and innovation of market value in the phases of start-up, growing-up, expansion and transformation/decline.
2. Analysis of your business friends: In the blank space of the map, write down the characteristics of your business friends' creation and innovation of market value in the phases of start-up, growing-up, expansion and transformation/decline.
3. Comparative analysis: Briefly analyze and compare the similarities and differences of the characteristics of creation and innovation of market value in the phases of start-up, growing-up, expansion and transformation/decline between your firm and your business friends.

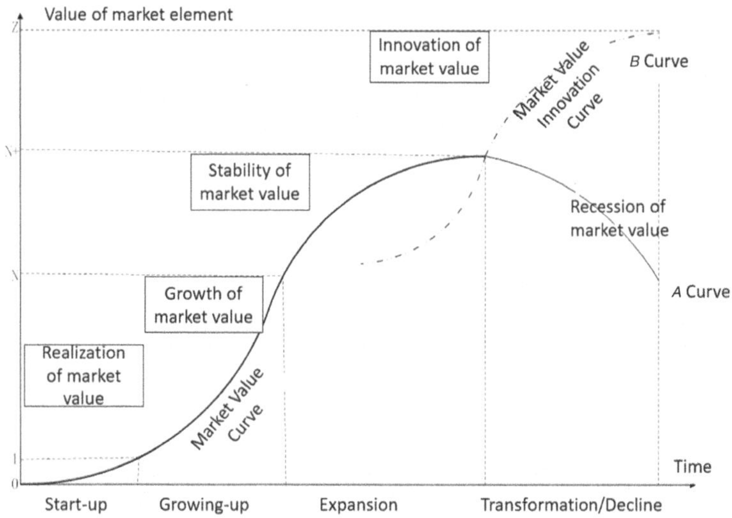

Firms and living organisms

We compare the firms to the living organisms.

The living organisms are composed of genes and organs, and the firms are also composed of some basic elements. The life cycle of a living organism has phases of birth, growth, maturity and aging, and a firm also has phases of start-up, growing-up, maturity, and decline/transformation.

Combining the four basic elements and the life cycle, there are four value curves: curve of user value element, curve of organization value element, curve of product value element and curve of market value element.

There are four thin S-shaped curved lines in the figure, which represent user value curve, organization value curve, product value curve and market value curve. Cooperating with these four S-shaped curved lines are four S-shaped curved lines, which represent the user value innovation curve, organization value innovation curve, product value innovation curve and market value innovation curve.

The combination of the value curves of these elements is the curve of enterprise value.

3.2 Double-S Curves of Market Value

What is enterprise value curve?

The connotation of "enterprise value curve" can be understood from three aspects, which are all implicit in the name "enterprise value curve".

The first is "enterprise", which is a comprehensive concept. An enterprise is a whole composed of four strategic elements. The enterprise value curve also includes the value curve of the four strategic elements. The enterprise value curve reflects the overall value of the enterprise.

The next is "value". The foundation of long-term development of an enterprise must be because of the creation of value, whether it is user value, organizational value, product value, or market value. The creations, transfer acquisition of value are the basic logic of strategic thinking.

The third is the "curve", which reflects the twists and turns of enterprise development, while the "innovation curve" reflects the leap of enterprise development. In terms of the twists and turns, an enterprise will undoubtedly meet good times and adversity, with highs and lows during its process of development. In terms of the leap, development of an enterprise must not be carried out along a curve from beginning to end, but at different time points, to achieve cross-cutting development between different curves.

3.2.1 From Start-up to Excellence

Can firms be built to last?

Jim Collins, a professor of management at Stanford University, was named one of the fifteen people who affect management in China by the World Manager magazine. He has published several best-selling books, including: Built to Last, Good to Great, How the Mighty Fall and Great by Choice.

The first of these four books is Built to Last published in 1994. This book focuses on large firms that were known by Collins as "visionary firms." Collins was very careful when choosing a research firm. The average founding year of the sample firms was 97 years before the book was published. In other words, Collins hoped to "discover the management principles that have not changed for hundreds of years."

After writing Built to Last, Collins wanted to study how to make a good firm great. So, in 2001 he wrote Good to Great.

After writing two books, the twenty-first century came. Unlike the twentieth century, the business environment faced by firms in the twenty-first century is more complicated. At the beginning of the twenty-first century, the 9–11 incidents occurred. When Sogou CEO Xiaochuan Wang mentioned "the forward-looking firms" in Built to Last in his speech at the annual meeting of the Chinese Future Star Firms in 2014, four of these forward-looking firms had already closed, and there were still several that are crumbling.

Collins apparently realized that only a small number of firms can really be built to last, and most "great" firms cannot escape the fate of decline. Therefore, Collins published the book How the Mighty Fall in 2009. Although the title of the book is "How the Mighty Fall", the subtitle of the book is "Why Some Companies Never Give In". Collins believed that the "bane" of firm's decline had been planted in the rapid growing-up phase.

After continuously studying "great", "good" and "declining" firms, Collins finally turned his attention to "high-speed-growth" companies in the "uncertain environment." In 2011, Collins published Great by Choice.

From the stage of enterprise development, Built to Last corresponds to the expansion phase, Good to Great corresponds to the growing-up phase, How the Mighty Fall corresponds to the decline phase, and Great by Choice corresponds to the start-up phase. If the enterprise value innovation curve is taken as the second choice, then Great by Choice can also correspond to the choice of the new enterprise value curve.

The question that Jim Collins spent 20 years studying, in the final analysis, is a question of "built to great".

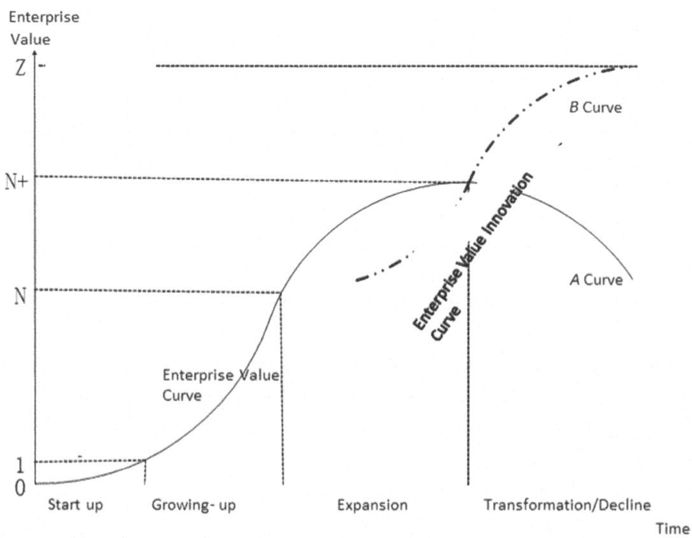

3.2.2 *Start-up from Failure*

3.2.2.1 Start-up from Failure

When Hang Zhou, who founded Yongche Inc, shared his entrepreneurial experience, he said: "Entrepreneurship is like a high jump game in a sense. If you are only trying to challenge, then the ultimate fate of such a business may be failure. Possibly failure is a kind of fate of entrepreneurship, and it is an inevitable thing. If we think that failure is inevitable, then the purpose of our failure to learn is not to avoid failure. Our purpose is first to face failure, then to accept failure, and solve failure, and let go of failure. The purpose of learning is to make life better."

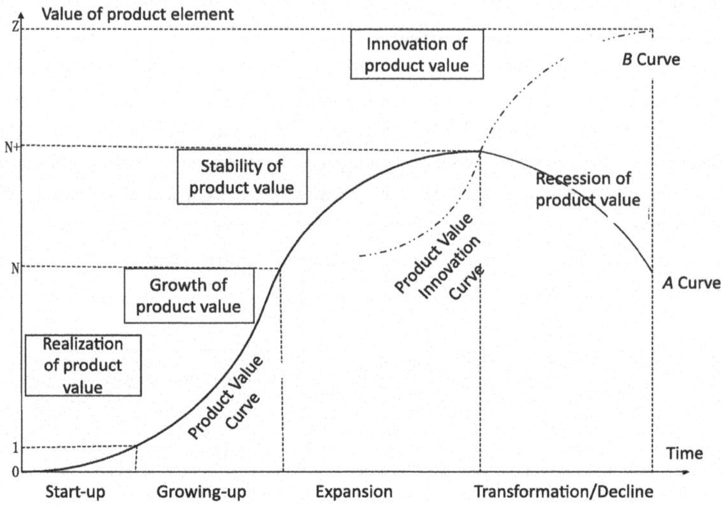

3.2.2.2 Success Gains Eternal Life in Failure

If the firm life cycle is divided into the start-up phase, the growing-up phase, the expansion phase and the transformation phase, then the entrepreneurs will experience four failures which are start-up failure, growing-up failure, expansion failure and transformation failure.

In the process of firm development, there are five key points related to failure.

① Desolation point. Most start-up firms will not enter the growing-up phase, but fail during the start-up phase. These entrepreneurial projects wither in the night without seeing the dawn of growth.

② Sweet point. The head of each golf club has an optimum point for hitting the ball, which can accurately hit the ball and lead to the farthest distance of the ball. It is the turning point from the start-up phase to the growing-up phase. At this point, entrepreneurs can largely be sure that the business model has been established, and next steps will be copying and zooming in.

③ Deceleration point. Even if a firm successfully passes the start-up phase and pulls out a beautiful growth curve during the growing-up phase, it will encounter a "deceleration point" one day. The reason for the deceleration may be the change of strategic elements such as users, organizations, products, and markets.

④ Decline point. The traditional business of a firm will inevitably enter a decline phase after a period of deceleration. The decline of traditional business is a natural. Faced with recession, firms need to be seriously prepared and actively treated.

⑤ Transformation point. No business is ever going to decline, so transformation is an eternal topic for firms. Great firms are looking for new directions in the ongoing transformation.

Looking for certainty in uncertainty,
and looking for continuity in discontinuity.

3.3 Core Algorithm of Life Code

4 phases

Start-up → Growing-up →

Expansion → Transformation

4 arithmetic operations
Subtraction → Multiplication → Addition → Division

4 elements
Users → Products → Market → Organizations

4 criteria of benefits
Lean → Focused → Amplifying → Upgrading

4 dimensions of space
Precision → Depth → Width → Dimension

4 patterns
"Point" → "Line" → "Surface" → "Body"

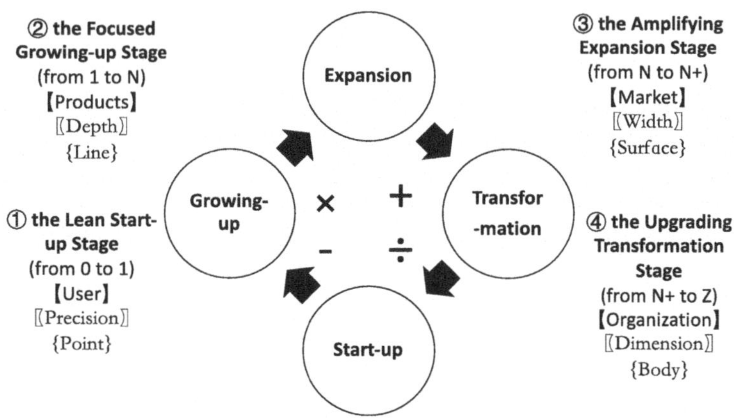

3.3.1 4 Phases and 4 Arithmetic Operations

4 phases
Start-up → Growing-up →
Expansion → Transformation

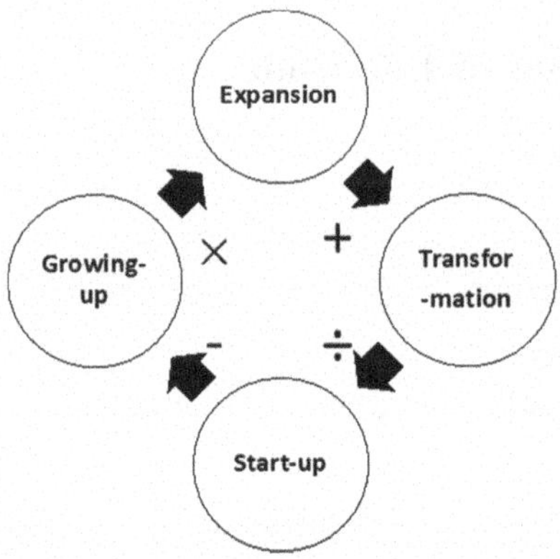

Enterprise life cycle is divided into four phases: start-up, growing-up, expansion and transformation, which respectively correspond to four cases: "from 0 to 1", "from 1 to N", "from N to N + ", and "from N + to Z".

"From 0 to 1" means that the firm starts from nothing to something, "from 1 to N" means that the initial business users grow from less to more, "from N to N + " means diversification around the core business, and "from N + to Z" means the firm switches or establishes new runways and then takes off again.

At each stage of development, the importance of each element is different, and the main driving force for promoting firm development is also different. These differences can be compared to the different strategic operation rules at each stage.

4 arithmetic operations
Subtraction → Multiplication → Addition → Division

During the start-up phase, use subtraction. Start-up means "doing complicated things in a simple way." How can you make complicated things simple? You have to use "subtraction"—subtracting uninterested needs of the users, subtracting unnecessary functions of the products, subtracting unnecessary duties of the organization, and subtracting unnecessary processes in the market.

During the growing-up phase, use multiplication. Growing-up means "doing simple things again and again". How can you repeat doing simple things? You have to use "multiplication"—multiplying the core user value by a larger quantity of users, multiplying the small organization by greater organizational energy, multiplying a single product by more significant sales, and multiplying a niche market by the more resource equivalents.

During the expansion phase, use addition. Expansion means "doing repetitive things seriously". How can you take repetition seriously? You have to use "addition"—exploring diversified needs around core users, building a cooperative platform around the core organization, developing related products around core products, and establishing cooperative networks around the core market.

During the transformation phase, use division. Transformation means "doing serious things in innovate ways". How can you do things attentively and creatively at the same time? You have to use "division"—removing the reliance on the original users, removing the inertia accumulated in the present organization, removing the outdated functions of the old products, and removing the unreasonable factors in the existing market.

3.4 4 Elements and 4 Criteria of Benefits

4 elements
Users → Products → Market → Organization

We know that the four basic elements of firm strategy are users, organization, products, and market. These four elements play a fundamental role in all stages of enterprise development. However, each element plays a different role in stages of development.

During the start-up phase, users are the most important element. To start up, you must first find the needs of users. Only when users have demands will the entrepreneurship have goals and meaning.

During the growing-up phase, products are the most important element. To grow up, you must make quality products in the first place. Only when the products have value will growth be possible and have a sound foundation

During the expansion phase, market is the most important element. To expand, you must first acquire market resources. With market resources, there is room for expansion.

During the transformation phase, organization is the most important element. To transform, you must first solve the problem of organizational inertia. Only when the organization can innovate will the transformation be hopeful.

4 criteria of benefits
Lean → Focused → Amplifying → Upgrading

Four key words of start-up, growing-up, expansion and transformation phases are lean, focused, amplifying and upgrading. Being lean means simplifying; being focused means concentrating; amplifying stresses efficiency; and upgrading stresses dimensions.

Be lean in the start-up phase. The lean start-up stage emphasizes the excellence of users' demand.

Focus in the growing-up phase. The focused growing-up stage emphasizes the focus of product quality.

Amplify in the expansion phase. The amplifying expansion stage emphasizes the pursuit of efficiency for market space.

Upgrade in the transformation phase. The upgrading transformation phase emphasizes on upgrading the dimensions of organizational capabilities.

3.4.1 *Start-up Stage: User-Centric Capability*

3.4.1.1 Introduction

Be lean in the start-up phase. The lean start-up stage emphasizes the excellence of users' demand.

"精(jing)" is composed of "米(mi)" + "青(qing)", and 青(qing) is the simplified form of "倩(qian)", which means pretty and beautiful. Therefore, "精(jing)" refers to the screened superior rice. Besides, "精(jing)" is the most advanced form of life energy.

Refining the users means to accurately grasp the demand of users.

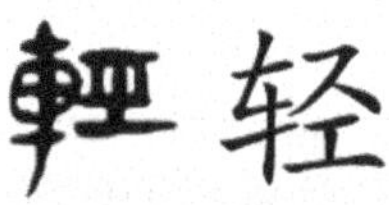

"轻(qing)" is composed of "车(che)" and "巠", and "巠" is the simplified form of "径(jing)", which means pathways. "轻(qing)" means small chariots that can run freely on pathways.

Lightening the organization means the start-up organization should operate freely.

"磨(mo)" is composed of "麻(ma)" and "石(shi)". "麻(ma)" means roughness, "石(shi)" means burrstone mill, and the combination of the two characters means burrstone mill with rough grooves. "磨(mo)" means the processing of food using two stone tools made of burrstone mill with staggered pockmarks.

Polishing the products means constantly bettering the products during the start-up phase.

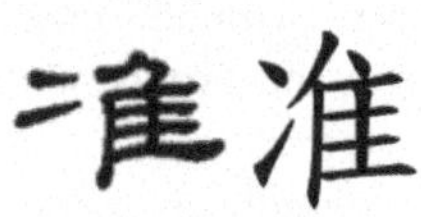

"准(zhun)" is composed of "冫 " and "隼". "冫 " originally refers to ice, and the meaning can be extended to "solidification". "隼" refers to the saker, and the meaning can be extended to "cusp". The combination of "冫" and "隼" means the solidification of the cusp. The original meaning of the character is that the craftsman narrows one eye to make sure the line or surface of the building material is level.

Identifying the market accurately means accurately identifying the market segments during the start-up phase.

Start-up stage: user-centric capability

The dominant element in the start-up stage is "users".

To start up, you must start from the users' needs. You should research the users' needs earnestly, follow them to establish a light organization, polish the fine products with the light organization, and enter the market accurately with fine products to achieve precise matching between users' needs and the market.

Therefore, the start-up phase is called "the lean start-up stage", and the core capability of this stage is user-centric capability.

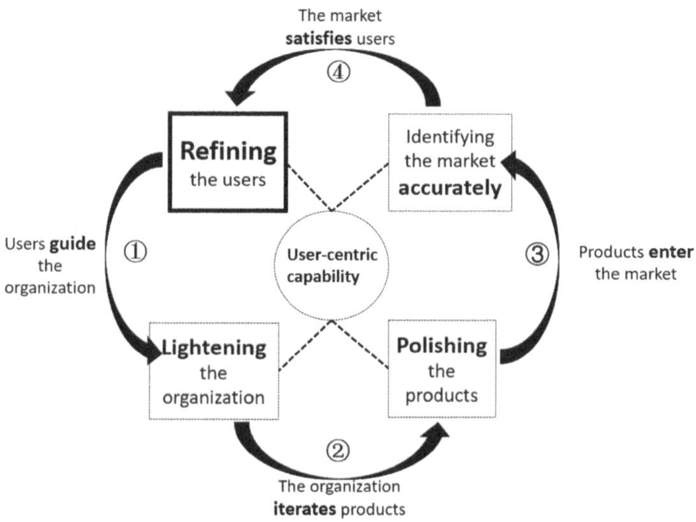

3.4.1.2 Model of Start-up Stage: User-Centric Capability

Usage of the tool

1. Analysis of your own firm: In the blank space of the map, analyze the experience and improvement space in 4 aspects as "refining the users", "lightening the organization", "polishing the products" and "identifying the market accurately" of your firm in the start-up phase.
2. Analysis of your business friends: In the blank space of the map, analyze 4 aspects as "refining the users", "lightening the organization", "polishing the products" and "identifying the market accurately" of your business friends in the start-up phase. And analyze what aspects of your business friends are worth learning.

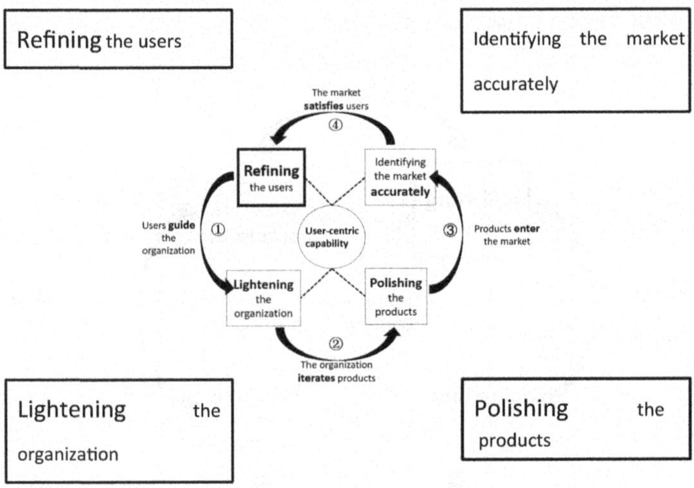

3.4.2 *Growing-up Stage: Product-Iteration Capability*

3.4.2.1 Introduction

Focus in the growing-up phase. The focused growing-up stage emphasizes the focus of product quality.

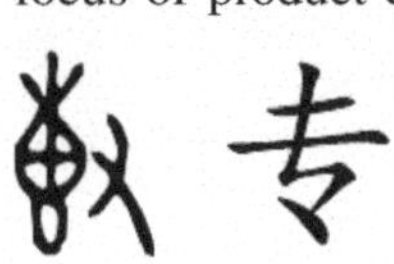

"专(zhuan)" is the original character of "转(zhuan)", which is divided into two parts. "车(che)" means the yarn hammer and the wheel wound around by the thread, and "专(zhuan)" means the two hands holding the yarn hammer and the wheel.

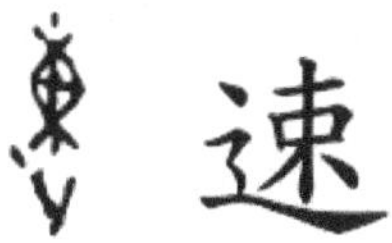

"速(su)" is composed of "辵" and "东(dong)", "辵" means marching forward, "东(dong)" means the travelling bag, and the original meaning of the character is marching forward with **the travelling bag. Since you want to travel far, you must have speed**.

Occupying the market rapidly means the firm should rapidly enter the market, rapidly acquire resources, and rapidly establish its competitive and cooperative position.

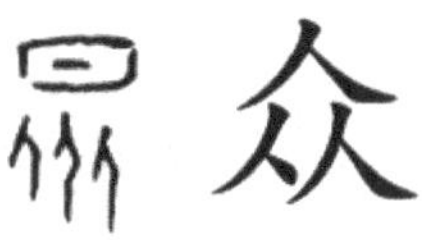

"众(zhong)" is composed of three "人(ren)", which means a group of people who are accompanied by each. There is a "日(ri)" on the Chinese old-style character "众(zhong)", and the original meaning of the character is the broad mass of people living under the blue sky and red sun.

Multiplying the users means expanding from "人(ren)"—a few innovators, to "从(cong)"—early users, and then to "众(zhong)"—the initial majority.

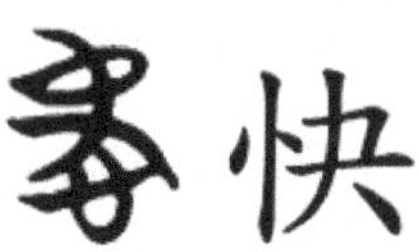

"快(kuai)" is composed of "心(xin)" and "夬", "心(xin)" means the mood, while "夬" means expression. The combination of the two characters means expressing your mood directly.

Accelerating the organization means the organization in the growing-up stage should not only act quickly, but also adopt direct internal communication.

The dominant element in the growing-up stage is "products".

Growth must be based on products. Firms should focus on continuous innovation of products, use products to detonate the market, quickly gain market development space, win public users, and establish an organization that responds and communicates quickly.

Therefore, the growing-up phase is called “the focused growing-up stage”, and the core capability of this stage is the “product-iteration capability”.

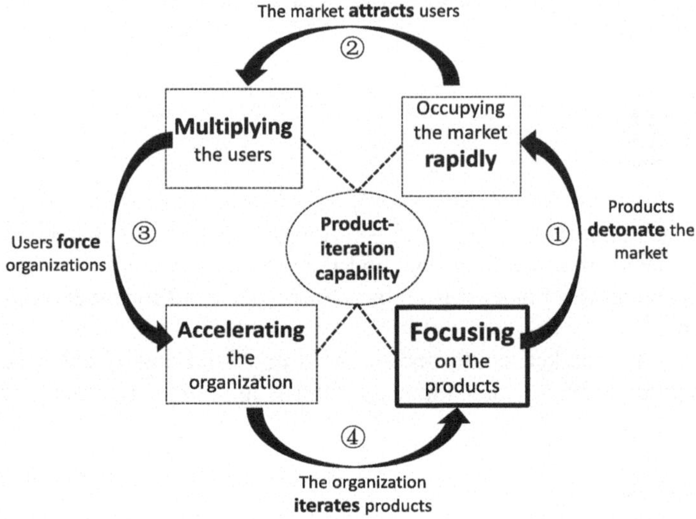

3.4.2.2 Model of Growing-up Stage: Product-Iteration Capability

Usage of the tool

1. Analysis of your own firm: In the blank space of the map, analyze the experience and improvement space in four aspects as “multiplying the users”, “accelerating the organization”, “focusing on the products” and “occupying the market rapidly” of your firm in the growing-up phase.
2. Analysis of your business friends: In the blank space of the map, analyze four aspects as “multiplying the users”, “accelerating the organization”, “focusing on the products” and “occupying the market rapidly” of your business friends in the growing-up phase. And analyze what aspects of your business friends are worth learning.

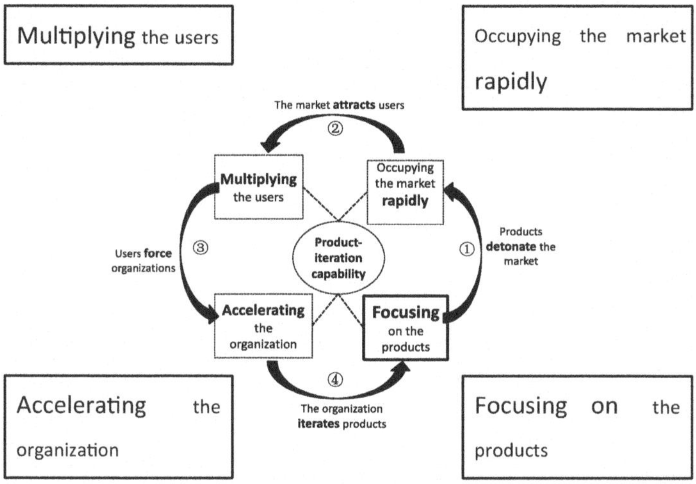

3.4.3 Expansion Stage: Market- Entry Capability

3.4.3.1 Introduction

Amplify in the expansion phase. The amplifying expansion stage emphasizes the pursuit of efficiency for market space.

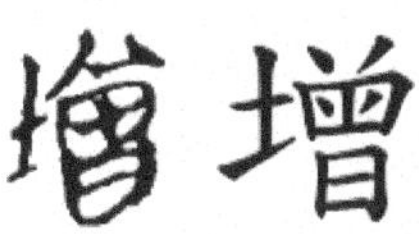

"增(zeng)" is composed of "土(tu)" and "曾(zeng)". "曾(zeng)" means adding or expanding things, so "增(zeng)" means adding soil, bricks and tiles.

Extending the market methodically means firms should expand its market step by step, rather than "rob Peter to pay Paul".

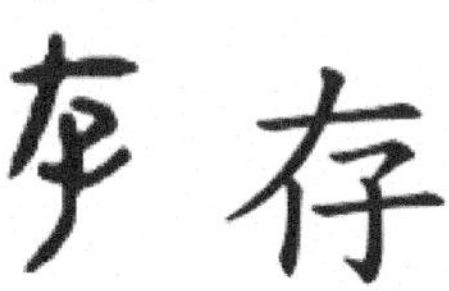

"存(cun)" is composed of "才(cai)" and "子(zi)". "才(cai)" means house pillars and beams, referring to the residence; "子(zi)" means descendants. Thus the original meaning of "存(cun)" is living and working in peace, carrying on the family line and keeping generations continuing.

Retaining the users means that firms should dig deep into the existing users rather than blindly emphasize on expanding the number of users during the maturity phase.

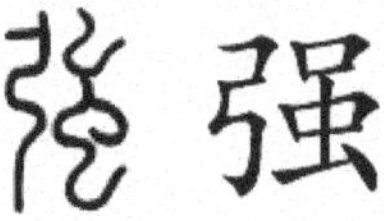

"强(qiang)" is composed of "弘(hong)" and "虫(chong)", "弘(hong)" means loud volume, "虫(chong)" means reptiles, and the combination of the two characters means large reptiles with thunderous roar.

Strengthening the organization is the purpose and foundation of expansion. Strengthening the organization is necessary during the maturity phase.

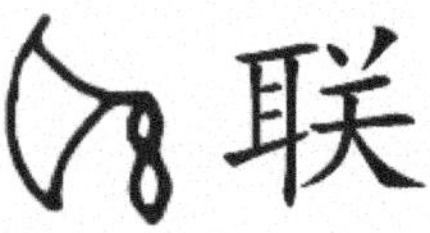

"联(lian)" is composed of "耳(er)" and "关(guan)", "耳(er)" means ears, and the original meaning of the character is chains attached to ears, which emphasizes pairwise connections.

Connecting the products means products should be related to each other during the expansion phase.

The dominant element in the maturity phase is the "market".

Firms face the biggest challenges from the market during the maturity phase. On the one hand, they may go up, and on the other hand, they may go down. During the maturity phase, attention must be paid to the incremental market and the existing users, strengthen the organizations, and occupy the incremental market with related products.

Therefore, the maturity phase is called "the amplifying expansion stage", and the core capability of this stage is market-entry capability.

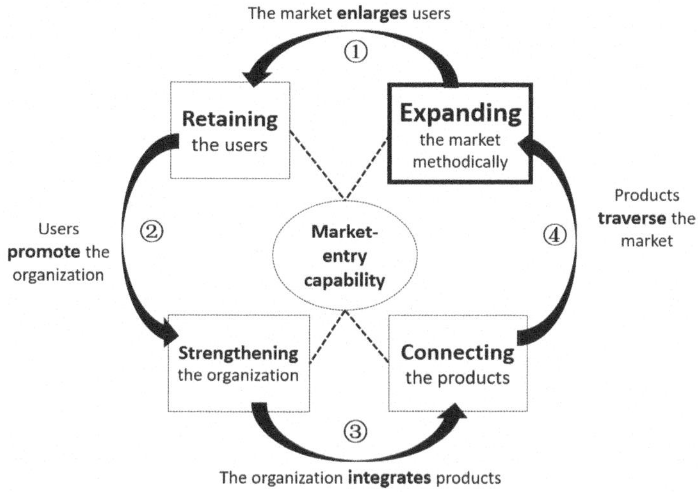

3.4.3.2 Model of Growing-up Stage: Market-Entry Capability

Usage of the tool

1. Analysis of your own firm: In the blank space of the map, analyze the experience and improvement space in four aspects as "retaining the users", "strengthening the organization", "connecting the products" and "extending the market methodically" of your firm in the expansion phase.
2. Analysis of your business friends: In the blank space of the map, analyze four aspects as "retaining the users", "strengthening the organization", "connecting the products" and "extending the market methodically" of your business friends in the expanding phase. And analyze what aspects of your business friends are worth learning.

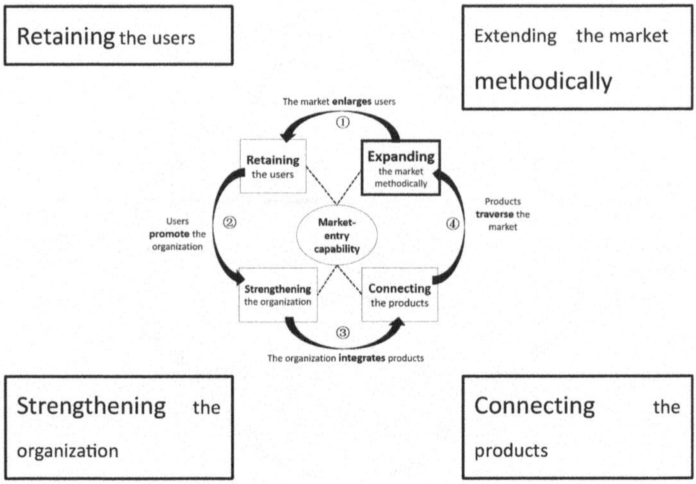

3.4.4 Transformation Stage: Organization-Upgrading Capability

3.4.4.1 Introduction

Upgrade in the transformation phase. The upgrading transformation phase emphasizes on upgrading the dimension of organizational capabilities.

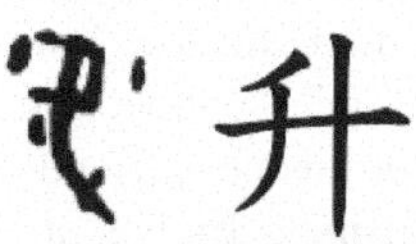

The old-style character of “升(sheng)” is “昇(sheng)”, which is composed of “日(ri)” and “升(sheng)” (to pick up a wine bucket) and represents the sun’s moving upwards from the horizon.

Upgrading the organization is to get the organization upgraded, rising from the original level to a higher level.

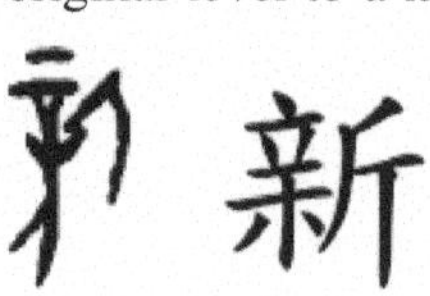

"新(xin)" is composed of "辛(xin)", "木(mu)" and "斤(jin)". "辛(xin)" refers to a ▼ shaped iron bar to chop firewood, "木(mu)" refers to stumps, and "斤(jin)" refers to axes. "新(xin)" then means using axes, iron bars and other tools to chop firewood. Each time you chop it, new wood is exposed.

Updating the products means that in the transformation stage, it is required to cut off some unnecessary functions on the basis of the original products and add some new elements, destroying the old and establishing the new.

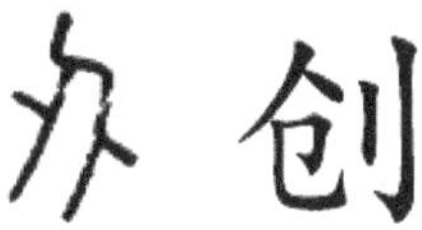

"创(chuang)" is composed of "仓(cang)" and "刀(dao)", meaning that the carpenter swings at the wood with an axe to cut a tree and build houses. Therefore, "创(chuang)" also has the meaning of destroying the old and establishing the new.

Viewing the market innovatively means that the difficult point of the transformation stage is to jump out of the original value network and see the market from a bigger picture and a further perspective.

"非(fei)" is a pictographic character. Two people are back to back, indicating that they have opposite thoughts, conflicting ideas, and mutually exclusive behavior.

Expanding the users means to discover new demands and enter new value networks.

The dominant element in the transformation phase is the "organization". After long-term development, the company has given birth to many "fortresses", and a fortress usually needs to be broken through from the inside. Therefore, the transformation must start from the inside of the organization to stimulate the vitality of the organization. Thus, the upgraded organization will innovate products, and innovative products will be used to reform the market, guiding the development of the market to create user needs.

Therefore, the transformation phase is called "the upgrading transformation stage", and the core capability of this stage is the "organization-upgrading capability".

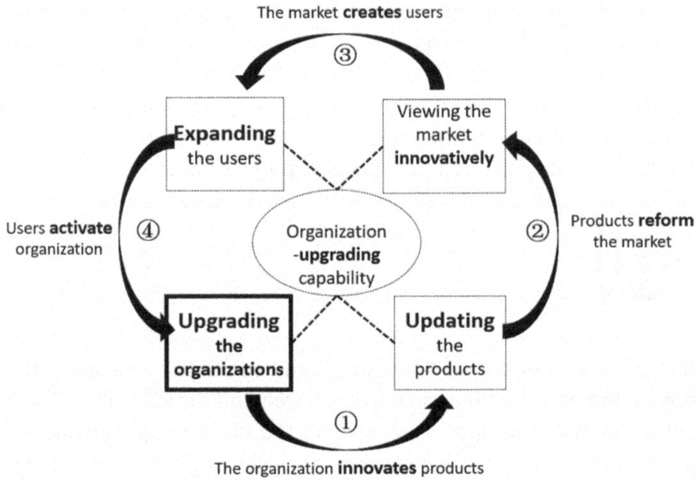

3.4.4.2 Model of Transformation Stage: Organization-Upgrading Capability

Usage of the tool

1. Analysis of your own firm: In the blank space of the map, analyze the experience and improvement space in 4 aspects as “expanding the users”, “upgrading the organizations”, “updating the products” and “viewing the market innovatively” of your firm in the transformation phase.
2. Analysis of your business friends: In the blank space of the map, analyze 4 aspects as “expanding the users”, “upgrading the organizations”, “updating the products” and “viewing the market innovatively” of your business friends in the start-up phase. And analyze what aspects of your business friends are worth learning.

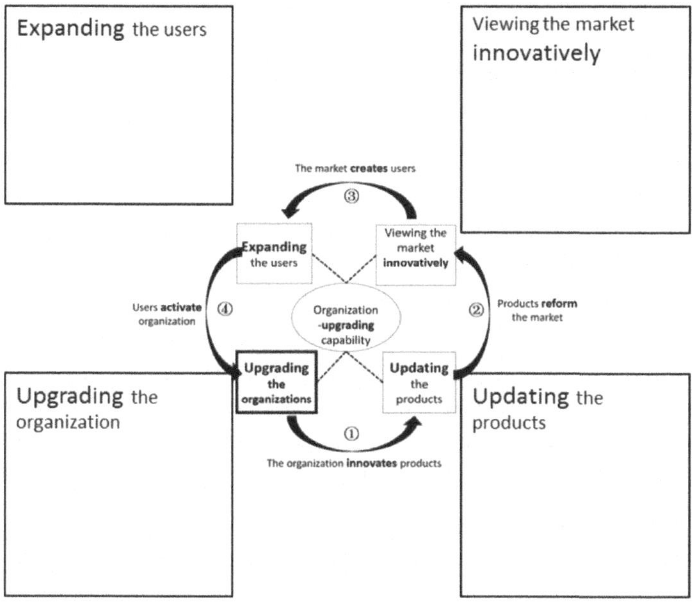
Expanding the users
Viewing the market innovatively
Upgrading the organization
Updating the products
The market creates users
③
Expanding the users
Viewing the market innovatively
Users activate organization
④
Organization -upgrading capability
②
Products reform the market
Upgrading the organizations
Updating the products
①
The organization innovates products

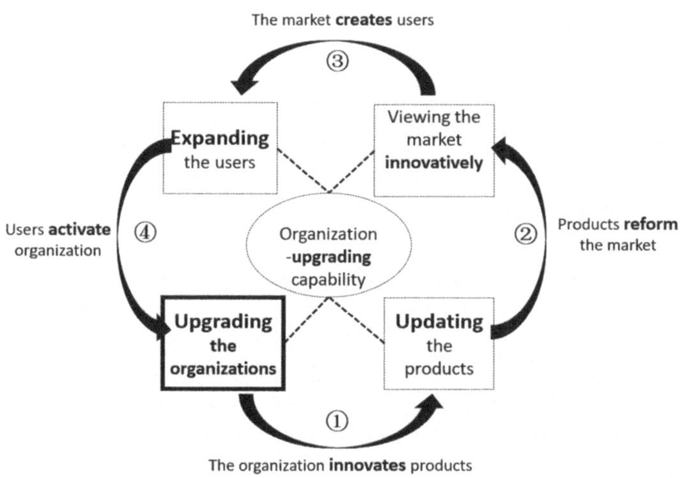
The market creates users
③
Expanding the users
Viewing the market innovatively
Users activate organization
④
Organization -upgrading capability
②
Products reform the market
Upgrading the organizations
Updating the products
①
The organization innovates products

3.5 4 Dimensions of Space and 4 Patterns

3.5.1 4 Dimensions of Space + 4 Patterns

3.5.1.1 4 Dimensions of Space

Precision → Depth → Width → Dimension

The evolution of the character "丁(ding)" Initially, inscriptions of the "丁" character on ancient bronze objects presented as a circle. Then in its seal script, the upper body changed into a horizontal, while the lower body changed into a vertical. The lower body curved to the left in its clerical script afterwards, and then evolved into a leftward hook in its regular script.

The implied meaning of the character "丁(ding)". In the start-up circle, entrepreneurs should look for a market that is "one centimeter wide and one kilometer deep".

"One centimeter wide", which relates to the horizontal stroke of "丁(ding)", refers to precision. Its implied meaning is to accurately find the entry points of the market.

"One kilometer deep", which relates to the vertical stroke of "丁(ding)", refers to depth. There is a leftward hook connecting to the vertical stroke of "丁(ding)", which means digging deep demand and hooking users.

The horizontal stroke of "丁(ding)" is not particularly short compared to its vertical stroke. This means that early entry points can be extended laterally to become a market with width.

The vertical stroke of "丁(ding)" goes deep underground. This means that if a firm has strong vitality, it will take root and sprout, grow into a leafy bamboo forest, and then become an ecosystem with multiple dimensions.

Behind the Xiaomi ecological chain is the logic of bamboo forest. Just like a bamboo shoot, one initial product breaks into the ground, goes deep down, takes root and sprouts, then quickly iterates and expands to multiple dimensions to form a bamboo forest.

3.5.1.2 4 Patterns

"Point" → "Line" → "Surface" → "Body"

The business model of the start-up phase is characterized by a "point" pattern. The interest relationship of related parties grow from nonexistence to existence, the trading relationship from 0 to 1, and the structural relationship from blank to scattered.

The business model of the growing-up phase is characterized by a "line" pattern. The interest relationship of related parties grow from small to medium, the trading relationship from low frequency to high frequency, and the structural relationship from scattered to connected.

The business model of the expansion phase is characterized by a "surface" pattern. The interest relationship of related parties grows from medium to large, the trading relationship from unidirectional to multidirectional, and the structural relationship from value chains to value networks.

The business model of the transformation phase is characterized by a "body" pattern. The interest relationship of related parties grow from large to huge, the trading relationship from multidirectional to multidimensional, and the structural relationship from value networks to ecosphere.

3.5.2 *Enterprise Value Model Tool*

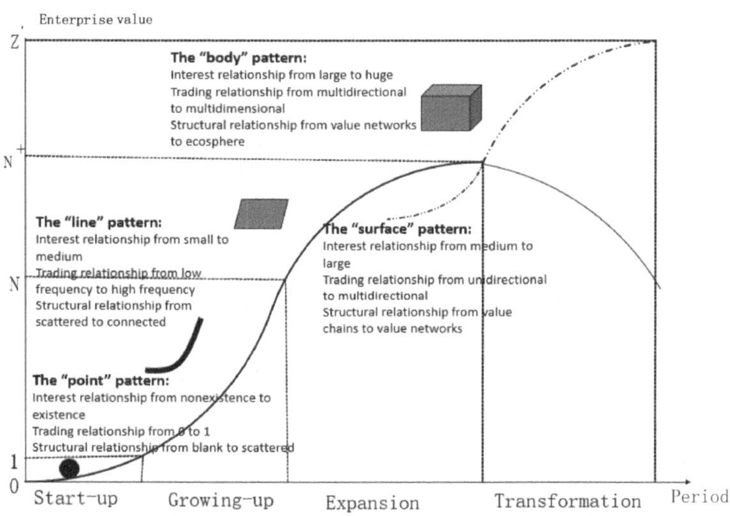

Point → Line → Surface → Body

Usage of the tool

1. Analysis of your own firm: In the blank space of the map, analyze the mechanism for the formation of the "point, line, surface and body" business model of your firm in the phases of start-up, growing-up, expansion and transformation.
2. Analysis of your business friends: In the blank space of the map, analyze the mechanism for the formation of the "point, line, surface and body" business model of your business friends in the phases of start-up, growing-up, expansion

and transformation. And analyze what aspects of your business friends are worth learning.

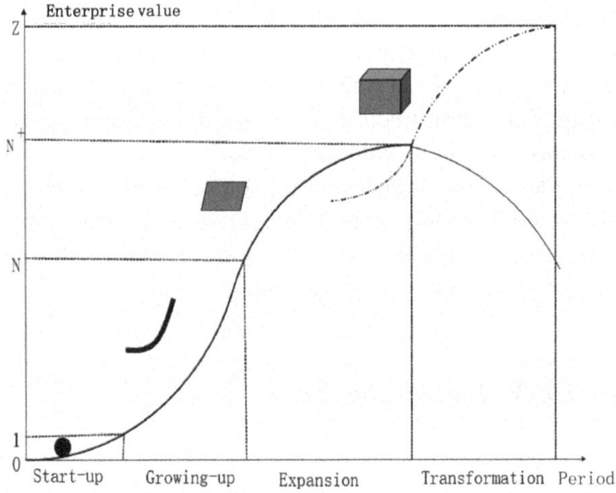

3.5.3 *Championship in the 4 Strategic Phases and 4 Major Martial Arts*

3.5.3.1 Championship in the 4 Strategic Phases

Innovate → Cultivate → Diversify → Recreate

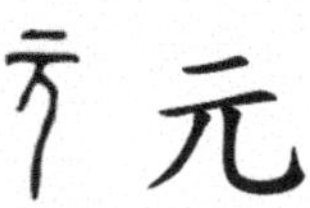

The dot on the top of the character "元 (Yuan)" indicates the source of all things. How to write this dot is very important. The starting point and initial focus of a startup is here.

With the initial dot, then the "—(One)" under the "dot" will be born, which is the so-called "Tao begets One". "The Doctrine of the Mean" has a saying, "The way of the sky and earth can be said in one word." This "One" is the sky and earth.

After the sky and earth, then "human" was born.
"Tao", "sky", "earth" and "human" constitute the "Yuan".

During the start-up phase, a firm should "innovate".
During the growing-up phase, a firm should "cultivate".
During the expansion phase, a firm should "diversify".
During the transformation phase, a firm should "recreate".

3.5.3.2 4 Major Martial Arts

One Sun Finger → Overlord Spear → Shaolin Stick → Yi Jin Jing

"One Sun Finger". A lost martial arts skill in wuxia novels. Its essence is to attack the acupoint with index finger, sometimes as slowly as wind, sometimes as fast as lightning, exactly hitting the nail on the head.

During the start-up phase, to have the power of "One Sun Finger", the key word is "accurate".

"Overlord Spear". According to legend, a meteorite fell from the sky before Xiang Yu rose an army, and was forged into a giant chiselled gold tiger-head gun, which was called "Overlord Spear".

During the growing-up phase, to have the power of "Overlord Spear", the key word is "resolute".

"Shaolin Stick". The stick is one of the most common and conventional weapons used by warrior monks in Shaolin. When talking about Shaolin martial arts, one must refer to Shaolin stick fighting. A spear can pierce a line of enemies, but a stick can hit a crowd.

During the expansion phase, to have the power of "Shaolin Stick", the key word is "stable".

"Yi Jin Jing". "Yi" means change. "Jin" means bones and muscles. "Jing" means guide. "Yi Jin Jing" is a method to change muscles and bones and dredge the channels and collaterals of the whole body through the cultivation of genuine qi (breath) in the elixir field.

During the transformation phase, to have the power of "Yi Jin Jing", the key word is "thorough".

Chapter 4
Start-Up

Gain a foothold before you start

Starting a business, is just like the birth of a human being, which is full of uncertainty and discontinuity.

As an entrepreneur, one must stay true to the mission, and focus on user demand.

J. Y. Lu, *Co-evolution Strategy Canvas*,
https://doi.org/10.1007/978-981-15-5988-4_4

4.1 4 Questions for Start-Up

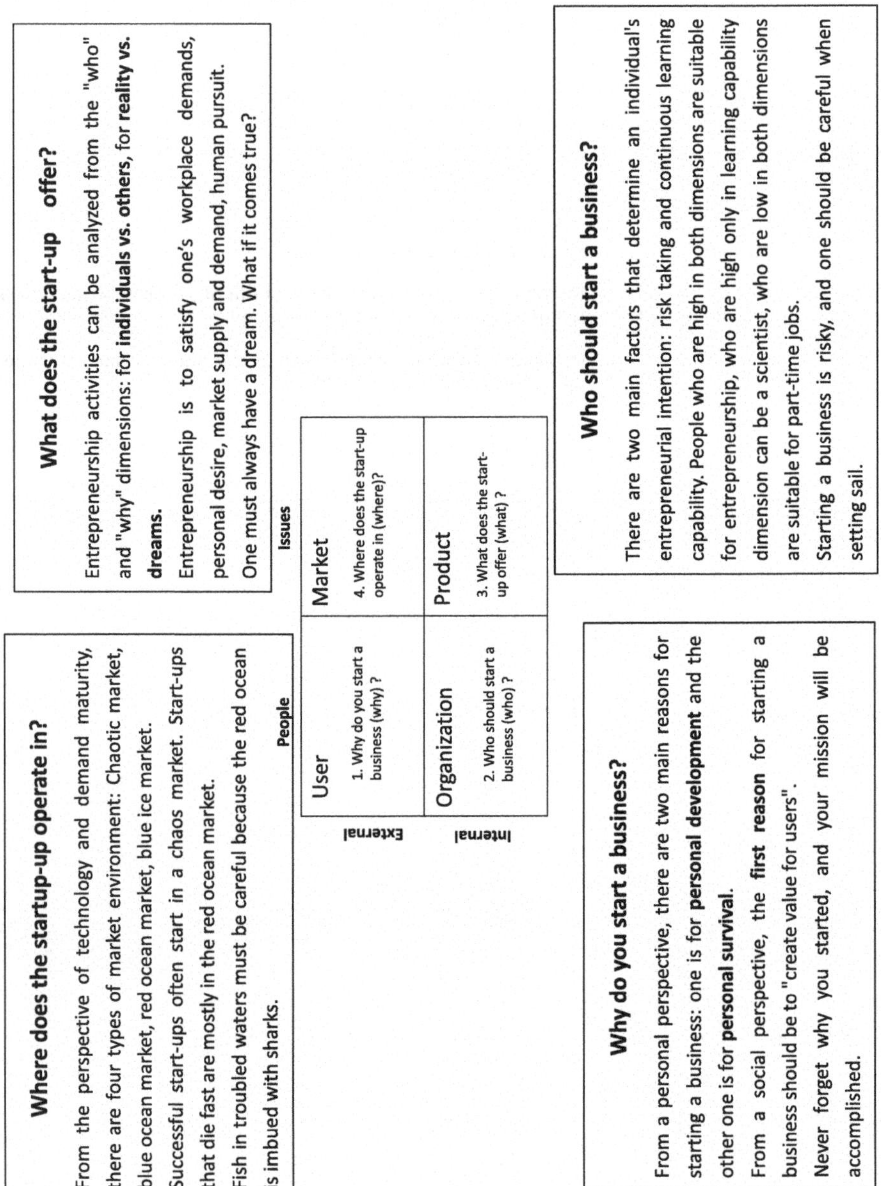

4.1.1 4 Questions for Start-Up Tools

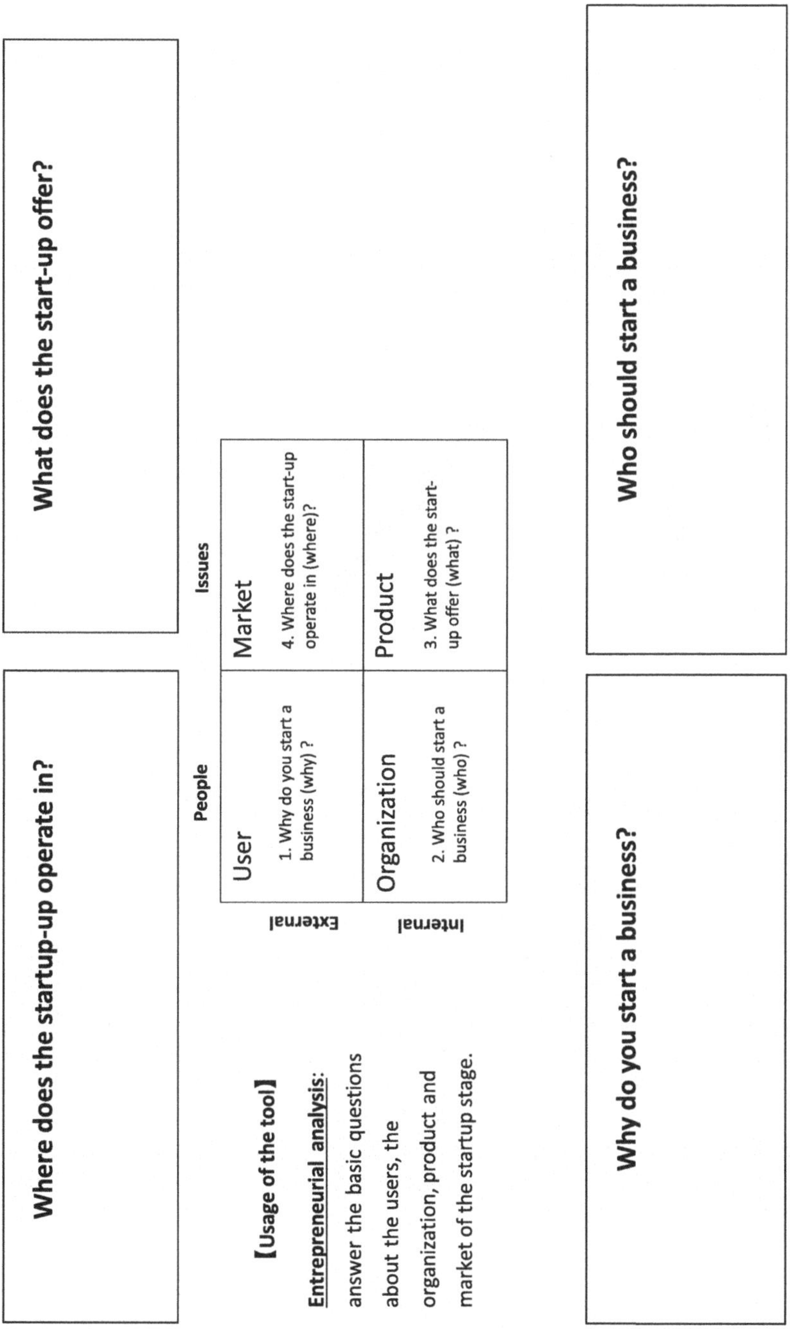

4.1.1.1 Users: Starting Point of Start-Ups

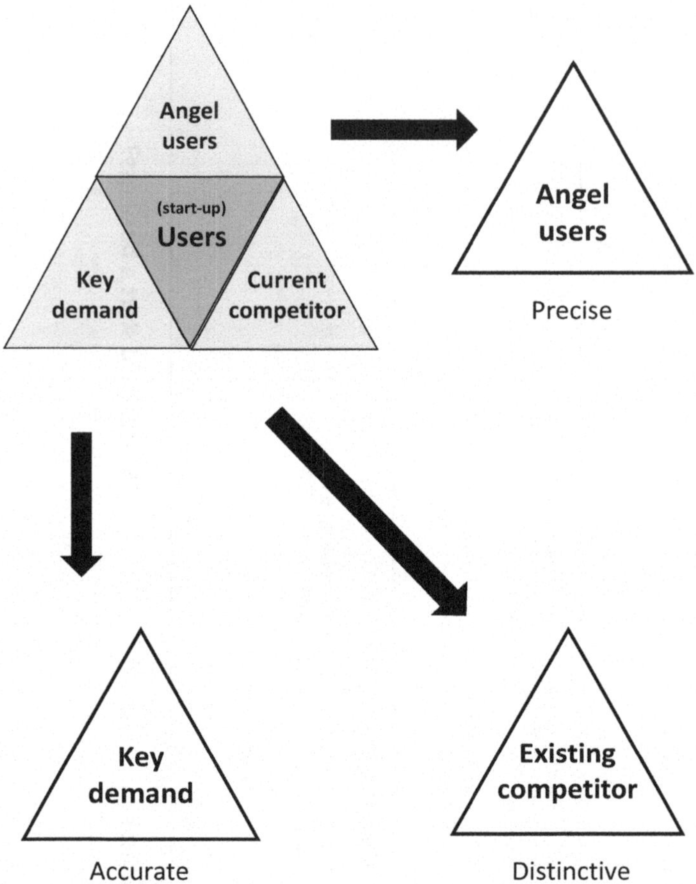

Users

(start-up stage).

The general characteristics of start-ups' users are "precise, accurate and distinctive".

"Precise" means that angel users should be fewer but better.

"Accurate" means that start-ups need to focus on the key demand of users.

"Distinctive" means that users should be different from that of existing competitors.

Angel users are the earliest group of users who acknowledge a product and want more people to acknowledge it. They are of great importance for the product and the firm.

Angel users can help start-ups to identify the key demands of users, grasp the direction of development, focus on MVP's function, and realize technology innovation.

Key demand

The first question for founders is why users should buy our products?

People spend money on two things: fighting pains and pursuing happiness.

Identify key demands of users can help start-ups to distinguish themselves from other competitive products, focus on most important things, achieve a single point of breakthrough, and find the direction for future development.

Existing competitor

The highest form of competition is monopoly.

Existing competitive products can be analyzed from two dimensions of user overlap and demand overlap.

Analyzing the difference of existing competitors from start-ups is helpful for start-ups to capture the demand of users, build competitive teams, develop MVP products and apply innovative technologies.

4.1.1.2 Organization: The Foothold of Start-Ups

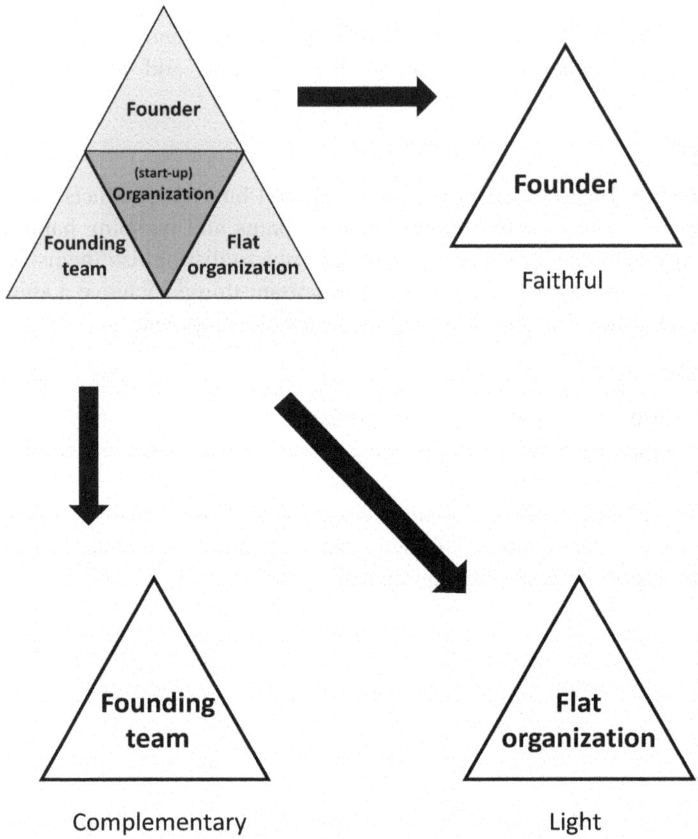

Organization

(start-up stage)

The general characteristics of start-ups' organization are "faithful, complementary and light".

"Faithful" means that founders should believe in the direction of development.

"Complementary" means that members of founding teams should have complementary capabilities with each other.

"Light" means that start-ups should develop with a flat organizational structure.

Founder

Most successful firms can attribute their success to founders' ambitious visions in their early days.

Founders' spirit includes:

A strong sense of mission;
A strong sense of ownership;
Attach importance to front-line business;
Be strategic.

Founding Team

Founding teams should have three types of people.

First, people who have the ability to find and analyze problems; second, people with technical expertise; third, people with management expertise.

Sun taoran also believes that there should be three complementary types of people in founding teams:

The first are leaders;
The second are sales people;
The third are technicians.

Flat Organization

Flat organization is the natural form of organization in start-up stage.

A flat organization can help startups interact closely with angel users, reduce the burden of managing teams, make MVP development smoother, and help startups find opportunities in a chaotic market.

4.1.1.3 Product: The Power for Shot of Start-Ups

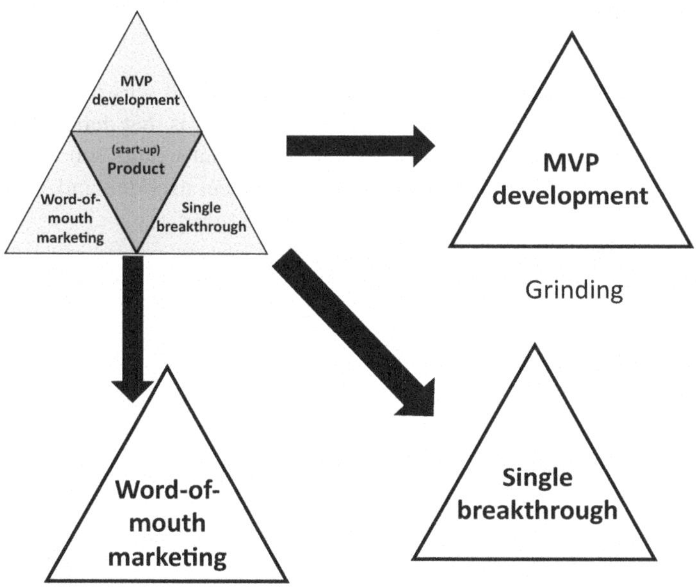

Product (start-up stage)

The general characteristics of start-ups' product are "grinding, small, and focused".

"Grinding" means iterative grinding of MVP product development.

"Small" means that word-of-mouth marketing in a small scale.

"Focused" means focusing on a a single-point breakthrough.

MVP development

The basic idea of MVP development is to build a workable product prototype in the fastest, most concise way. The prototype expresses the expected function of your product, and can be refined through iterations.

MVP development is important for start-ups to achieve a single breakthrough, to capture users' key demands, to form a flat organizational structure, and to find a direction in a chaotic market.

Word-of-mouth marketing

There are three effects of word-of-mouth marketing on start-ups:

First, to save marketing costs;

Second, to improve marketing efficiency;

Third, to verify the match between products and markets.

Word of mouth marketing is very important for start-ups to achieve a single breakthrough of products, to capture users' key demand, to help enterprises to establish a flat organization and to make start-ups better positioned in the chaotic market.

Single breakthrough

Entrepreneurs can ask themselves a few "one" questions:

If you can only choose one user, who is that person and why?

If you can only satisfy one demand of your users, what is that demand and why?

If you had only one chance to convince the user, what would you do and why?

If a product can only have one feature in order to meet user demand, what is that feature and why?

4.1.1.4 Market: The Goal of Start-Ups

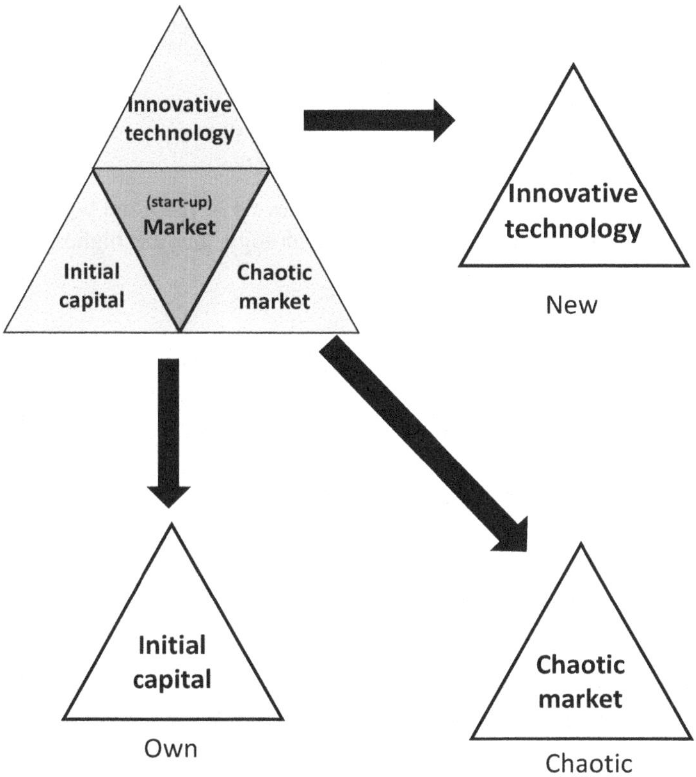

Market

(start-up stage).

The general characteristics of start-ups' market are "new, own, and chaotic".

"New" means that technology needs to be new and innovative.

"Own" means that founders should invest their own money.

"Chaotic" means that the direction in a chaotic market is unclear.

Innovative technology

Technology can be divided into four types according to its innovation level and application level.

(1) Conventional application of mature technology.
(2) Innovative application of mature technology.
(3) Conventional application of innovative technology.
(4) Innovative application of innovative technology.

The four types of technology have different levels of risks and benefits, of which the innovative application of innovative technology has the highest risk but the greatest potential.

Initial capital

The initial capital may come from both inside and outside of the founding team.

Capital from the founding team includes both personal savings and personal borrowings. Capital from other outside sources includes venture capital and government funds.

To gain trust from outside capital, the founding team must invest a fair amount of its own money.

Chaotic market

To break the chaotic market and find orders in it is an important way for start-ups to "achieve 1 from 0".

For firms in start-up stage, the chaotic market is of great significance for them to acquire innovative technologies, capture users' demands, build flat organizations and achieve single breakthrough of products.

4.2 12 Key Points for Start-Up Stage

Market

Innovative technology: analyze how start-ups can capture the market trend

Initial capital: analyze how start-ups can better leverage their own capital

Chaotic market: analyze how start-ups deal with the market of high uncertainty and discontinuity, and find a direction in such a chaotic market

Product

MVP development: focus on the development of MVPs and iterate products quickly

Word-of-mouth marketing: validate demand at low cost and in a quick way through word-of-mouth marketing

Single breakthrough: Concentrate all your efforts to achieve a single breakthrough

【Usage of the tool】

Think about users, organization, product, and market in start-up stage from the perspective of the 12 key points. Use "Co-evolution strategy canvas for start-up stage" (next page) to do deep analysis.

	People	Issues
External	Users Angel user Key demand Existing competitor	Market Innovative technology Initial capital Chaotic market
Internal	Organization Founder Founding team Flat organization	Product MVP development Word-of-mouth marketing Single breakthrough

Users

Angel user: understand the features of angel users deeply

Key demand: dig into the key demands angel users

Existing competor: analyze what demands are unsatisfied by existing competing products and launch products that are distinctive from the those competitors.

Organization

Founder: analyze founders' features and their advantages/ disadvantages as a founder

Founding team: analyze individual characteristics of each team member and the complementarity of the whole team

Flat organization: analyze how the flat organization can achieve light operations and high efficiency

4.2.1 Co-evolution Strategy Canvas for Start-Up Stage

Angel user	**Founder**	**MVP development**	**Innovative technology**
Key demand	**Founding team**	**Word-of-mouth marketing**	**Initial capital**
Existing competitor	**Flat organization**	**Single breakthrough**	**Chaotic market**

4.2.2 *Case Analysis: Alibaba*

Angel user	Founder	MVP development	Innovative technology
- In October 1999, the number of registered users of Chinese and English websites exceeded 20,000. - In December 2001, it's B2B business had 1 million members. - From Hope Translation to the Chinese yellow pages, Jack Ma and his team had accumulated experience to understand users' key demands.	- We're going to do a great thing, our B2B is going to revolutionize Internet services. Don't need to be panic, you have more than a dozen people work together. - 35 years old, 3 failed experiences as an entrepreneur, being called "liar" - Strategic vision: the Internet; the accession to the WTO; the electronic commerce	- In 1999, Alibaba decided not to advertise for 6 months but focused on making the website better. - In October 2000, Alibaba launched "China supplier" products: displayed products, collected information, and provided knowledge guidance for them. - In 2001, cxt 1688.com: pre-negotiation authentication, RMB 2,300 per year.	- Free (basic display) + fee (member value-added service, cxt 1688.com). Membership fee (RMB 40,000-80,000); Value-added services for golden products (millions RMB). - Internet + (cross-border) trade (innovative application of innovative technologies).
Key demand	**Founding team**	**Word-of-mouth marketing**	**Initial capital**
- SMEs with import and export demand can obtain order information. - Cxt 1688.com was launched to address 87% users' worry about credit problems. - "A firm must solve problems for the society in order to achieve sustainable growth."	- A team of 18 members who climbed the Great Wall and met in lakeside garden - Joseph Tsai gave up his one million dollar's annual salary to join Alibaba, with a salary of only 500 RMB per month.Team members complement each other in skills, 4 Os and 4 nationalities. - A culture of martial arts; Feng Qingyang.	- Post on various websites and BBS. In 2000, the lecture in German provided 1,500 seats but only three people came. - In September 2000, Alibaba organized the first West Lake to attract media attention. - The strategy in 2002 was to earn 1 RMB.	- The founding team contributed RMB 500,000; failed to receive external capital. - In October 1999, after rejecting 38 institutions' investment, Alibaba accepted Goldman Sach's investment of 5 million dollars - In January 2000, softbank plans to invest 30 million dollars and Alibaba accepted 20 million dollars.
Existing competitor	**Flat organization**	**Single breakthrough**	**Chaotic market**
- Offline trade (high advertising cost, low frequency, no training service, no daily interaction) - Take the advantage of West Lake to huddle together for warmth.	- Improved the ESOP system at the beginning of the business. - "Go to practice, practice outside th e bones skin." - In early stage, Alibaba invited many many MBA and international elites, but later it began to develop talents internally.	- In early 2000, after receiving the money, Alibaba relocated the office and expanded rapidly, built the R&D Center in the Silicon Valley, set up branches in Japan, South Korea and Taiwan. - After the burst of Internet bubble, it went "back to China" and "back to Hangzhou"	- 1999 is the first year of the Chinese Internet. Alibaba was finding orders in chaos.

Co-evolution strategy canvas for start-up stage
(Case Analysis: Alibaba, 1999-2003)

Chapter 5
Growing-Up

Prospering while singing all the way Growing up, just like the youth of a person, is full of hope and dreams.
As a cultivator, one must believe in the vision, and focus on the products.

J. Y. Lu, *Co-evolution Strategy Canvas*,
https://doi.org/10.1007/978-981-15-5988-4_5

5.1 4 Questions for Growing-Up

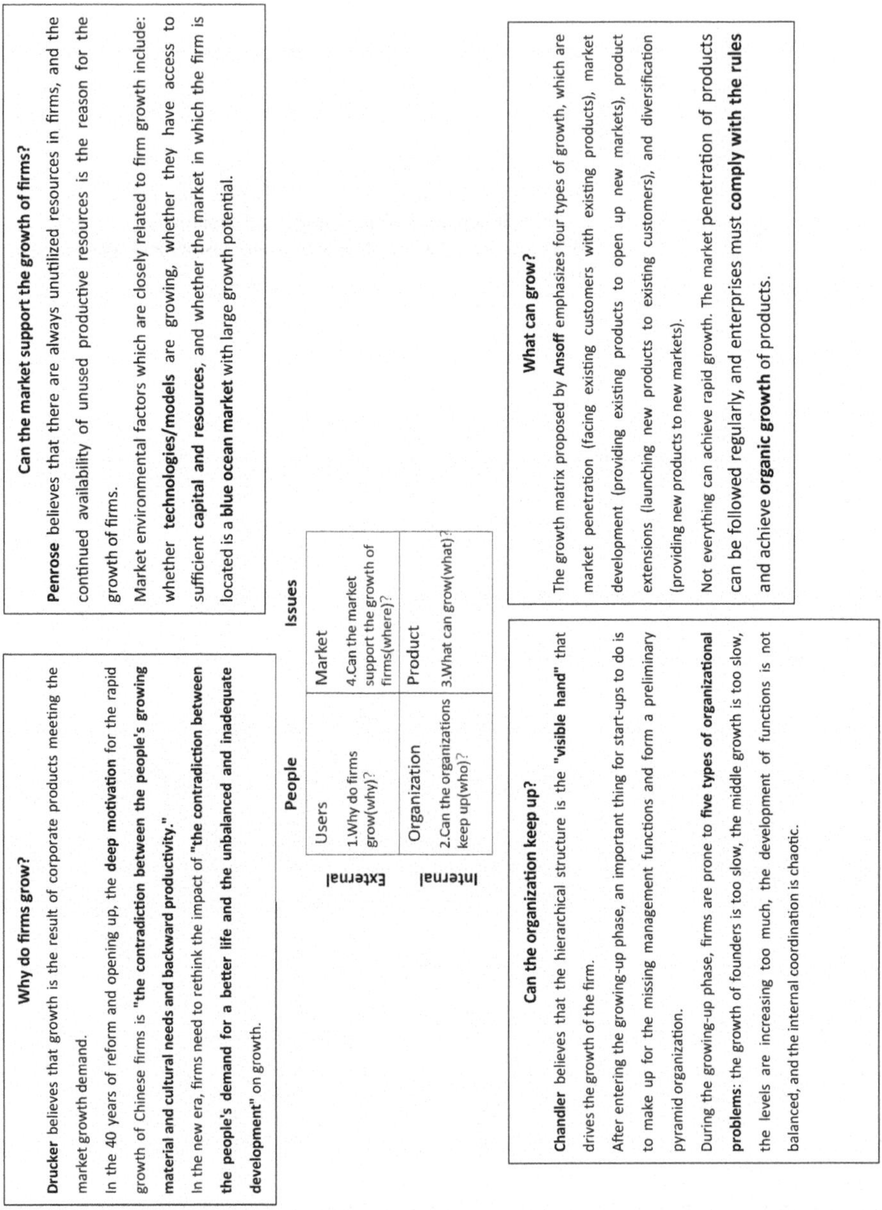

5.1.1 *4 Questions for Growing-Up Tools*

Usage of the tools

Growth analysis: Answer the basic questions about users, organization, product and market of the growing-up stage.

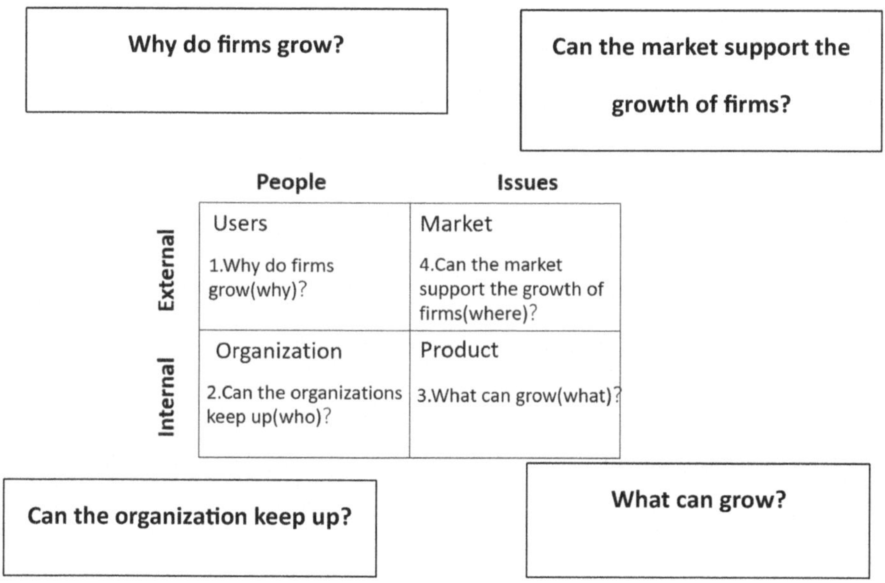

5.1.1.1 Users: The Reasons of Growing-Up

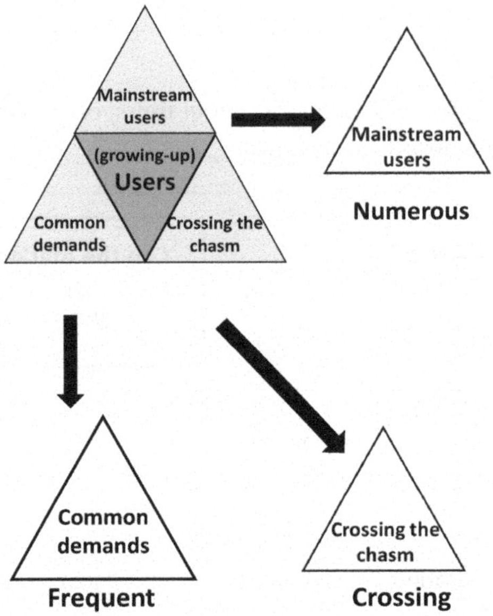

Users (growing-up stage)

The overall characteristics of users in the growing-up stage are "numerous, frequent and crossing."

"Many" means that there are a large number of public users.

"Frequent" means that the common demands are daily.

"Crossing" means that the demand chasm is difficult to cross.

Mainstream users

When firms enter the growing-up stage, the first problem to be faced is the change of users, that is, the transition of user groups from angel users to mainstream users.

The mass users are quite different from the angel users in terms of physiological, psychological and social characteristics.

Many firms "died" on the road to growth because they could not get mainstream users.

Common demands

The common demands are demands that a large number of users have in common, which are opposed to the differentiated demands of few individual users.

The universality of demands is influenced by two factors: the number of users in the group and the similarity of user demands.

The success of WeChat payment is due to the large number of WeChat users and the fact that the payment scenario involves many aspects of life.

Crossing the chasm

The key to crossing the chasm is to target a highly specific market segment in the mainstream market, pooling all forces and then conquering that segment. Subsequently, this market segment was taken as a position to gradually expand the results to the entire mainstream market.

Tencent has always wanted to develop its payment business, but Tenpay, which was previously cut from e-commerce, is always tepid until the WeChat red envelope appears. It gradually increases the user's tie-in rate, expands the offline payment scenario, and eventually becomes the main mobile payment mean.

5.1.1.2 Organization: The Bottleneck of Growing-Up

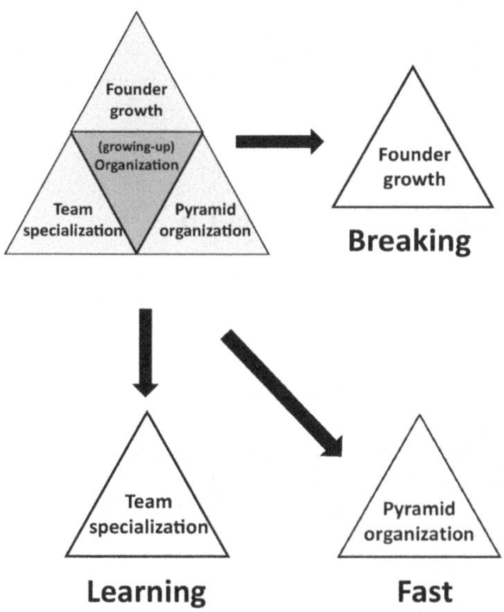

Organization (growing-up stage)

The overall characteristics of the organization in the growing-up stage are "breaking, learning and fast."

"Breaking" means that the founders should pursue self-breakthrough.

"Learning" means that the team should become more specialized in learning.

"Fast" means that the pyramid organization aims at fast speed.

Founder growth

As a popular saying in the start-up community goes, "the cognitive boundary of the founder is the development boundary of the start-ups."

The growth of founders can greatly stimulate the growth of the team, help the firm to capture the general needs, enable the firm to achieve efficient marketing, and attract important capital resources investment for the firm.

Team specialization

The formation of a start-up team can be basically divided into three modes: relationship-driven, factor-driven, and value-driven.

No matter which mode it is, a team's specialized division of labor is critical to the rapid development of a start-up firm.

Team specialization can be considered in two dimensions: team composition and member development. It is particularly divided into four modes: re-dividing, learning while working, introducing new members and training future stars.

Pyramid organization

There are usually two types of relationships between management growth and business growth. The first is "first business, then management", and the second is "first management, then business".

Start-ups usually adopt a "first business, then management" mode, but if management fails to keep up, business development will be constrained.

Many start-ups died early on the road to growth because their management couldn't keep up.

5.1.1.3 Product: The Foundation of Growing-Up

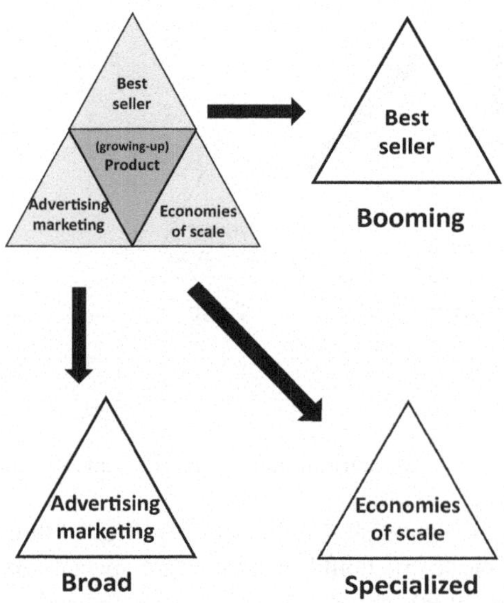

Product (growing-up stage)

The overall characteristics of the product in the growing-up stage are "booming, broad and specialized."

"Booming" means that product development should create best sellers.
"Broad" means that advertising marketing should be widely publicized.
"Specialized" means that the business model should be professional and focused.

Hugely popular product

The theory based on the logic of the hugely popular product is the "winner-take-all" theory, which holds that "the industry leader can gain an ultrahigh market share".

Jun Lei once said: "In today's Internet era, if you want to succeed, you must make hugely popular products, and have products and strategies that will detonate the market. Even if you heat the warm water to 99 °C, it is still useless. It must be 100 °C."

Advertising marketing

Entering the growing-up stage, firms can no longer rely on word-of-mouth marketing as in the start-up stage, but need to do some advertisement marketing.

The marketing 1.0 era is a product-centric era, the marketing 2.0 era is a relationship-centric era, and the marketing 3.0 era is a value-driven era.

Advertisement marketing in the new era should also be value-driven.

Economies of scale

The economies of scale are the source of competitive advantage that firms dream of during the growing-up stage.

Economies of scale come mainly from the amortization of fixed costs. With the rapid growth of business, the cost of unit business is rapidly decreasing.

Only by being professional and focused on the product can the firm achieve economies of scale.

5.1.1.4 Market: The Space of Growing-Up

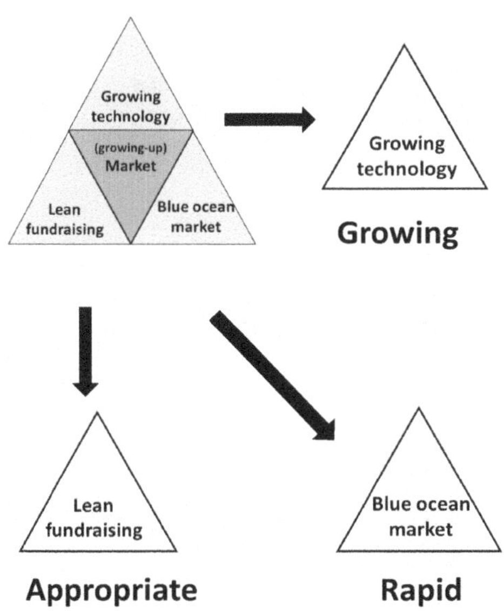

Market (growing-up stage)

The overall characteristics of the market in the growing-up stage are "continuous, appropriate and rapid."

"Continuous" means that technology growth should continue to be stable.

"Appropriate" means that external financing is just right.

Growing technology

The technical considerations of firms in the growing-up stage are mainly the growth and practicality of technology.

In fact, there is often a huge "expectation trap" between novelty technology and growth technology.

Successfully crossing the "expectation trap" of technology is another "chasm" that growing-up firms need to cross.

"Rapid" means that market space should expand rapidly.

Lean fundraising

The lean fundraising model is to sell "the most appropriate" shares of the firms in stages and in batches.

It includes two main points: setting stage goals and taking fast and small steps.

Fundraising should have long-term as well as short-term goals. Taking small steps means that fundraising can not be achieved at once; going fast means that designing a time window for fundraising.

Blue ocean market

Going out of the chaotic market and opening up the blue ocean market has opened up a vast world for the rapid growth of firms in growing-up stage.

To explore the blue ocean market, firms need to:

Go beyond the existing needs;

Overcome organizational barriers;

Innovate product value;

Rebuild market boundaries.

5.2 12 Key Points of the Focused Growing-Up Stage

Users

Mainstream users: understand the difference between mainstream users and angel users.

Common demands: think about the shift path from key demands to common demands.

Crossing the chasm: crossing the chasm from angel users to mainstream users, and from key demands to ordinary demands.

Market

Growing technology: only by using growing technology can the firm adapt to market trends.

Lean fundraising: fundraising is not about more or quicker, but about lean: at the right time, getting the right money, doing the right thing.

Blue ocean market: only by avoiding pointless competition can the firm grow rapidly.

【Usage of the tool】

Think about users, organization, product, and market in growing-up stage form the perspective of the 12 key points.

Use "strategy canvas for the focused growing-up stage"(next page) to do deep analysis.

	People	Issues
External	Users Mainstream users Common demands Crossing the chasm	Market Growing technology Lean fundraising Blue ocean market
Internal	Organization Founder growth Team specialization Pyramid organization	Product Best seller Advertising marketing Economies of scale

Organization

Founder growth: obstacles, paths, and abilities in the process of the founder's self-growth.

Team specialization: whether and how the start-up team can grow quickly through learning.

Pyramid organization: how to establish a suitable organizational structure in the process of growth, and use organizational growth to support business growth.

Product

Best seller: create hugely popular product and establish the foundation of growth.

Advertising marketing: let products be widely known through advertisement.

Economies of scale: reduce the cost of per unit of product through economies of scale.

5.2.1 Co-evolution Strategy Canvas for the Focused Growing-Up Stage

Mainstream users	Founder growth	Best seller	Growing technology
Common demands	Team specialization	Advertising marketing	Lean fundraising
Crossing the chasm	Pyramid organization	Economies of scale	Blue ocean market

5.2.2 *Case Analysis: Alibaba*

Mainstream users	**Founder growth**	**Best seller**	**Growing technology**
- From small and medium-sized trading firms to individual consumers, from B2B to B2C, C2C	- It is proposed that Alibaba's mission is "to make sure there isn't difficult business in the world" - In the process from losing of expansion to contraction, experiencing the cognitive upgrade from inductive to deductive thinking, and then to rational intuition. - The interaction with important investors accelerates the growth of the firm.	- In March 2002, B2B was fully charged. In 2003, it earned a daily income of 1 million yuan. In 2004, it earned a daily profit of 1 million yuan. In 2005, it paid a daily tax of 1 million yuan. - Taobao has no profit pressure and it concentrates on refining products. Free charge + Alipay makes Taobao an explosive.	- The popularity of Internet and PC - Platform products such as Taobao and Alipay have the characteristics of high economies of scale and low marginal cost.
Common demands	**Team specialization**	**Advertising marketing**	**Lean fundraising**
- The trend ofi ncreased consumer demand has accelerated e-commerce. - In 2004, Taobao had 4.5 million users.	- Special team, secret development - Full mobilization: point and return - From guerrillas to regular army - From believing in new members to training internal future stars (learning while working)	- The countryside encircles the city (small and medium-sized websites, "The World Without Thieves") - Ready to launch 100 million ads, be preempted by eBay, froze the market budget for 7 months, "let the opponents first educate the market" - Defeating the biggest competitor is the best advertisement	- In July 2003, Sun Zhengyi **convinced** Ma Yun to accept an investment of 82 million US dollars. - In 2005, Yahoo invested Alibaba in a billion dollars (a huge amount of money allowed Ali to make a series of mistakes: entering the search field, cultural integration failed)
Crossing the chasm	**Pyramid organization**	**Economies of scale**	**Blue ocean market**
- In 2003, eBay invested in eachnet. - Users' complaints about eBay: charging mode and too high shipping costs. - Free beats fee - The payment system is not in line. Early trials of Alipay appeared in 2003. - Bearing the risks of both users and traders.	- SARS has reinforced the company's employees, and the company's culture has been strengthened. - Inverted culture (see differences); martial arts culture (interesting company, diluting the hierarchical concept, replacing "power" with "status", Feng Qingyang)	- In April 2003, preparing C2C project, declaring that it would be free of charge and would not be profitable for three years. - In 2005, an additional 1 billion investment was made and promised to continue free for 3 years. - In 2005, Alipay was free, and users suddenly increased.	- Concept Leading: hosting the Network Business Conference, the age of online business - Turning from small and medium-sized firms to individual consumers; planning ahead for future competitions - Alipay solved the trust and risk issues in the transaction

Co-evolution strategy canvas for the focused growing-up stage

(Case Analysis: Alibaba, 2004-2006)

Chapter 6
Expansion

Yellow Sand Wears the Gold Armor

Expansion, just like the prime of man's life, is full of dignity and responsibility.

As a spreader, one must resist the lure, and keep the mission in mind deeply.

J. Y. Lu, *Co-evolution Strategy Canvas*,
https://doi.org/10.1007/978-981-15-5988-4_6

Why do firms expand?

Firms have acquired some users in the start-up and growing-up stages and have met their specific demands.
However, after serving the user for a period of time, firms will find some unmet demands of users. **Meeting the unmet needs of users** is an important reason for business expansion.

Whether the market support the expand of firms?

Diversified market conditions can be considered from two dimensions: the availability of technology and resources (feasibility) and the competition and cooperation relationship of the market (necessity).
When the possibility of obtaining technology and resources from the market is high, and the market's main competition and cooperation relationship is dominated by competition, the feasibility and necessity of firm's diversification is high.

	People	**Issues**
External	Users 1.Why do firms expand(why)?	Market 4.Whether the market support the expand of firms(where)?
Internal	Organization 2.Can the organization hold on(who)?	Product 3.Which direction will the firm expand for(what)?

Can the organization hold on?

There are three main mechanisms for maintaining organizational operations: **coordination, supervision, and standardization.**
The main mechanism in the start-up stage is coordination, and the monitoring mechanism is introduced during the growing-up phase. When the scale of the firm grows further, it is not enough to rely solely on coordination and supervision. **Work efficiency needs to be improved by standardizing** work inputs (beforehand), workflow (in-process), and work output (afterwards).

Which direction will the firm expand for?

According to the analysis of the two dimensions of "whether it have been done" and "whether it should be done", the direction of diversification can be divided into four categories: what should be done and have been done, what should be done but have not been done, what should not be done but have been done, and what should not be done and have not been done. The direction of expansion should be based on "what should be done but have not been done" and avoid expanding in the direction of "what should not be done and have not been done".
As for what is "what should be done", it can be considered from the future growth of the business and the importance to the current financial.

6.1 4 Questions for Expansion

6.1.1 4 Questions for Expansion Tools

Usage of the tool

Expansion analysis: Answer the basic questions about users, organization, product and market of the expansion stage.

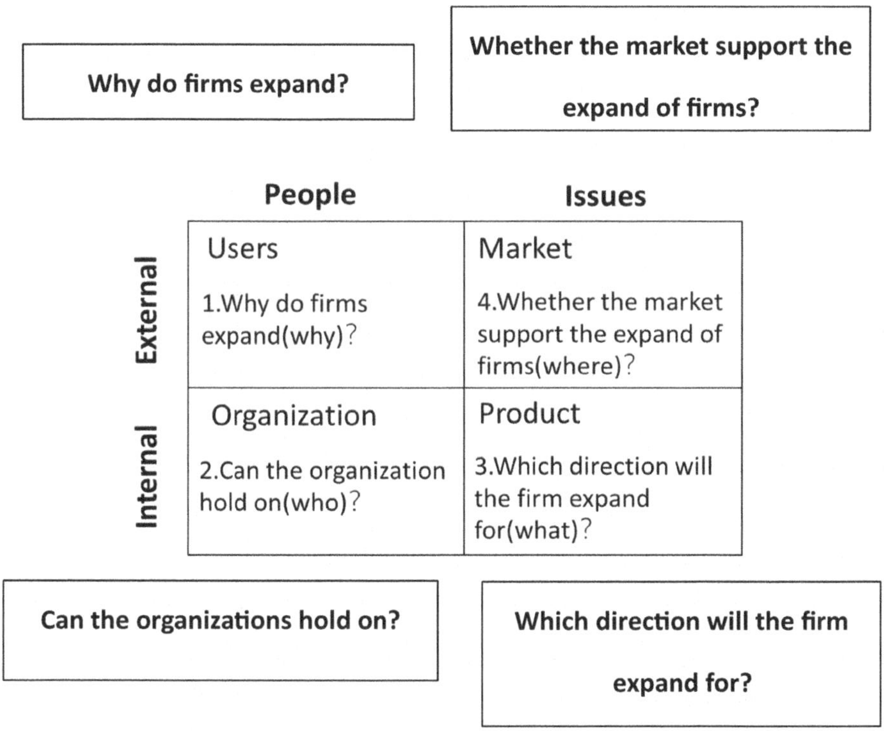

6.1.1.1 Users: The Motivation for Expansion

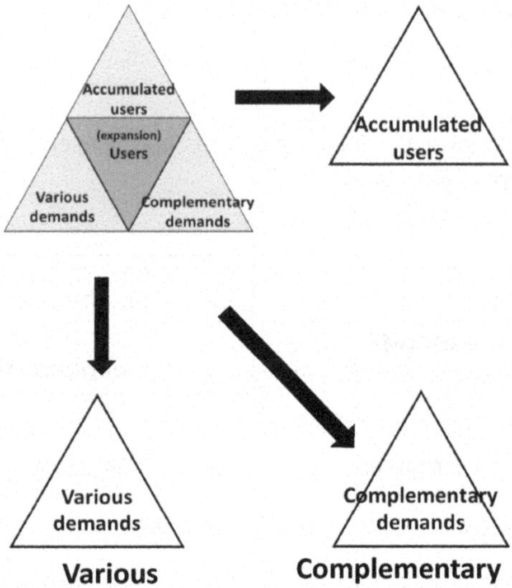

Users (expansion stage)

The overall characteristics of users in the expansion stage are "preservative, many and complementary."

"Preservative" means the concept of accumulated users.

"Various" means that various demands induce expansion.

"Complementary" means the importance of complementary demands.

Accumulated users

As data and Internet technologies mature, more and more firms are beginning to value the lifetime value of their users.

There are two main factors that affect the user's lifetime value. One is the length of time that the user has a transaction relationship with the firm, and the other is the breadth of the transaction relationship.

Various demands

In 1985, Michael Porter proposed the concept of "value chain". For more than 30 years, readers have focused on the "value chain of firms" but neglected the "value chain of buyers".

"Enter users' demand chain" is an important strategy of Xiaomi.

If the user's various demands are linked to the firm's product structure, the firm can gradually meet the user's relevant various demands.

Complementary demands

Complementary demands mean that two or more requirements are often generated in the same scenario. When firms diversify around the same user group's demands in the same scenario, the demands are the most complementary.

For example, when a user travels, there may be demands for transportation, accommodation and shopping.

6.1.1.2 Organization: The Vitality of Expansion

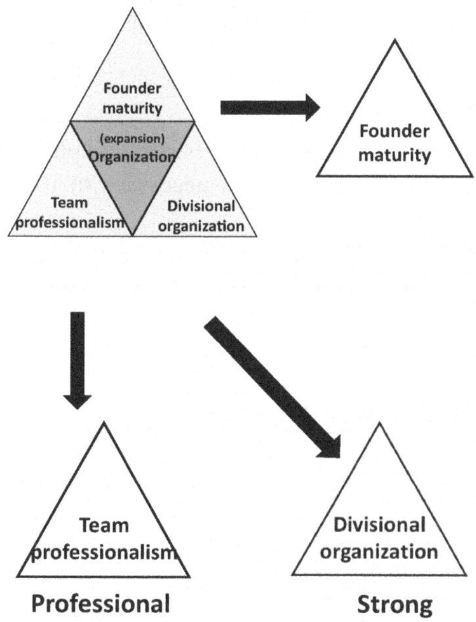

Founder maturity

The maturity of the founders mainly depends on two aspects, one is the grasp of external opportunities, and the other is the handling of internal management.

When the firm develops to the expansion/maturity stage, the founders usually adopt the "middle way" development strategy and the "grayscale" management method. They find the direction of business development by balancing the gap between conservation and risk.

Organization (expansion stage)

The overall characteristics of the organization in the expansion stage are "stable, professional and strong."

"Stable" means that the founders have become mature and steady.

"Professional" means that the team enters the professional stage.

"Strong" means that the organization must have a strong foundation.

Divisional organization

The key principle of the design of the divisional department system is: using "concentration policy, decentralized management" in the vertical relationship, and using "independent accounting, equivalent exchange" in the horizontal relationship.

The key to the success of the divisional department system is the proper division of organizational authority and the appropriate balance of centralization and decentralization.

The divisional department system is the basic organizational structure for diversified firms, and the amoeba organization is also changed from the divisional department system.

Team professionalism

When the firm develops to a certain stage, it is not enough to lead its development by the growth of the founding team. It is necessary to introduce a professional executive team.

The relationship between professional executives and founders should be seen in terms of both competence and vision. The best way to cooperate is to complement each other's abilities and share the same vision.

6.1.1.3 Product: The Ability of Expansion

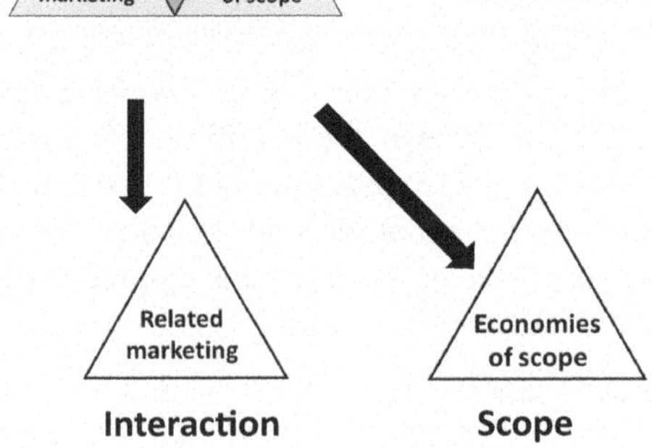

Related products

The logic behind the related products is "round income."

Xiaomi uses the cost-effective products to meet the core needs of users (mobile phones), form a traffic portal, and then profit by meeting the additional needs of users (mobile phones derivatives). With the generation of user upgrade requirements (intelligent hardware), a further traffic entry is formed, which in turn meets the user's associated demands (intelligent hardware consumables).

Product (expansion stage)

The overall characteristics of the product in the expansion stage are "correlation, interaction and apportion."

"Correlation" emphasizes the relevance among products.

"Interaction" emphasizes the interactivity of marketing.

"Apportion" emphasizes that the mode can dilute costs.

Economies of scope

Users, organization, products, and market factors all bring economies of scope.

Users are willing to pay a higher price for products that are more efficient to integrate.

Organization management experience and employee production experience can save costs.

The results of product development techniques can be used to produce a variety of products.

Market partnerships, capital advantages, etc. can support the sale of a variety of products.

Related marketing

As the types of firm products increase, it is necessary to establish links between different products in the minds of users. By using related marketing, the products of the firm are uniformly displayed through various channels, and the overall concept of the multi-products of the firm is formed in the mind of the users.

Haier's smart home solution involves multiple life scenes in different physical spaces in the living room, kitchen, bathroom and bedroom. It is related marketing around the family scene.

6.1.1.4 Market: The Potential of Expansion

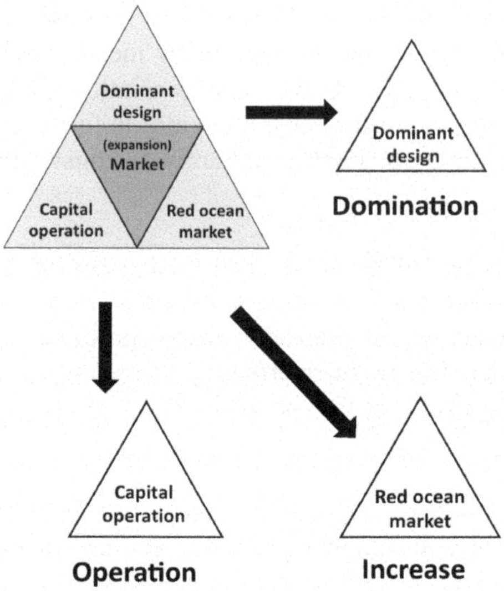

Market (expansion stage)

The overall characteristics of the market in the expansion stage are "domination, operation and increase."

"Domination" means the leading position of dominant design.

"Operation" means the operation of the capital market.

"Increase" means the increasing potential of market space.

Dominant design

When the industry develops to a certain stage, the dominant design will emerge. Dominant design is a widely accepted technology that interacts with technological choices and market choices.

Being the industry-leading design maker can help firms achieve a relative monopoly in the red sea competition, enabling firms to build related products around the dominant design, and to organize the divisional department system around the leading design, and to meet the complementary demands of users.

Capital operation

In the expansion phase, firms acquire external organizations, technologies, products, and users by investment, mergers and acquisitions. They transform these external elements into organizational, technical, product, and user elements within the organization through transformation and absorption.

Market

Dominant design: The emergence of dominant design reduces technical uncertainty and improves the economics of the technology.

Capital operation: Capital operation is a necessary market means for firm expansion.

Red ocean market: With the expansion of major firms, market competition is becoming increasingly fierce.

Product

Related products: Developing related products can better meet the complementary demands of users.

Related marketing: The related products have their own flow, and the accumulated user acceptance barrier is low.

Economies of scope: Related products can dilute relevant cost of R&D, marketing, etc., to achieve economies of scope.

【Usage of the tool】

Think about users, organization, product, and market in expansion stage form the perspective of the 12 key points.

Use "strategy canvas for the amplifying expansion stage"(next page) to do deep analysis.

	People	Issues
External	Users Accumulated users Various demands Complementary demands	Market Dominant design Capital operation Red ocean market
Internal	Organization Founders maturity Team professionalism Divisional organization	Product Related products Related marketing Economies of scope

Users

Accumulated users: Instead of developing new users, it's better to develop lifetime value of accumulated users.

Various demands: Explore the diverse needs of accumulated users and find new growth points.

Complementary demands: Meeting the complementary demands of accumulated users can do more with less.

Organization

Founders maturity: The founders have experienced the process of starting a business and growing up.

Team professionalism: If the start-up team can't keep up with the development of the firm, it needs to introduce a professional executive team.

Divisional organization: As the business diversifies, the divisional department structure is gradually formed.

Capital operation can help firms rapidly expand the number of accumulated users, gain a dominant design position in the market, accelerate the professionalization of corporate teams, and enjoy the benefits of economies of scope.

Red ocean market

The degree of competition in the market depends on the size of the market space and the number of competitors in the market.

If the users in a market increase rapidly, then the potential space in this market is relatively large. If the number of firms in a market increases rapidly, competition among firms will be fierce even in a large market space.

6.2 12 Key Points of the Amplifying Expansion Stage

6.2.1 Co-evolution Strategy Canvas for the Amplifying Expansion Stage

Accumulated users	Founder maturity	Related products	Dominant design
Various demands	Team professionalism	Related marketing	Capital operation
Complementary demands	Divisional organization	Economies of scope	Red ocean market

6.2.2 *Case Analysis: Alibaba*

Accumulated users	Founder maturity	Related products	Dominant design
- In June 2007, Ali had 24.6 million registered users, 255,000 paid members, an increase of 83% in 2005 and a 55% increase in 2006. Ali's accumulated users drive its listing and B2C. - The accumulated users of Taobao promoted the arrival of the C2B era.	- Grasping the timing of the listing. - Judging the big trend. For example, the judgment that a third-party payment enterprise must be 100% domestic. - Dismantling Alipay's VIE structure without the agreement of the board of directors and shareholders. - Establish a balance between business growth and standard management.	- Alibaba, Taobao, Alipay, Alisoft, Yahoo, Aliyun, Wanwang. - When the business grows in a large amount, the business must be developed in a controlled manner. - 2013, arranged logistics, CAINIAO. - 2013, developed Yu E'bao.	- "You don't know technology, but you need to understand how to judge technology." - CAINIAO has become the dominant design in the logistics industry. - Taobao becomes the dominant design of the C2C industry. - Tmall becomes the dominant design of the B2C industry.
Various demands	**Team professionalism**	**Related marketing**	**Capital operation**
- "Double Eleven" discovers, creates, pulls, and fulfills demands between consumers and merchants. - Taobao, Tmall,etao, Juhuasuan, koubei.	- "Because I don't know technology, our company's technology is the best." - In 2010, the partner system, "The majority of directors on the board of directors are nominated by partners". - Integrity and anti-corruption in 2011, CEO Wei Zhe resigned.	- The countryside encircles the city (small and medium-sized websites, "The World Without Thieves"). - Ready to launch 100 million ads, be preempted by eBay, froze the market budget for 7 months, "let the opponents first educate the market".	- In November 2007, Ali B2B listed in Hong Kong, listed before the financial crisis, raised a lot of money. - In 2010, Alipay was capitalized and the VIE structure was demolished.
Complementary demands	**Divisional organization**	**Economies of scope**	**Red ocean market**
- Transaction flow, capital flow, data flow, information flow, logistics. - "Big Taobao Strategy" meets the demand for complementarity. - Large supply platform reduces the diversification demands of small firms.	- In 2011, Taobao was split into three parts (Taobao Mall, etao, Taobao); Ali Group was split into seven parts (Taobao, Yitao, Tmall, Juhuasuan, International Business, Small Business, Aliyun). - In 2013, 7 was split into 25.	- In 2009, created Double 11 Festival. - Added options for Tmall, Poly cost, and Amoy on the shopping page. - Increase rookie logistics options. - Promote Laiwang in the Ali user group.	- Faced with the challenges of various vertical e-commerce from Jingdong, Dangdang, Amazon, Suning, and the challenges of e-commerce in NetEase Koala and Vipshop, the competition in e-commerce is increasingly fierce.

Co-evolution strategy canvas for the amplifying expansion stage

(Case Analysis: Alibaba, 2007-2013)

Chapter 7
Transformation

Ten thousand saplings shoot up beyond the withered tree
Transformation, just like the rebirth of a person, is a combination of suffering and glory. As a change-maker, one must review the situation, and keep moving forward.

J. Y. Lu, *Co-evolution Strategy Canvas*,
https://doi.org/10.1007/978-981-15-5988-4_7

7.1 4 Questions for Transformation

Why do firms transform?

Any business will inevitably enter the recession stage. Some firms are able to prosper, not because they are "**built to last**", but because they will transform at the right time.

The prerequisite for a successful transformation is to understand **the "real" and "potential" demands** of users. For example, Apple redefined the phone by treating the phone as a mobile computing center rather than a communication device.

How is the market environment of transformation?

Firms do not exist in isolation, and the market environment of firms can be expressed by "**value network".** Value network is the network formed by firms in the process of creating, transmitting and acquiring value. The stakeholders in this value network are not only the firms themselves, but also their **suppliers, users, competitors, and complementors**.

Transformation of firms should **be coordinated with the value network**. This is also the reason why many firms reshape the business ecosystem while transforming.

	People	**Issues**
External	Users 1. Why do firms transform? (why)?	Market 4.How is the market environment of transformation(where)?
Internal	Organization 2.Can the organization transform(who)?	Product 3.What is the direction of transformation(what)?

Can the organization transform?

Organizational inertia is a force that solidifies in the organization to maintain or preserve the patterns and habits of existing work activities. It shows that the internal vitality and innovation ability of the organization is declining, and the members of the organization lack a sense of ownership.

In the transformation stage, the urgency of organizational inertia and strategic change is often at a high level. Organizations need change, but have no motivation for change.

What is the direction of transformation?

There are two basic directions for transformation: **technological innovation** and **business model innovation**.

Technological innovation is the application of developing new technologies or innovating existing technologies. Business model innovation is the innovation of the structure and process of creating, delivering and acquiring value. The transformation of many firms is a combination of technological innovation and model innovation.

7.1.1 4 *Questions for Transformation Tools*

Usage of the tool

Transformation analysis: answer the basic questions about users, organization, product and market of the transformation stage.

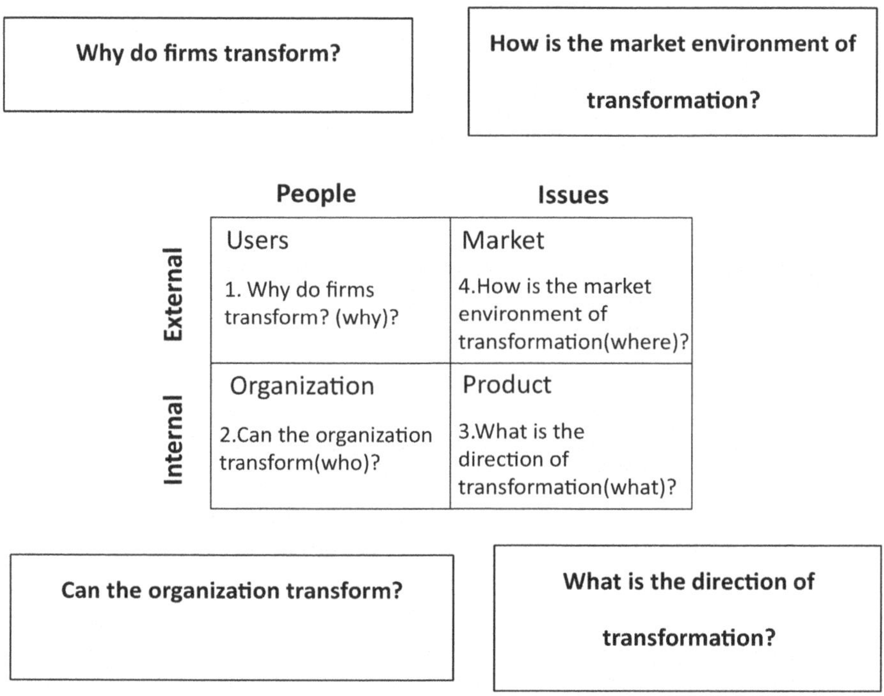

7.1.1.1 Users: The Reasons of Transformation

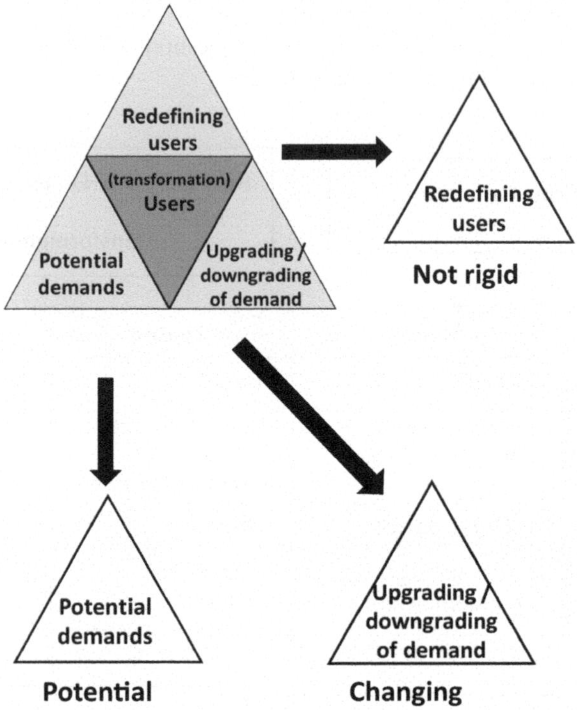

Users (transformation stage)

The overall characteristics of users in the transformation stage are "not rigid, potential and changing."

"Not rigid" emphasizes redefining users rather than sticking to old perceptions.

"Potential" emphasizes the importance of tapping potential needs.

"Changing" means the constant change of ups and downs of the demand.

Redefining users

The most important thing in the transformation phase is to redefining users.

After experiencing start-up, growing-up, expansion and other stages, firms are often very familiar with existing users, but may also be "locked" by users, while ignoring the "non-user" group.

Transforming firms need to redefine existing users and re-examine non-users' demands.

Upgrading/downgrading of demand

The mismatch between supply and demand is the fundamental source of business opportunities. In many cases, the mismatch is not the lack of total supply or demand, but the mismatch of structure.

On the one hand, the matching can be achieved through downgrades in demand or upgrades in supply (e.g. smartphones replace traditional phones). On the other hand, it can be matched by upgrades in demand (e.g. creating a fashion to wear a diamond in marriage) or a downgrade of the supply (e.g. Pinduoduo).

Potential demands

The actual demand is the user's demand in case that the users have purchasing power and the firms have the product capability. While the potential demand is the user's demand in case that the users have purchasing power but the firms have no product capability.

Focusing on actual users and demands, it is hard to balance low-cost and differentiated strategies. However, if you focus on the potential demands of potential users, it is possible to achieve both.

7.1.1.2 Organization: The Key of Transformation

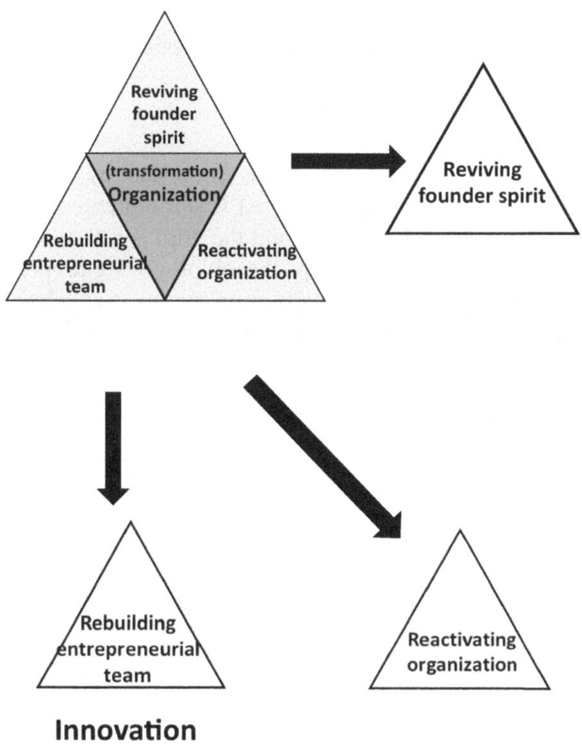

Organization (transformation stage)

The overall characteristics of the organization in the transformation stage are "revival, innovation, entropy".
"Revival" emphasizes the re-emphasis on the spirit of the founders.
"Innovation" emphasizes team innovation and entrepreneurship.
"Entropy" emphasizes the removal of the organization's inertia.

Regaining founder spirit

In the start-up stage, the spirit of the founders is good because of the positive development of the firm.
In the growing-up stage, with the rapid growth of the firm, the spirit of the founders began to be ruined by the tedious management work.
In the expansion stage, the spirit of the founders has been reduced to a lower level.
In the transformation stage, how to regain the spirit of the founders is the primary task of the founders.

Reactivating organization

The concept of "dissipative structure" comes from the second law of thermodynamics. In the "dissipative structure", the system continuously generates energy exchange with the outside world, generate "negative entropy" and maintain the continuous operation of the system.
Ren Zhengfei has very clearly proposed to establish a "dissipative structure" within Huawei. Ren said that Huawei must dissipate the surplus capacity generated in management. This is like exercising every day, dissipating excess energy in the body and turning it into muscle.

Rebuilding entrepreneurial team

"Rebuilding entrepreneurial employees" was proposed by Haier CEO Ruimin Zhang. It is divided into three aspects: the first is self-entrepreneurship, the second is online and on-the-job entrepreneurship, and the third is self-evolving mechanism. Similar to the entrepreneurial leadership, the employee's entrepreneurial spirit is relatively high in the stage of start-up and growing-up, and relatively low in the stage of expansion and decline. Stimulating the employee's entrepreneurial spirit is a key step in the transformation stage of the firm.

7.1.1.3 Product: The Footstone of Transformation

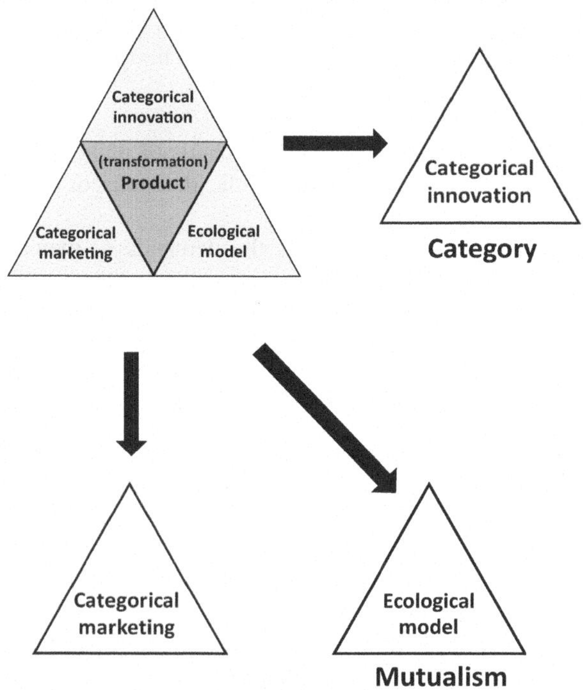

Product (transformation stage)

The overall characteristics of the product in the transformation stage are "category, mind and togetherness'.
"Category" emphasizes the ability of products to innovate.
"Mind" emphasizes that marketing must occupy the users' minds.
"Mutualism" emphasizes that business models must achieve a win–win situation.

Categorical Innovation

Product innovation in the start-up stage is "I have something that no one else has";
Product innovation in the growing-up stage is "I do what others have done better";
Product innovation in the expansion stage is "I make things that others have done well cheaper‵";
Product innovation in the transformation stage is "I make things that others have done cheap more special'.

Ecological model

The business model of firms in the transformation stage is a "body" business model (see the "point, line, surface and body" model above).

Apple started with the point of computer business and formed a computer business line by producing different types of computers. With the computer as the platform, Apple has created iTunes, the copyright sharing platform, and launched the iPod to create an Apple-centric surface. Immediately, through the launch of iPhone, iPad, Apple TV and other products, the Apple ecosystem body was formed.

Categorical marketing

In the start-up stage, the product meets the demands of niche users for "taste";
In the growing-up stage, the product meets the demands of the mass users for "quality";
In the expansion stage, the product meets the demands of mainstream users for "brands";
In the transformation stage, the product meets the demands of new users for "category".

7.1.1.4 Market: The Environment of Transformation

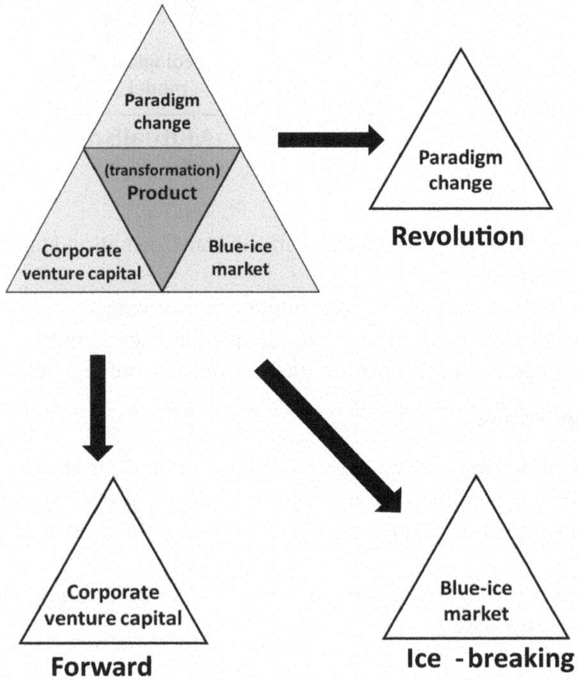

Market (transformation stage)

The overall characteristics of the product in the transformation stage are "revolution, forward and ice".
"Revolution" emphasizes the important and fundamental transformation of paradigm change.
"Forward" emphasizes that the corporate venture capital faces to the future.
"Ice" emphasizes that the blue-ice market has the potential to be explored.

Paradigm change

Scientific paradigm change refers to the transformation of science from one scientific paradigm to another. Similar to the transformation of the scientific paradigm, there are technological paradigm change, social paradigm change and business paradigm change.
The impact of technological/commercial paradigm change is relatively small, and the impact of scientific/social paradigm change is very large.

Corporate venture capital

Corporate venture capital has several important roles in corporate transformation. First, the firm meets the demands of new business users through new ventures. Second, investing in new ventures will help firms acquire new and innovative products. Third, startups are independent of the firm's own organizational structure and can take different incentives without affecting the firm's organization. Fourth, the firm can introduce external resources by setting up a venture capital institution.

Blue-ice market

The "Blue-ice Market" represents a new field that needs to be developed and has great potential for development. "Blue" refers to the huge development potential in this field. "Ice" refers to the field that requires a continuous investment of time, energy and resources to explore.
Once ice-breaking is successful, the blue ice market will become the next blue ocean market.

7.2 12 Key Points of the Upgrading Transformation Stage

Market

Paradigm change: Grasp the great opportunity of the paradigm change and conform to the general trend of market development.

Corporate venture capital: Invest in small firms and seize the great future.

Blue-ice market: "When you hoist the sails to cross the sea, you'll ride the wind and cleave the waves."

Product

Categorical innovation: Innovate product categories to form a market segmental monopoly.

Categorical marketing: Occupy users' mental awareness of new product categories.

Ecological model: Focus on the core products and capabilities of the firm to create a win-win situation.

【Usage of the tool】

Think about users, organization, product, and market in transformation stage form the perspective of the 12 key points.

Use "strategy canvas for the upgrading transformation stage"(next page) to do deep analysis.

	People	Issues
External	Users Redefining users Potential demands Upgrading / downgrading of demand	Market Paradigm change Corporate venture capital Blue-ice market
Internal	Organization Reviving founder spirit Rebuilding entrepreneurial team Reactivating organization	Product Categorical innovation Categorical marketing Ecological model

Users

Redefining users: Redefining existing users and rediscover non-users.

Potential demands: Focus on the potential demands of non-users and achieve value innovation.

Upgrading/downgrading of demand: Solve the mismatch between supply and demand and forming a new balance between the two.

Organization

Regaining founder spirit: Review the spirit of the founders and create greater success.

Rebuilding entrepreneurial team: Overcome organizational inertia and inspire employees' innovative and entrepreneurial spirit.

Reactivating organization: Establish an open system that dissipates excess energy from the organization.

7.2.1 Co-evolution Strategy Canvas for the Upgrading Transformation Stage

Redefining users	Reviving founder spirit	Categorical innovation	Paradigm change
Potential demands	Rebuilding entrepreneurial team	Categorical marketing	Corporate venture capital
Upgrading / downgrading of demand	Reactivating organization	Ecological model	Blue-ice market

7.2.2 Case Analysis: Alibaba

Redefining users	Reviving founder spirit	Categorical innovation	Paradigm change
- The development space of the C-end user market is getting narrower and narrower, from the transaction itself to the Internet + (Internet + finance, smart home, big health and big entertainment). - Change from serving consumers to providers.	- In the face of WeChat's challenge (I thought that Tencent would shake the operator, but I didn't expect it to shake us at the end), pushed "Laiwang" and then failed. - Retiring CEO, beyond strategy - *"Jack Ma wearing cloth shoes"*	- Yu E'bao (its legality is questioned and is suppressed by the traditional banking industry) - Alipay faces the challenge of WeChat payment. - Aliyun	- Large platform, big data, big calculation and big application - The advance layout of Aliyun and YunOS meets the technical and cost requirements for massive data processing in large-scale transactions such as Yu E'bao and Double Eleven.
Potential demands	**Rebuilding entrepreneurial team**	**Categorical marketing**	**Corporate venture capital**
- Supply and demand consumption upgrade - Poor users' demand for scattered funds - The demand for mobile services, the way consumers connect. - SMEs have convenient access to implement information technology with advanced technology, supply chain upgrade (enterprise SaaS).	- First-line business presidents are becoming 70 post-generation. - Young management team (the leaders born in 1960s exited and handed over to leaders born in the 1970s and 1980s). - Providing an imaginary space for young and thoughtful employees to rise channels. "It's better to consider staying behind to start a business than to jump out and start a business yourself."	- Become the benchmark and standard of "Internet + Business" and endorse new retail	- In 2014, Ali was listed in the United States. - M&A companies that are strongly associated with big data - Through Ali Capital, it has invested in Sina Weibo, Kuaidi Taxi, Momo, Amap, etc., in the form of investment, holding, and shareholding.
Upgrading demand	**Reactivating organization**	**Ecological model**	**Blue-ice market**
- From IT to DT - From the network to the mobile network - From information to AI	- Established wireless division - Break the large firm into smaller ones and set up strategic decision-making committees and strategic management executive committees - Created a networked ecosystem in the form of equity investment	- Ali cultivates an open, collaborative and prosperous e-commerce ecosystem which includes search, instant messaging, logistics, maps, group purchases, taxis, travel, department stores, film and television, music, education, smart hardware, data and other fields through corporate venture capital.	- Develop the blue-ice market such as Internet Finance (Yu E'bao) and Enterprise SaaS (Ali dingtalk) with the concept of the Internet and traditional industries

Co-evolution strategy canvas for the upgrading transformation stage

(Case Analysis: Alibaba, 2013-)

Chapter 8
Systematicness

Fighting together in the same boat
Riding the wind and breaking the waves
–Huai Nan Zi

8.1 Systematicness of Co-evolution Strategy

System

Any system consists of three components: elements, connections, and goals.

Co-evolution strategy system

Elements: The co-evolution strategy system has four strategic elements: users, organizations, products, and markets.

Connections: The connection relationship of the co-evolution strategy system is divided into two categories, the connections between the elements and the connections between the internal points of the elements.

Goals: The elements and points of the co-evolution strategy are linked together to achieve the strategic goals of the company.

Microsoft's "road to the future"

Bill Gates wrote in The Road to the Future that in the early days of Microsoft's development, there were three operating systems on the market for pre-installation on IBM personal computers—Microsoft's PC-DOS, CP/M-86, and UCSD Pascal P-System. Only one of the three systems will succeed.

In order to succeed, Microsoft has worked on every aspect of the four elements of strategy.

J. Y. Lu, *Co-evolution Strategy Canvas*,
https://doi.org/10.1007/978-981-15-5988-4_8

Users: Make MS-DOS the best product for users.

Organization: Help other firms write MS-DOS-based software.

Product: Reduce the cost of MS-DOS by using economies of scale.

Market: bundled with IBM's interests to promote MS-DOS with IBM.

Initially, IBM tried to offer three operating systems: the UCSD Pascal P-System, priced at $450; the CP/M-86, priced at $175 and the MS-DOS, priced at $60.

In the end, Microsoft's systemic strategic thinking mode played a role. The positive feedback loop between users, organization, product, and market elements has made Microsoft the dominant PC software producer.

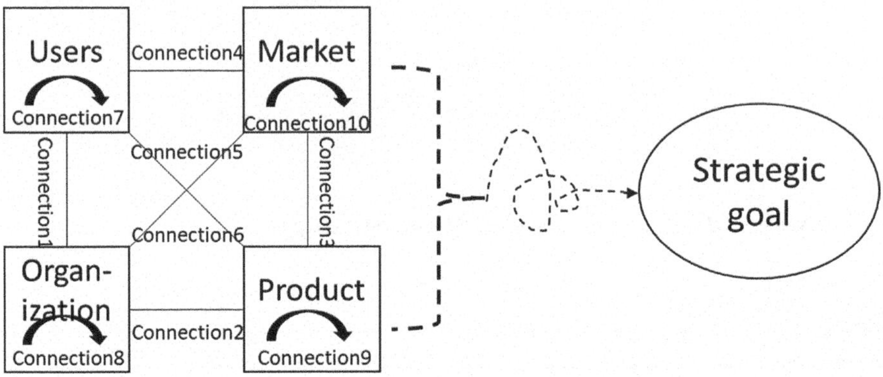

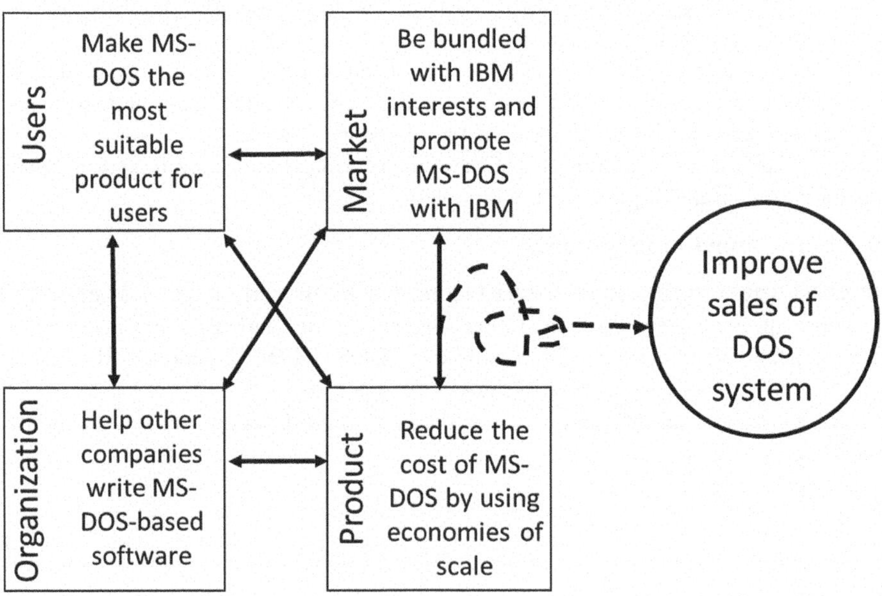

8.1.1 Feedback: The Operating Mechanism of the System

8.1.1.1 Dynamic Feedback Loop Mechanism

The operation of the system mainly relies on the dynamic feedback loop mechanism. A dynamic feedback loop is a closed causal chain. Starting from a certain stock, and according to the current situation of the stock, after a series of decisions and actions, it affects the flow associated with the stock, which in turn changes the stock.

As shown in the figure, there is a feedback mechanism between the stock and the inflow, and between the stock and the outflow. Once the actual stock level is lower than the preset level, the system will initiate a process of correcting the adjustment, or increase the inflow quantity, or reduce the outflow quantity.

8.1.1.2 Feedback Loop of Co-evolution Strategy System

In the co-evolution strategy system, information, resources, and value will flow between strategic elements such as users, organization, product, and market. The subsystems between the elements consist of stock, flow, and feedback loops.

For example, employees flow out of organization element and into different aspects of product element (e.g. product development, marketing, and business models). Organization element and product element have a stock of employees. As the deviation between the current stock and the target stock changes, the information will be fed back to the relevant parts of the system to adjust the flow.

For another example, a firm creates user value through products, and user value flows out of product element and flows into user element. If the user value inventory is too high, or the user demands are over-satisfied, the information will be fed back into the exchange mechanism between the user element and the product element, reducing excessive user value and preventing the firm from being overturned due to excessive satisfaction of the user's demands.

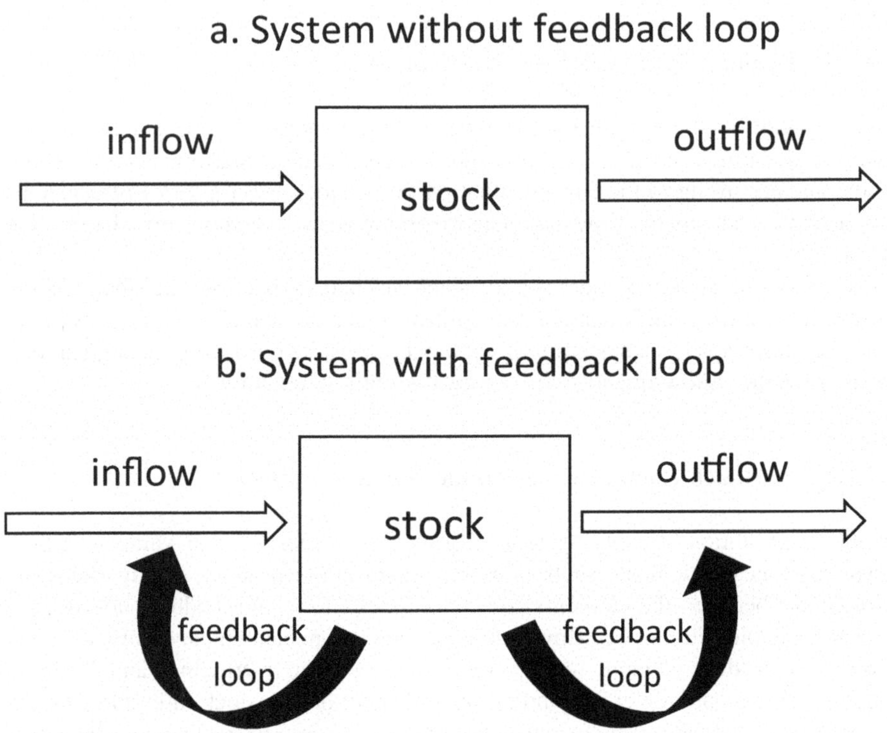

8.1.2 Enhanced Loop and Regulative Loops

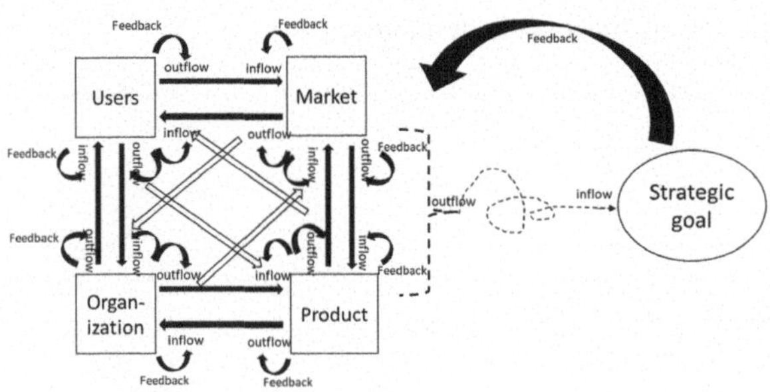

8.1.2.1 Two Feedback Loops

There are generally two feedback loops in the system, one is the enhanced loop and the other is the regulative loop.

The role of the enhanced loop is to constantly enlarge and reinforce the original development situation, self-replicating just like snowballing. For example, if the quality of TV programs is good, it will increase the ratings, thereby increasing the satisfaction of advertisers and generating more revenue. Program producers will also increase their investment due to rising incomes to further improve the quality of TV programs.

The role of the regulative loop is to keep the stock level stable and tend to adjust or correct for a target. For example, when you pour coffee into a cup, there will be a target water level. Your eyes will always pay attention to the rise of the water level in the cup, and at the same time evaluate the difference between the target water level and the actual water level, and control the body movements while pouring coffee.

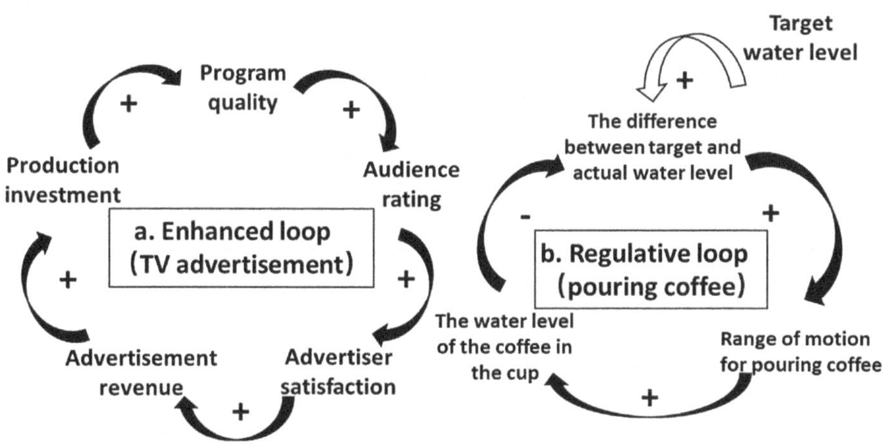

8.1.2.2 Wintel Alliance

The Wintel alliance between Microsoft and Intel has brought long-term high profits to the two giant companies, and the enhanced loop effect plays an important role.

The core of Microsoft's business model is to expand the installed base of Microsoft operating systems and applications. The core of Intel's business model is to expand the use of Intel chips. Microsoft and Intel formed the Wintel Alliance, which built an enhanced loop between the business systems of the two companies. That is to say, the rise of hardware level will bring users the need for software performance upgrade, and the software upgrade in turn will cause users to have new demands for hardware.

Each company's business system is also an enhanced loop inside. For example, Microsoft's system software adopts a strategy of low pricing levels, because the decline in system software prices will lead to an increase in software sales, providing Microsoft with high profits, which are used to invest in new operating systems. After users updated the operating systems, the stock and performance of the Microsoft operating system have been increased, and the development of supporting software has been stimulated, which attract more users, then the operating software can be sold at a lower price.

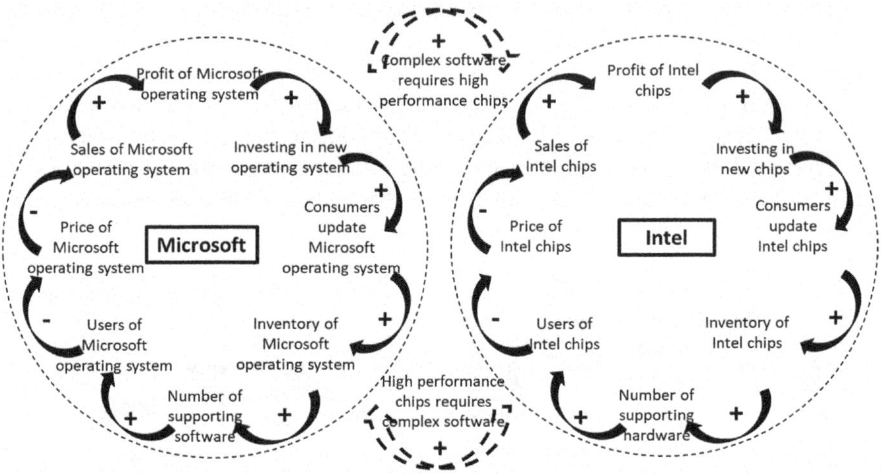

8.1.3 Synergies Among Four Elements

Logical relationship between four elements

First, the relationship between the co-evolution strategy elements should be understood from the users, and entrepreneurs can judge the future trend of economic development according to the demands of users.

Second, identify market gaps and opportunities by understanding what products and services are already on the market.

Third, choose the opportunities that you can grasp in the market and determine the general direction of the future development of the company.

Fourth, implement the determined direction of enterprise development into the specific actions of employees and teams to form a corporate action plan.

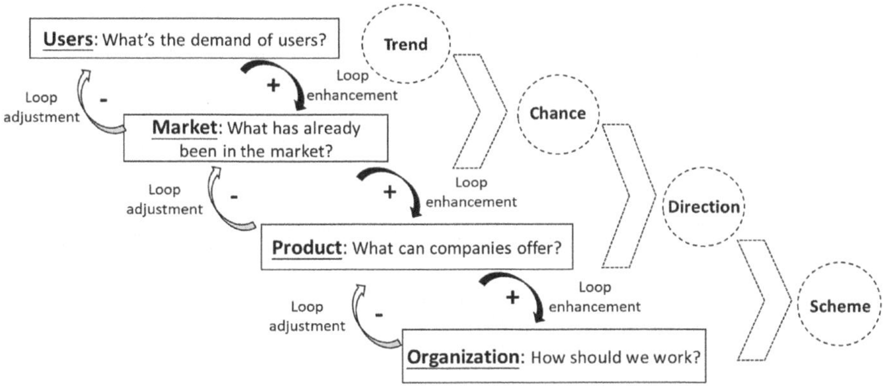

Alibaba case

The state of users' demand depends on the trend. At the beginning of the business, Yun Ma realized in a negotiation with a US company that the Internet can help people search for information, and then realized the trend that users need the Internet.

Market supply depends on opportunities. When Yun Ma first used the Internet in Seattle, USA, he found that he could not search for any information about China at that time. He realized that China did not have the Internet. The opportunity door of the Internet opened to him.

The ability of firms decides the direction. In 1995, Yun Ma established China's first commercial website "China Yellow Pages", whose main business is to promote the Internet to domestic firms. In the following years, Jack Ma clearly realized that e-commerce is a capable thing for him and found the direction after a series of exploration.

Develop the scheme after the implementation of the organization. After determining the direction, what Yun Ma did next is to organize the team. In addition to the 18 Luohan who worked with him at the time of start-up, Jack Ma quickly attracted some key talents and gradually developed a series of business.

8.1.3.1 The goal of synergy of co-evolution strategic elements.

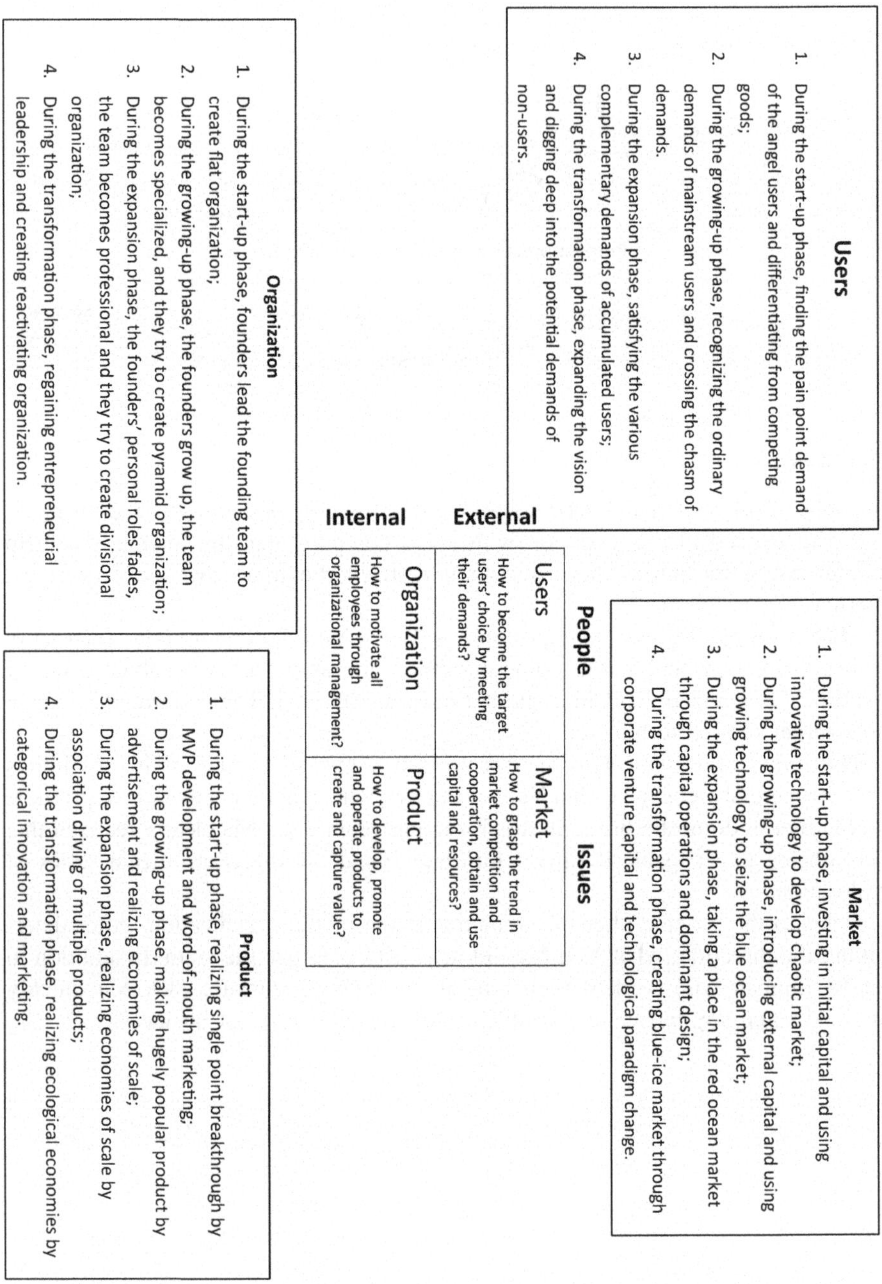

8.1.3.2 Internal synergy of user elements

The three main points of user elements include user characteristics, user demands, and user choice. The goal of internal synergy of user elements is to become the choice of target users by meeting the demands of users, so that user characteristics, requirements and choices can be consistent.

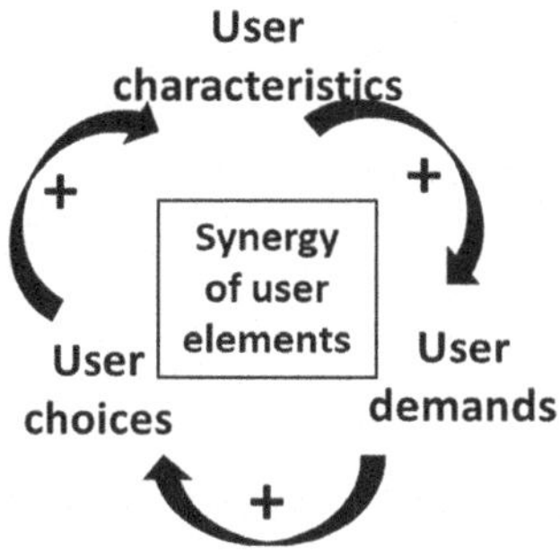

Internal synergy of user elements at different stages.

The synergy between user characteristics, user needs, and user choices changes at different stages of firm development.

In the start-up stage, the users of the firm are mainly angel users who are few and fine. The products are mainly aimed at the users' refreshing or pain point demand. The grasp of the demand must be precise and accurate, and the emphasis mainly lies on the existing difference form existing competing goods.

In the growing-up period, the firm need to take advantage of the mainstream users' herd mentality, meet the ordinary demands of a large number of mainstream users who pay attention to practicality, cross the chasm between angel users and mainstream users, and form economies of scale.

During the expansion stage, the firm has accumulated a certain number of users and gained the trust of them. On the basis of satisfying the basic practical demands of users, the firm must also tap the various demands of accumulated users and form economies of scope through the evolution of demand and mutual reinforcement of various demands.

In the transformation stage, the user demand basis for the development of the firm may have undergone a qualitative change. The firm needs to dig deep into the potential demands of users, be alert to the limitations imposed by the accumulated users on the development of the firm, avoid over-satisfying the needs of users, seize the big trend of upgrading of demand, and complete the leap to the next user demand curve.

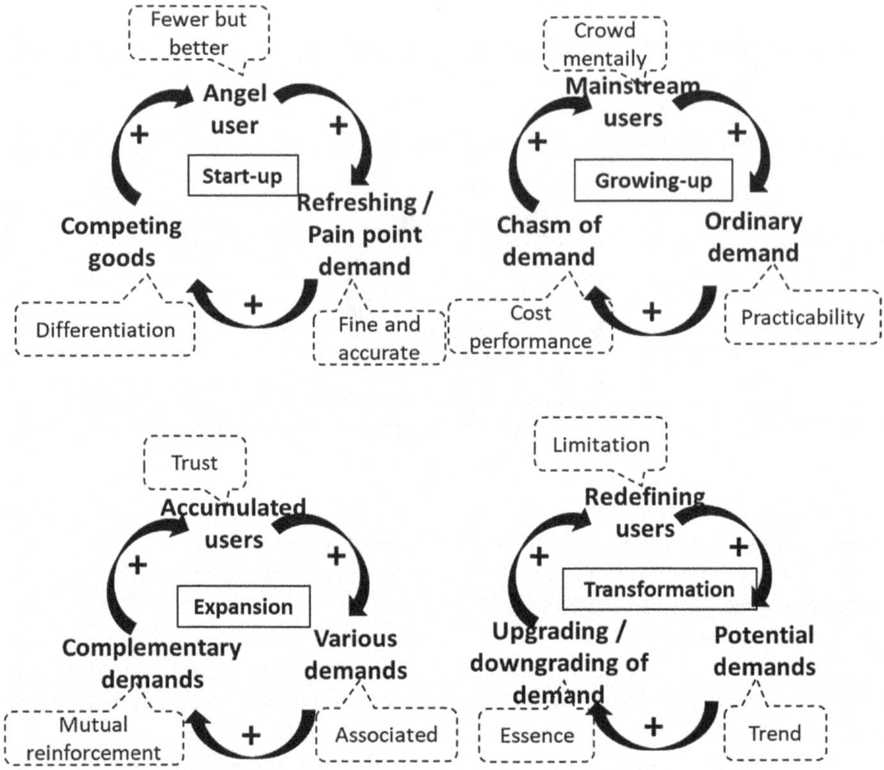

Case Analysis: Xiaomi

Internal synergy of user elements at different stages in Xiaomi

At the different stages of Xiaomi's development, the internal synergy of user characteristics, user demands and user choices have changed a lot.

During the start-up stage, Xiaomi's angel users are mainly some mobile phone enthusiasts who became big fans because of the ease of use and sense of participation of Xiaomi MIUI. These users have high requirements for the experience, but they can also actively participate in the interaction with Xiaomi and achieve self-propagation in the process of roasting.

During the growing-up stage, Xiaomi's mainstream users are the young who use smartphones for the first time, and Xiaomi organizes young people together by building communities. These users have high requirements on cost performance ratio, so they prefer the middle or low priced phones. At the same time, young people pursue fashion, which promote the fashion style of Xiaomi.

During the expansion stage, Xiaomi expanded the user base to the middle class in some first, second and third tier cities, providing them with high-quality and low-priced smart devices. These users like high-quality products that are easy to choose, and Xiaomi's self-built channels play an important role.

During the transformation stage, Xiaomi noticed the limitations of the pure Internet model and the original product positioning. Then it began to push smart hardware products for middle-to-high-income people to meet the requirements of high-end or middle-end users for product quality instead of simply stressing the cost performance ratio. In this case, Xiaomi has also begun to make up its own technical shortcomings, launching full-screen mobile phones and other mobile phones with its own chips.

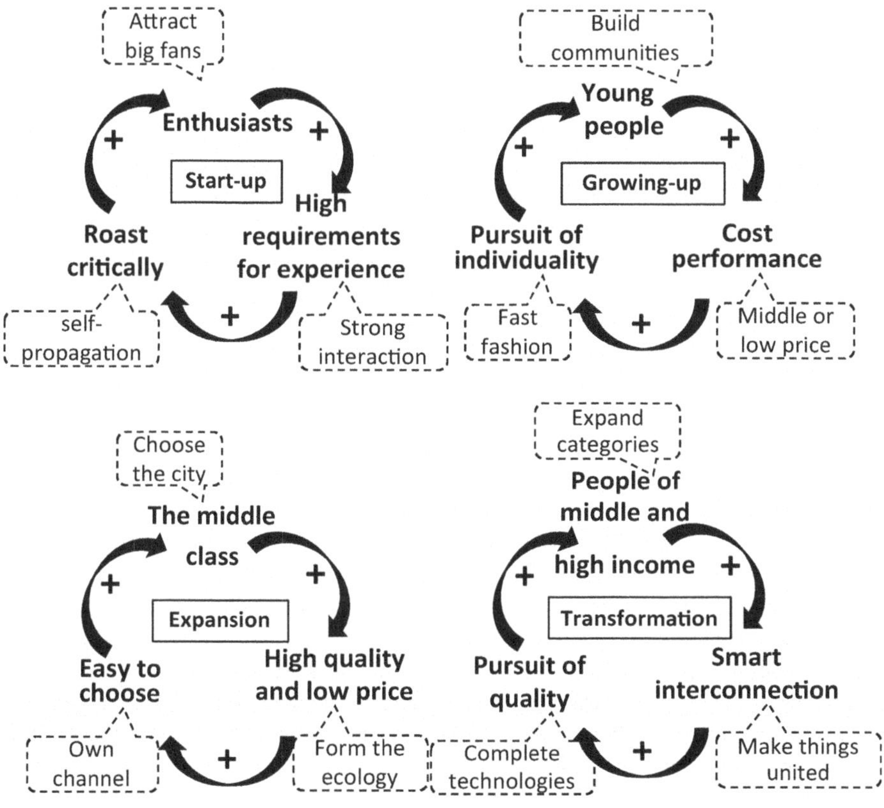

8.1.3.3 Internal synergy of organization elements

Organization elements include three main points: leaders, team employees, and organizational management. The synergy goal within the organization elements is to motivate all employees, including leaders, teams, and employees, through appropriate organizational design.

Internal synergy of organization elements at different stages.

Synergy between leaders, team employees, and organizational management changes at different stages of business development.

In the start-up stage, the founders started their own business with their own abilities and high-risk commitments, attracting entrepreneurial partners and early-stage employees with mutual trust and complementary capabilities. The founders lead a flat entrepreneurial team that relies on personal charisma and entrepreneurial passion to drive organizational growth.

In the growing-up stage, the team gradually realized specialization through learning, and the hierarchical organizational structure gradually formed. The cognitive upgrade of the founders is the main driving force for the development of the firm.

In the expansion stage, the scale of the firm is expanding. It is unrealistic to rely on the founders' personal ability to promote the development of the firm. The growth of the founding team may not be able to meet the development of the firm. It is necessary to introduce a professional manager team. With the development of business, firms tend to present the organizational form of divisional organization.

In the transformation stage, due to the changes and challenges of the external environment, regaining founder spirit is usually an important force for leading firms to overcome the obstacles of transformation, and the rigid and closed organizational structure that tends to become rigid and closed has been replaced by a flexible and open organizational structure after transformation stage. They overcome organizational inertia through rebuilding entrepreneurial team and reactivate organization.

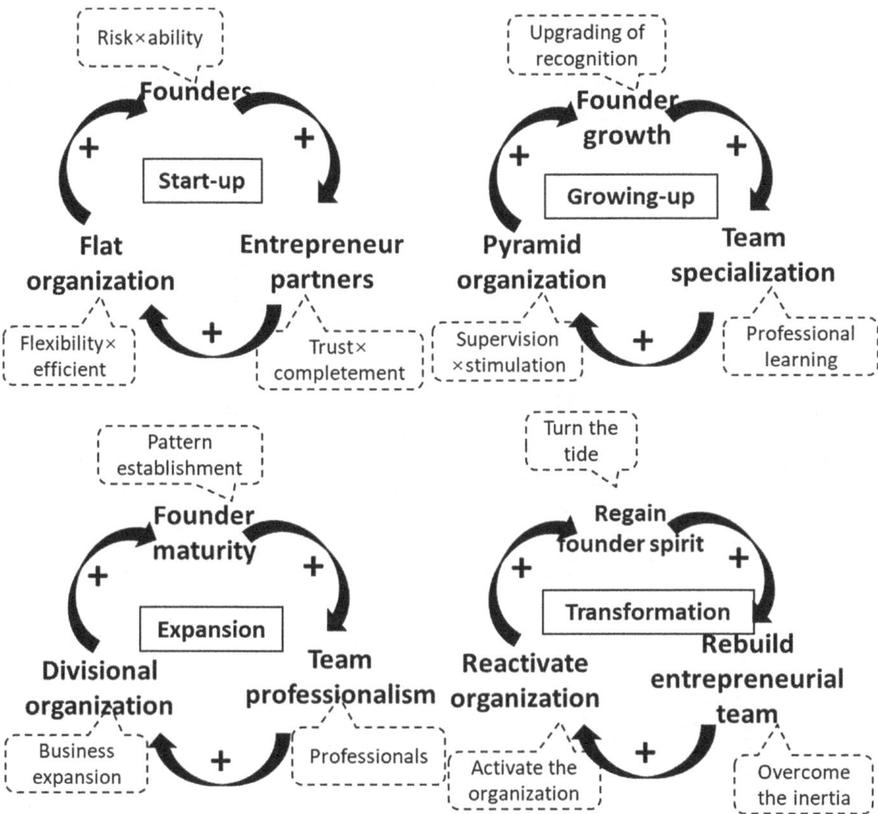

Case Analysis: Xiaomi

Internal synergy of organization elements at different stages in Xiaomi

At the different stages of Xiaomi's development, the internal synergy of founders, team employees and organizational management have changed a lot.

During the start-up stage, Xiaomi was founded by seven "old boys" over 40 years old. The early team was self-motivated, and the management fully authorized the employees to create a struggle atmosphere for the brothers.

In the growing-up stage, partners work on the basis of mutual trust and independently have the decision-making power to take charge of the project. The company continues to introduce professional talents to fill the shortcomings in management. The three-tier organization of partners, management and employees has gradually formed, which played a role in material incentives.

During the expansion stage, the cooperation mode of the Xiaomi ecological chain was used to lay out some potential directions in the future. Although it is expanding rapidly, it is not mainly managed in the form of KPIs. In the process of expansion, organizations also face the dilemma of rapid expansion.

During the transformation stage, Xiaomi re-adjusted its strategy and seized the core products such as mobile phones to fill the shortcomings of offline channels and supply chains. More than 10,000 people have been organized, and some management communication barriers have begun to emerge, and various incentives have been used to stimulate organizational vitality. The form of ecological organization was initially formed, and refined management was put on the agenda.

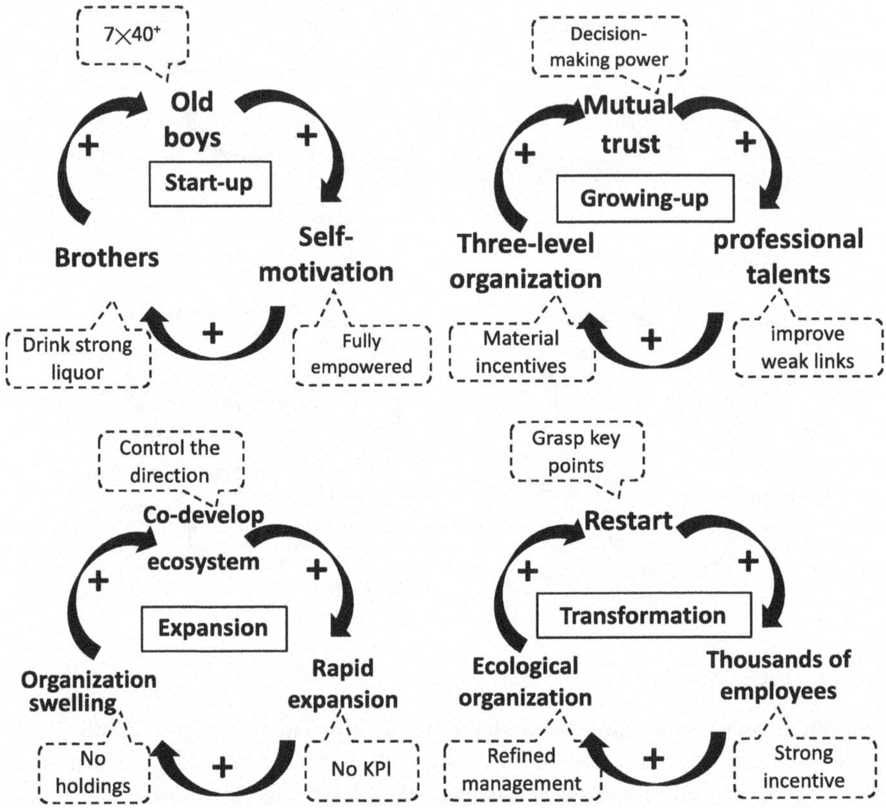

8.1.3.4 Internal synergy of product elements

Product elements include product development, marketing and business models. The synergy goal within the product elements is to create and capture business value through the development, promotion and operation of the business.

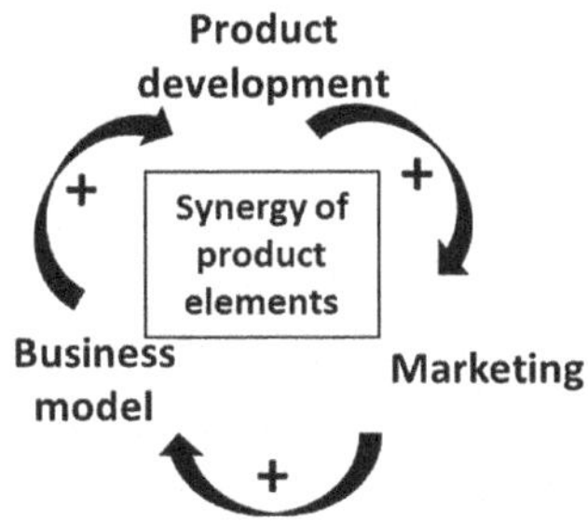

Internal synergy of product elements at different stages.

The synergy between product development, marketing and business models changes at different stages of business development.

In the start-up stage, firms often need to create a minimum viable product (MVP) through rapid iteration, and through word-of-mouth marketing to verify the matching of products and market demand, to create a single point breakthrough business model around the core product.

In the growing-up stage, in order to seize the development opportunities, firms often use the marketing and promotion methods to make core product into huge popular product, rapidly expand the number of users, amortize fixed costs, and achieve economies of scale.

In the expansion stage, it is difficult to maintain the continuous development of the firms by relying only on the core products formed when they started up. At this time, firms needs to diversify around the core products and use the product linkage to achieve economies of scope.

During the transformation stage, firms need to find new products that can help them to enter the next development cycle, complete industrial upgrading, enter new value networks, and play a positive feedback effect of products, and strive to achieve ecological economy.

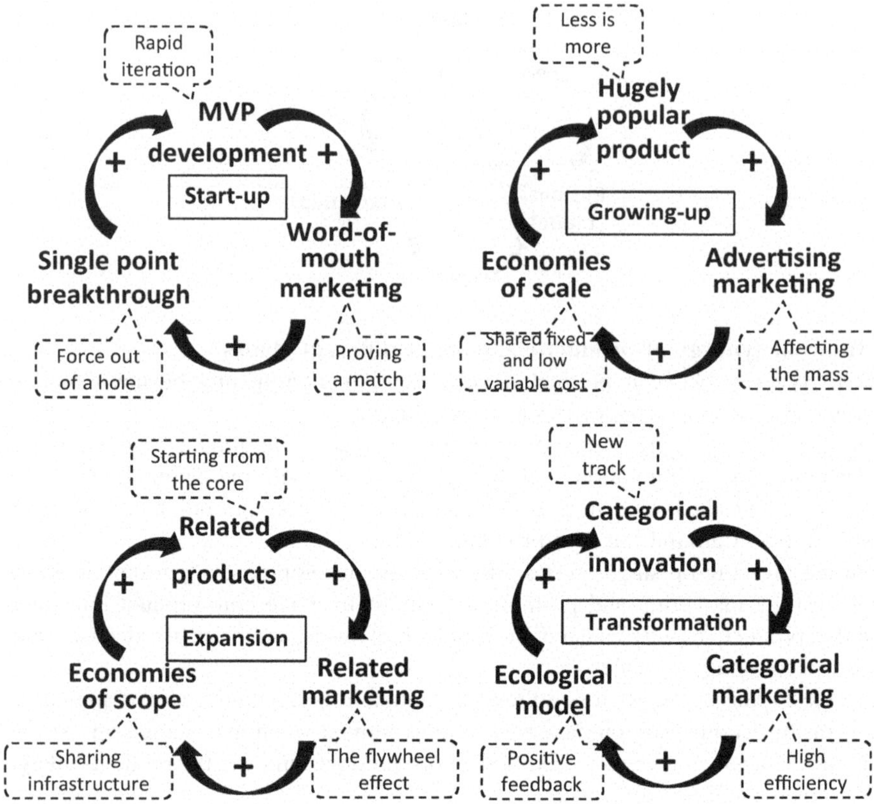

Case Analysis: Xiaomi

Internal synergy of product elements at different stages in Xiaomi

At the different stages of Xiaomi's development, the internal synergy of product development, marketing and business models have undergone great changes.

During the start-up stage, Xiaomi products are mainly based on MIUI, and the products are developed through rapid iteration. The products in the start-up stage are mainly promoted by word of mouth in the fan community. After cutting in from the software, Xiaomi gradually turned to hardware development.

During the growing-up stage, Xiaomi mobile phone cut through the mid-end products, and later covered the low-end market in order to seize the young man's first smartphone. Due to limited production capacity, the impression of a single hugely popular product and "hunger marketing" is formed.

During the expansion stage, by creating a model of the ecological chain product line, Xiaomi cut into a number of single product mass market. It accumulated data through self-built marketing channels to lay the foundation for data transformation.

The flywheel effect business model has established a good correlation between products for Xiaomi.

In the transformation stage, Xiaomi began to develop relatively high-end mobile phones, while complementing the weakness of offline channels to enhance the user experience. The direction of Xiaomi's commercial transformation is to create a scene of intelligent IoT, which allows Xiaomi's products to be interconnected in life and work scenarios.

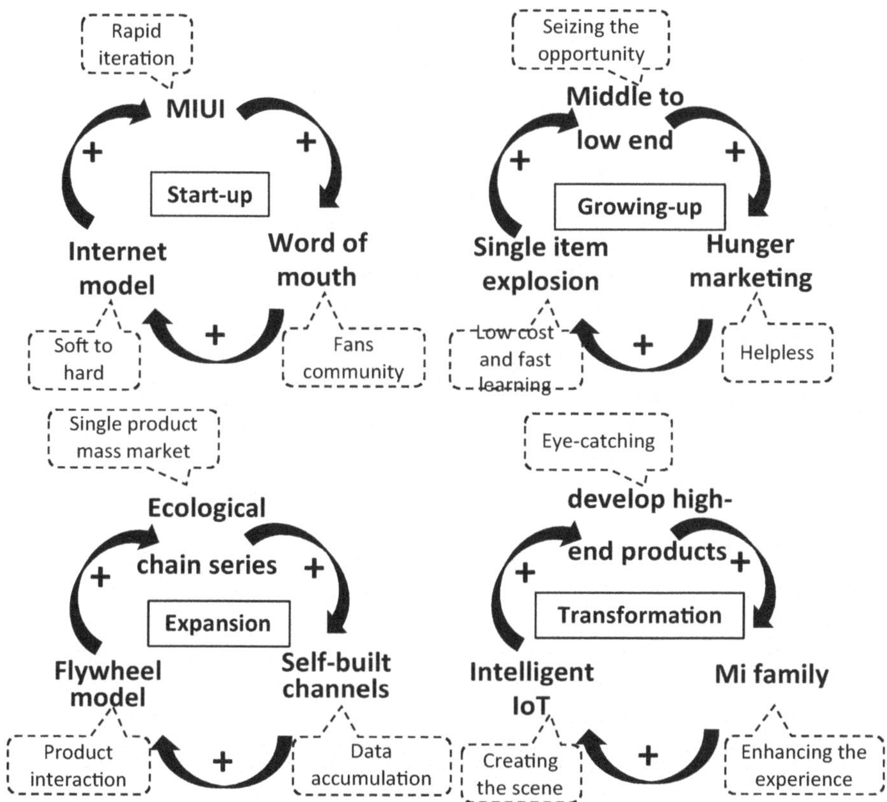

8.1.3.5 Internal Synergy of Market Elements

Market factors include key points such as tech trend, capital and resources, and market competition and cooperation. The synergy goal within the market element is to obtain the required capital, resources and technology in the market, and is in a favorable position in market competition and cooperation.

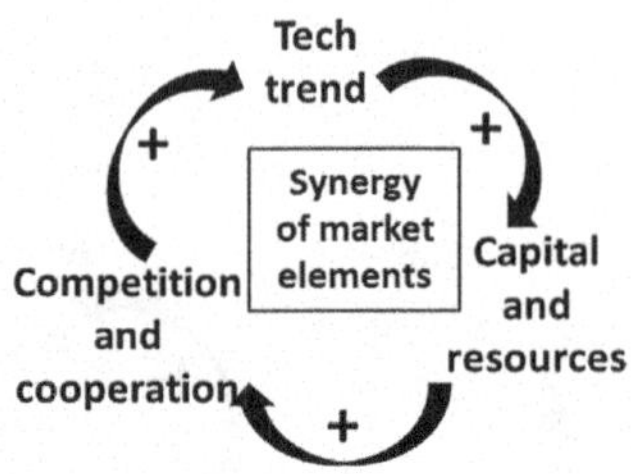

Internal synergy of market elements at different stages.

At different stages of business development, synergy between tech trends, capital and resources, and market competition and cooperation will change.

During the start-up stage, firms use innovative technology to cut into the market and use the initial capital to occupy a place in the chaotic market.

During the growth stage, firms use the rising trend of growing technology to achieve exponential growth, and through the small-step fast-running lean fundraising to achieve the rapid development of the industry in the blue ocean market.

During the expansion stage, the firm's goal is to occupy a monopoly position in the market segment, and by virtue of its dominant position in the market, through mergers and acquisitions to expand, and to win competition in the red sea market.

During the transformation stage, firms often need to adopt paradigm changes to seize large development opportunities, and invest in future possible development tracks through the form of corporate venture capital, and use the firm's physical strength to break through the ice in the blue ice market and open up new channels.

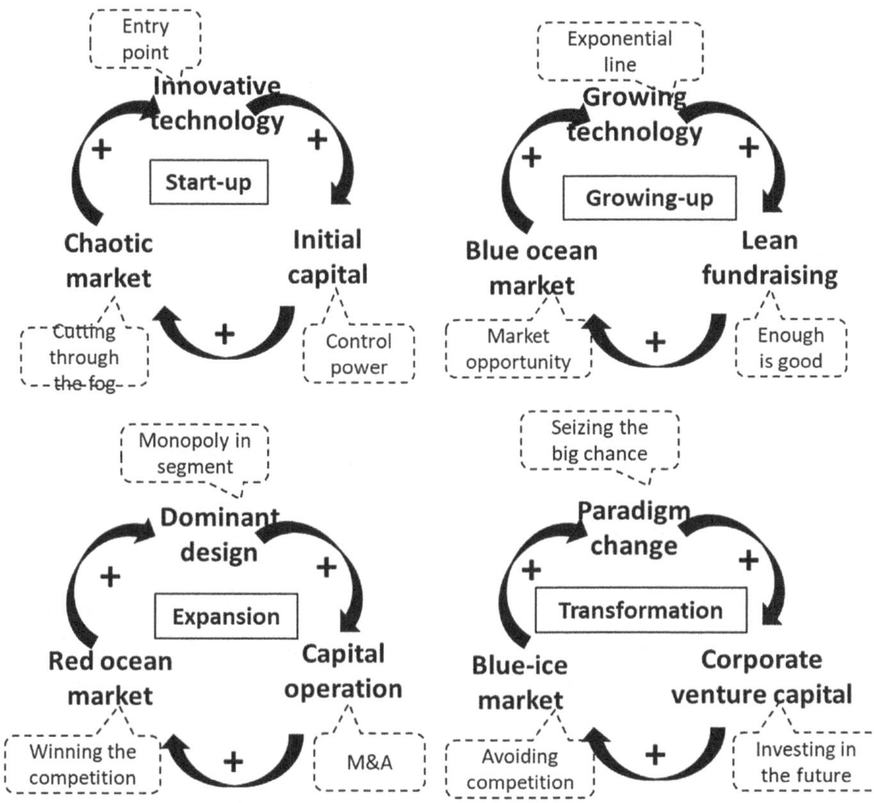

Case Analysis: Xiaomi

Internal synergy of market elements at different stages in Xiaomi

At different stages of business development of Xiaomi, synergy between tech trends, capital and resources, and market competition and cooperation have changed a lot.

During the start-up stage, the arrival of the mobile internet era is the most obvious technology trend. The background of Lei Jun's entrepreneurial star and the blessing of Morningside Venture Capital have provided sufficient funds for the early development of Xiaomi. At that time, the low-end smartphone market had a big gap, which provided valuable space for the development of Xiaomi.

During the growing-up stage, Xiaomi's early MIUI experience has provided the advantage of software and hardware integration for manufacturing mobile phones. With the rapid development of mobile phone business, Xiaomi has shown strong financing capabilities. At the same time, it has cooperated with key suppliers such as Foxconn to lay the foundation for high-quality and low-priced products.

During the expansion stage, Xiaomi seized the opportunity of smart interconnection, and the valuation once reached 45 billion US dollars, which made it a global unicorn enterprise. At the same time, the development of the ecological chain provides a broad network of cooperative relationships for Xiaomi.

During the transformation stage, Xiaomi began to adapt to the trend of consumption upgrading, providing young users with a new generation of mobile phones. In the period when the capital market is getting colder, Xiaomi uses operating profit to achieve endogenous development. At the same time, due to the increasingly fierce competition in the mobile phone industry, the advantages of the Xiaomi ecological chain began to emerge. In May 2018, Xiaomi submitted a listing application.

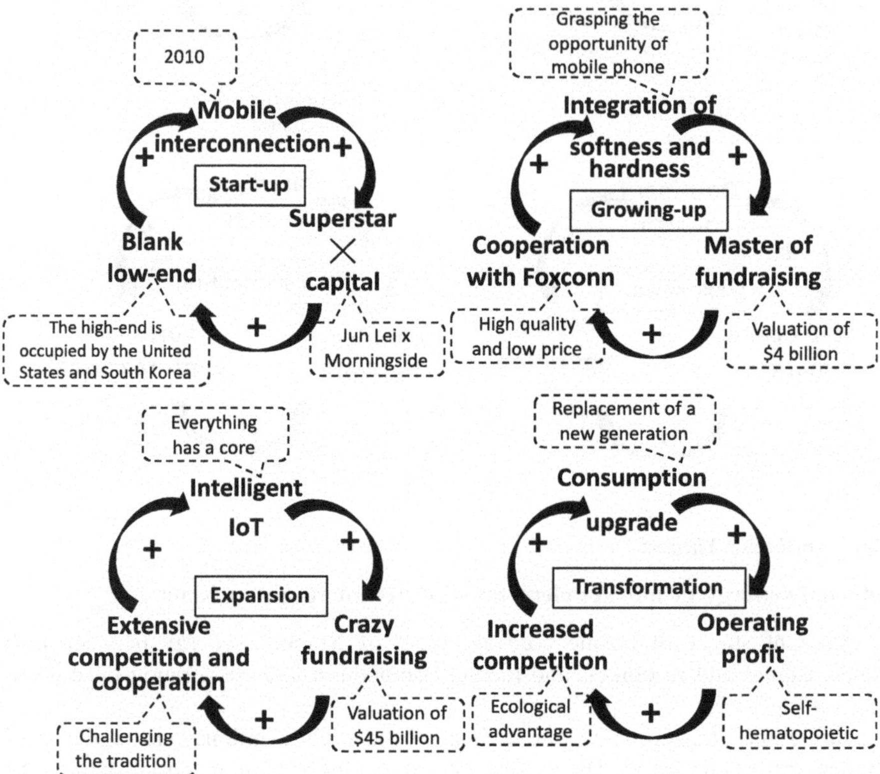

8.1.4 Basic Principles of Synergy Between Elements

4 principles

In all stages of firm development, the synergy between the four elements of users, organization, product, and market requires four principles.

① User-centered principle. The development of organization, product and market elements should be consistent with and coordinated with user elements, user-centered, in line with user characteristics, meet user needs, and become the users' choice.
② Principle of entropy reduction of organization. In the process of development, firm must constantly dissipate organizational inertia, "regarding users as friends", "regarding market as the mirror", and "regarding products as the origin".
③ Product-oriented principle. In the process of firm development, we must adhere to the ingenuity to build products, and to meet the needs of users with high-quality products, support organizational development and win market position.
④ Market-oriented principle. Whether the firm can meet the needs of users, whether the product can win the competition, whether the organization can last for a long time, these questions will ultimately be tested by the market.

4 mechanisms

The synergy between the four elements of users, organization, product and market is as follows:

① User versus organization: The only goal of an organization is to create user value.
② User versus product: Products are the primary means of creating user value.
③ User versus market: Consider the creation of user value from a market perspective.
④ Organization versus product: Promote business innovation with organization change
⑤ Organization versus market: Adapt to changes in the market environment through organization change.
⑥ Product versus market: The market is the only standard for testing products.

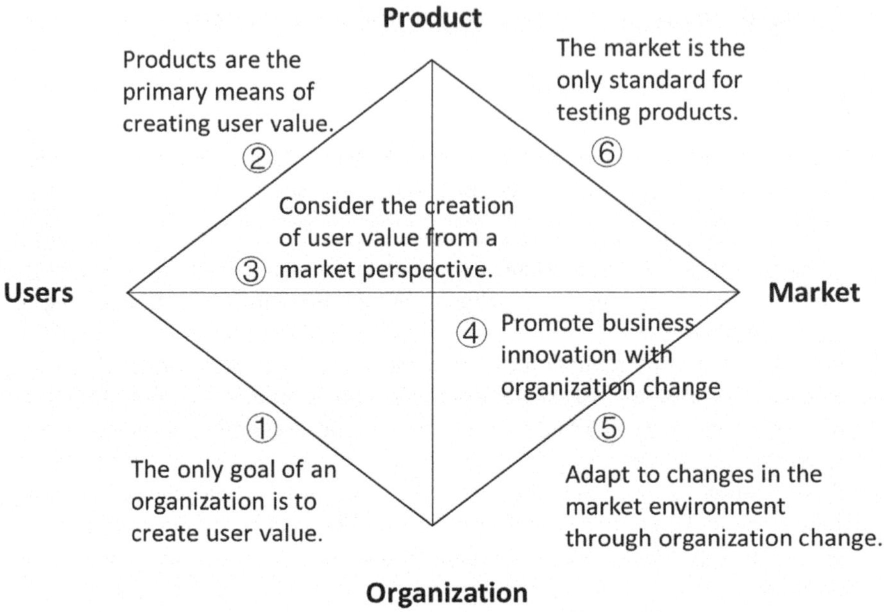

8.1.4.1 Logic of Synergy Between Elements

(User elements and other elements)

Goal of synergy between elements	Logic of synergy between elements
User and organization synergy	• During the start-up stage, the leaders personally study user characteristics, needs and choices, and the team employees interact closely with the users to establish user-centered organizational management • During the growing-up stage, the leaders help the firm to gain the recognition of the mass. The team members provide excellent services for the rapidly increasing users, and the organizational structure strikes a balance between cost and quality • During the expansion stage, the leaders determine the diversification direction according to the complementary needs of users, and the team members of each business department work closely together • During the transformation stage, leaders adjust organization management to changing user needs, and team members maintain a user-centric spirit

(continued)

(continued)

Goal of synergy between elements	Logic of synergy between elements
User and production synergy	• During the start-up stage, according to the needs of users, rapidly iterate products and develop products, and acquire users with the appeal of the products themselves, not the main goal of the products themselves • During the growing-up stage, the firm continues to optimize the "fist" products and uses the word-of-mouth to quickly promote the growth of users and stabilize cash flow • During the expansion stage, the products are developed around the users' multiple needs, and the growth is achieved by using the inter-product correlation effect. The firm distinguishes the traffic business that attracts users and the cash cow business that contributes profits • During the transformation stage, the firm taps the potential needs of potential users and existing users, and tries the disruptive innovation of business and technology
User and market synergy	• During the start-up stage, exploit the capital, resources and technology that angel users can provide, and try to avoid competing with existing firms for core users • During the growing-up stage, ensuring that the capital and resources obtained can support the rapid growth of the number of users, the technology can support the mainstream users at a decreasing cost, and cooperate with relevant firms to avoid competition • During the expansion stage, use resources and technologies that meet the diverse demands of users, and focus on the complementary role of products to meet user needs and avoid self-competition • During the transformation stage, pay attention to unmet and over-satisfied user demands and adjust capital and resources, technology and competitive and cooperation relationship accordingly to help firms develop new user markets

8.1.4.2 Logic of Synergy Between Elements (Organization\Product \Market Elements)

Goal of synergy between elements	Logic of synergy between elements
Organization and product synergy	• During the start-up stage, the leader usually plays the role of product manager. The team members work closely to develop, promote products and explore business models. The product team and the management team have a high degree of overlap • During the growing-up stage, leaders began to shift their focus from developing products to exploring business models. Team employees continue to focus on the products themselves, and product teams often exist as development teams

(continued)

(continued)

Goal of synergy between elements	Logic of synergy between elements
	• During the expansion stage, the leaders pay attention to the product relevance. The team employees are specialized around the product line, and the product team exists in the form of a business unit • During the transformation stage, leaders focus on subverting the threat of their products, and team employees and organization management adjust around the direction of exploring new products
Organization and market synergy	• During the start-up stage, the leaders focus on the grasp of technology trends. Team employees need technical talents, and organizational management is designed around technical personnel • During the growing-up stage, the leaders focus on the acquisition of capital and resources. The staff of the team needs to add people of financing and public relation experience, and the importance of organization management increases • During the expansion stage, the leaders focus on market competition and cooperation, and the team members and organizational structure are adjusted according to market segments • During the transformation stage, the leaders focused on discovering new market opportunities, and the teamwork and organizational structure were adjusted to the new market direction
Product and market synergy	• During the start-up stage, capital and resources to support product development, promotion and business models are limited, and product characteristics and business models should focus more on market cooperation than competition • During the growth stage, it is necessary to continuously invest capital resources for product development and promotion. Product differentiation should support firms to cope with competition from the market • During the expansion stage, resource input, technical stability, and market cooperation play an important role in the development and promotion of related products • During the transformation stage, it is necessary to balance the resources, technologies and market resources invested in the development and promotion of existing products and new products

8.1.4.3 Canvas for Synergy of User and Organization Elements (Case Analysis: Xiaomi)

Stage	Users elements	Organization elements	Synergy of user and organization elements
Start-up	Technical enthusiasts; high demand for mobile phone experience; dissatisfied with the original android system	Jun Lei and other mobile phone enthusiasts founded Xiaomi; employees jointly invested; flat organization mode	Jun Lei personally researched user characteristics, needs and choices. The team staff interacted closely with the enthusiast users. Employees worked overtime day and night to update products according to user demands
Growing-up	Young people who use smartphones for the first time; high cost performance; less choice in the market	Executives responsible for hardware joined in; employee self-driven; three-tier organizational structure	Jun Lei helped Xiaomi to establish the image of "new domestic products" and "national mobile phones" and gained the recognition of the masses. The team members provided high-quality services for the rapidly increasing users, while controlling costs by self-driving and restraining
Expansion	Smart device + middle class; cost-effective + time scarcity; market gap	More executives joined; creating Mi's culture; group intelligence and middle-level decision making	Jun Lei determined the diversified direction according to the user's complementary needs of smart devices, and created a corporate culture of participation and respect, emphasizing the cooperation between the team members of the divisional organization and the members of the "non-control" eco-chain

(continued)

(continued)

Stage	Users elements	Organization elements	Synergy of user and organization elements
Transformation	The user population is complicated; the demand for products varies greatly; there are many competing products, and the choice is difficult to make	Jun Lei personally controlled the supply chain; employees over 10,000; promoting exquisite management	Supply chain problems are caused by factors such as user demand complexity, product diversification, and increased competition. The founders personally controlled the supply chain, promoted team members to maintain the user-centered spirit, and gradually used KPI and other refined management methods

8.1.4.4 Canvas for Synergy of User and Product Elements (Case Analysis: Xiaomi)

Stage	Users elements	Product elements	Synergy of user and product elements
Start-up	Technical enthusiasts; high demand for mobile phone experience; dissatisfied with the original Android system	MIUI was iteratively developed; word of mouth by enthusiasts; first making software, then making hardware	According to the user's needs, the MIUI was rapidly and iteratively developed, and the user were attracted by the product itself. The main goal is not to profit from the product itself, but to lay the foundation for the subsequent product line expansion
Growing-up	Young people who use smartphones for the first time; high cost performance; less choice in the market	Release low-end mobile phones; word of mouth marketing; outsourcing production + Internet channels + single products	Continuously optimize MIUI, combine hardware and software to improve the cost performance of mobile phones, lay a good foundation for

(continued)

(continued)

Stage	Users elements	Product elements	Synergy of user and product elements
			the growth of mobile phone users, quickly promote by using user reputation and e-commerce channels, and become the third largest e-commerce platform after Ali and JD
Expansion	Smart device + middle class; cost-effective + time scarcity; market gap	Products of Xiaomi ecological chain series; Mi's platform; "Muji in the scientific and technological field"	Focusing on the users' diversified demand for smart devices, using the correlation effect between smart products and platform sales to achieve growth, highlighting the high cost performance which eliminating the trouble of users shopping. Some products depended on sales (basic power supply) to attract users, while some products contributed profit (high version of the power supply)
Transformation	The user population is complicated; the demand for products varies greatly; there are many competing products, and the choice is difficult to make	Release high-end mobile phones; Xiaomi's home experience store; star advertising, independent chip	Exploring the needs of potential high-end users and the potential needs of existing users, then the products and user needs are more closely matched. Through Xiaomi's Home, users can directly experience Xiaomi products, and continue to innovate with technology and channels to find sustainable growth points.

8.1.4.5 Canvas for Synergy of User and Market Elements (Case Analysis: Xiaomi)

Stage	Users elements	Market elements	Synergy of user and market elements
Start-up	Technical enthusiasts; high demand for mobile phone experience; dissatisfied with the original android system	On the eve of Android outbreak; Jun Lei invested in entrepreneurship; enthusiasts participated in MIUI development	Enthusiasts represent future user needs and technology trends, while providing some of the technology and testing capabilities needed to develop MIUI
Growing-up	Young people who use smartphones for the first time; high cost performance; less choice in the market	Software and hardware integration trend; B, C round of rapid financing; competition with low-end mobile phones	Hardware development requires a lot of capital, and rapid financing provides the capital needed for mobile phone R&D and mass production. As the price of mobile phone parts and components declined, the cost of the same mobile phone decreased in the later stage, ensuring a certain profit margin. The low-end positioning avoids the competition from strong manufacturers such as Apple and Samsung
Expansion	Smart device + middle class; cost-effective + time scarcity; market gap	Trend of smart Internet; D and E rounds of high financing; expanding cooperation and competition scope	Complying with the trend of intelligent Internet to meet the needs of users for smart products around mobile phones. A large amount of financing enabled Xiaomi to invest in eco-chain enterprises. At the same time, one type of products could only invest in one enterprise to avoid self-competition

(continued)

(continued)

Stage	Users elements	Market elements	Synergy of user and market elements
Transformation	The user population is complicated; the demand for products varies greatly; there are many competing products, and the choice is difficult to make	Data-driven consumption trends; using self-owned funds to supplement cash flow; competition and cooperation in high-end market	Based on the accumulated intelligent device users, use big data to refine user images, tap the unmet needs of users, provide different positioning products for different levels of users, cut into the high-end market, and obtain higher profits

8.1.4.6 Canvas for Synergy of Organization and Product Elements (Case Analysis: Xiaomi)

Stage	Organization elements	Product elements	Synergy of organization and product elements
Start-up	Jun Lei and other mobile phone enthusiasts founded Xiaomi; employees jointly invested; flat organization mode	MIUI was iteratively developed; word of mouth by enthusiasts; first making software, then making hardware	Founders like Jun Lei and Feng Hong personally played the role of product managers to develop MIUI. The team members worked closely on development, promotion, service and business model exploration, and the product team and management team had a high degree of overlap
Growing-up	Executives responsible for hardware joined in; employee self-driven; three-tier organizational structure	Release low-end mobile phones; word of mouth marketing; outsourcing production + Internet channels + single products	Pingguang Zhou and other executives with rich experience in mobile phone hardware development have accelerated the development of Xiaomi mobile

(continued)

(continued)

Stage	Organization elements	Product elements	Synergy of organization and product elements
			phones. The word-of-mouth communication of users has promoted the explosive growth of Xiaomi mobile phones, and the self-driving and flat management of employees has supported growth
Expansion	More executives joined; creating Mi's culture; group intelligence and middle-level decision making	Products of Xiaomi ecological chain series; Mi's platform; "Muji in the scientific and technological field"	With the establishment of the Xiaomi ecological chain, the eco-chain enterprises connected by capital and cultural ties relied on Internet marketing channels such as the Mi's home platform, and the activation and authorization of individual employees to support the related diversification of Xiaomi
Transformation	Jun Lei personally controlled the supply chain; employees over 10,000; promoting exquisite management	Release high-end mobile phones; Xiaomi's home experience store; star advertising, independent chip	With the intensification of competition from OPPO, VIVO and Huawei, Xiaomi has responded to the challenges through the organizational strategy of Jun Lei's personal supply chain, promotion of fine management and the release of high-end mobile phones, independent chips, offline channels, and star advertising

8.1.4.7 Canvas for Synergy of Organization and Market Elements (Case Analysis: Xiaomi)

Stage	Organization elements	Market elements	Synergy of organization and market elements
Start-up	Jun Lei and other mobile phone enthusiasts founded Xiaomi; employees jointly invested; flat organization mode	On the eve of android outbreak; Jun Lei invested in entrepreneurship; enthusiasts participated in MIUI development	The founders such as Jun Lei used their keen observation of industry and technology trends to create Xiaomi before the outbreak of smart phones, invested their own funds, showed entrepreneurial confidence, and inspired a group of employees with a common vision to join
Growing-up	Executives responsible for hardware joined in; employee self-driven; three-tier organizational structure	Software and hardware integration trend; B, C round of rapid financing; competition with low-end mobile phones	The founding team has a background in software, hardware and internet, which is in line with the trend of integration of mobile hardware and software. The team's financing ability, staff management ability and positioning ability help Xiaomi seize the historical opportunity of rapid growth of low-end mobile phones
Expansion	More executives joined; creating Mi's culture; group intelligence and middle-level decision making	Trend of smart Internet; D and E round of high financing; expanding cooperation and competition scope	Xiaomi introduces executives with richer backgrounds to meet the requirements of talents in the development of intelligent Internet. Through two rounds of high-funded financing, they seized the opportunity of investing in eco-chain enterprises and activated organizations through

(continued)

(continued)

Stage	Organization elements	Market elements	Synergy of organization and market elements
			group-sharing and decision-making
Transformation	Jun Lei personally controlled the supply chain; employees over 10,000; promoting exquisite management	Data-driven consumption trends; using self-owned funds to supplement cash flow; competition and cooperation in high-end market	Under the trend of big data-driven consumption, demand changes more rapidly, and it is difficult to adapt to the new trend by not controlling the supply chain and offline channels. Xiaomi has accordingly adjusted the organization management and market management

8.1.4.8 Canvas for Synergy of Product and Market Elements (Case Analysis: Xiaomi)

Stage	Product elements	Market elements	Synergy of product and market elements
Start-up	MIUI was iteratively developed; word of mouth by enthusiasts; first making software, then making hardware	On the eve of Android outbreak; Jun Lei invested in entrepreneurship; enthusiasts participated in MIUI development	The operating system has the role of leading the development of the mobile phone industry. Xiaomi has cut in from the MIUI system and developed it with enthusiasts. It has accumulated both the user base and made the preparation for developing hardware.
Growing-up	Release low-end mobile phones; word of mouth marketing; outsourcing production + Internet channels + single products	Software and hardware integration trend; B, C round of rapid financing; competition with low-end mobile phones	The MIUI system, which has advantages in user interface, helps Xiaomi to create cost-effective mobile phones. Word-of-mouth marketing, outsourcing

(continued)

(continued)

Stage	Product elements	Market elements	Synergy of product and market elements
			production, Internet channels, and single-explosive products all contribute to cost reduction. In addition, the continuous investment of funds makes it possible for Xiaomi to obtain a large amount of low-end mobile phone users
Expansion	Products of Xiaomi ecological chain series; Mi's platform; "Muji in the scientific and technological field"	Trend of smart Internet; D and E round of high financing; expanding cooperation and competition scope	The Xiaomi ecological chain series products are characterized by intelligent interconnection and are in line with the development trend of the industry. Eco-chain companies rely on Xiaomi's sales channels to create cooperative relationships, trying to become "the MUJI of the scientific and technological community"
Transformation	Release high-end mobile phones; Xiaomi's home experience store; star advertising, independent chip	Data-driven consumption trends; using self-owned funds to supplement cash flow; competition and cooperation in high-end market	Under the trend of big data-driven consumption, Xiaomi plans to develop high-end mobile phones, independent chips and cloud computing platforms in advance, and cooperate with the transformation of channels and marketing to strive for higher added value

8.2 Equation of Strategy

① Strategy = Co × Evolution	Enterprises are composed of a variety of elements, which co-evolve in the corporate life cycle to form the enterprise strategy
② Strategy = Insight × Vision	The development of enterprises depends on the insight and vision of entrepreneurs. Qualified entrepreneurs should be able to undertake the whole picture, predict the ending, understand the current position, and cope with changes
③ Strategy = Space × Time	Space and time determine the potential of enterprise development. Excellent enterprises can always expand their development space and extend their development time
④ Strategy = Systematicness × Dynamism	Strategy determines the overall development direction of the enterprise. Holistic means looking at strategy from a systemic perspective; Direction means looking at strategy from a dynamic perspective

Chapter 9
Dynamics

> There are talented people in every dynasty, each leading the way for hundreds of years.
>
> (Qing Dynasty) Yi Zhao

9.1 Dynamics of Co-evolution Strategy

Exponential growth in the growing-up stage

Exponential growth

Dr. Kreuz Kutzville (MIT) put forward the Kutzville theorem in the book "Singularity Approaching". The theorem states that all technological developments since the advent of humans have grown exponentially. That is to say, the development of technology at the beginning is slow, but once information and experience have accumulated to a certain foundation, development begins to grow rapidly and then grows in the form of exponential growth.

In fact, not only does technology have exponential growth, but there are exponential growth in users, organization, product and market in some growing-up stages.

Exponential growth of Wechat pay

Taking WeChat pay as an example. The WeChat pay project was established at the end of 2012 and officially launched on August 5, 2013. After that, WeChat payment has been tepid. In the Spring Festival of 2014, WeChat red envelopes were screened in Wechat moments, and 458 million people received and sent 1576 red envelopes on New Year's Eve. However, after the Spring Festival, the WeChat red envelope entered a period of silence again. In 2015, WeChat pay began to work. And during the Spring Festival, the "Spring Festival Evening Shake" campaign was launched. On New Year's Eve 2015, 104 million people sent and received 1.01 billion red envelopes. Later, with the WeChat red envelope becoming a "everyday social tool", 420 million people sent and received 8.08 billion red envelopes on New Year's Eve 2016.

J. Y. Lu, *Co-evolution Strategy Canvas*,
https://doi.org/10.1007/978-981-15-5988-4_9

The growth of WeChat pay is actually driven by the four elements of users, organization, product and market.

User-driven: First grab the refreshing point demand for red envelopes, and then for the general payment demand.

Organization-driven: Establish new teams and small teams with flexible mechanisms, relying on Tencent organization.

Product-driven: Red envelope, shake, transfer, change and other functions continue to innovate.

Market-driven: Cooperate with CCTV and offline merchants to build an open ecosystem.

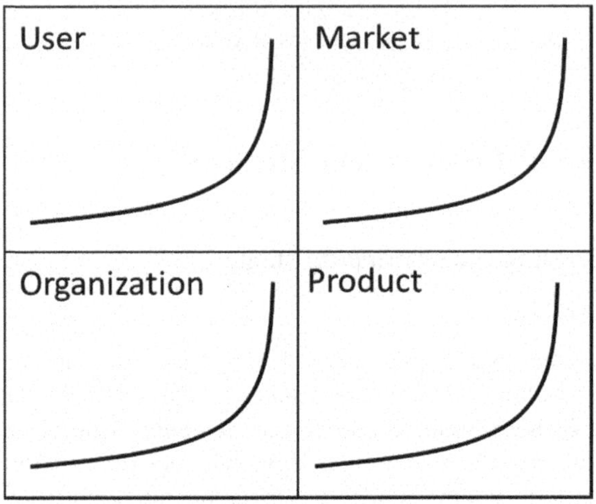

Exponential growth of Wechat pay

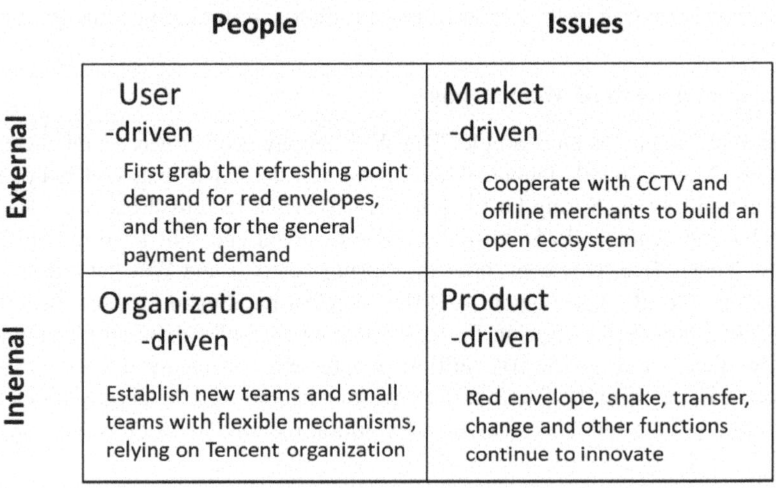

Exponential recession in the decline stage

Exponential recession

Similar to exponential growth, many companies experience exponential recession. There are many reasons for a company's decline, at least from the four aspects of users, organizations, products and markets.

Although the basic needs of users will not change greatly, there are many ways for users to meet their needs. Some specific products may be quickly eliminated due to increased user choices or products that better meet user needs. In terms of organization, it may also cause organizational disintegration due to unexpected events of founders or key figures. In the market, external events such as new technological paradigm changes or financial crises may also cause an exponential recession.

Exponential recession of Kodak film

In 1975, Kodak engineers developed the world's first digital camera. In 1991, Kodak had a 1.3 megapixel digital camera. However, in 2002 Kodak's product digitization rate was only about 25%, while its competitor Fuji had reached 60%. The sales profit of Kodak's traditional imaging division dropped sharply by $10 billion between 2000 and 2003. In 2004, Kodak announced a layoff of 20% of its employees. In 2009, Kodak continued to implement a strategic restructuring with a 50% layoff. In 2012, Kodak filed for bankruptcy protection.

Kodak's exponential recession is also driven by four elements: users, organization, product and market.

User-driven: It failed to understand that the deeper user needs than recording "wonderful moments" are sharing happiness.

Organization-driven: Organizations are bloated, decision-making efficiency is low, the market is global, and decision-making is at headquarters.

Product-driven: It ignored digital product innovation, over-expanded print shops, and was lack of model innovation.

Market-driven: It underestimated the digital trend and regarded digital cameras as rivals rather than partners.

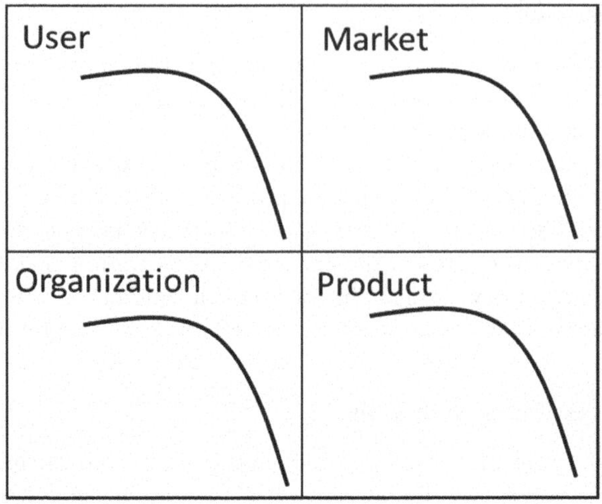

Exponential recession of Kodak film

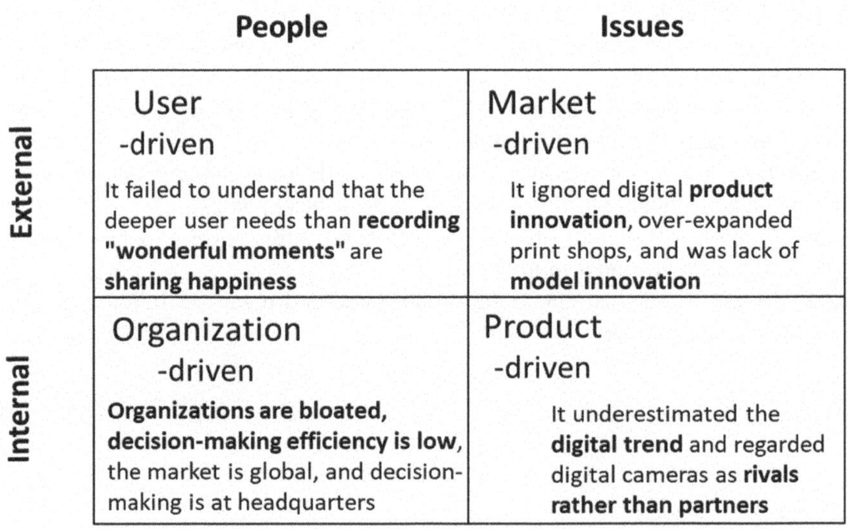

9.1.1 *Enhanced Feedback Loop for Changes in Strategic Elements*

Enhanced feedback loops are the main cause of a company's exponential growth or exponential recession. The enhanced loop is also divided into a positive enhanced loop and a negative enhanced loop. The positive enhanced loop is also called a benign loop, and the negative enhanced loop is also called a vicious loop.

9.1.1.1 Enhanced Feedback Loop of 4 Elements

User elements On the one hand, as the users flow in, the number of users' increases, and the increased number of users may have a positive enhanced loop effect on user inflow, thereby accelerating the speed of user inflow. On the other hand, with the loss of users, the number of users decreased, and the reduced number of users may have a negative enhancement loop effect on the user outflow, thereby accelerating the speed of user outflow.

Organization elements On the one hand, as the vitality of the organization increases, the organizational energy increases, and the increased energy may have a positive enhanced loop effect on the source of organization vitality, thereby accelerating the increase of organization vitality. On the other hand, as organization inertia increases, organization energy decreases, and decreased organization energy may have a negative enhanced loop effect of increased organization inertia, thereby increasing organization inertia level.

Product elements On the one hand, with the increase of product innovation, product quality is improved, and the improved product quality may have a positive enhanced loop effect on the source of product innovation, thus accelerating the speed of product innovation. On the other hand, as products become obsolete, product quality declines, and declining product quality may have a negative enhanced loop effect on the product obsolescence, thereby accelerating product obsolescence.

Market elements On the one hand, with the increase of market cooperation, the market capacity increases, and the increased market capacity may have a positive enhanced loop effect on market cooperation behavior, thereby increasing the possibility of market cooperation. On the other hand, as market competition intensifies, market capacity declines, the declining market capacity may have a negative enhanced loop effect on market competition, thus exacerbating market competition.

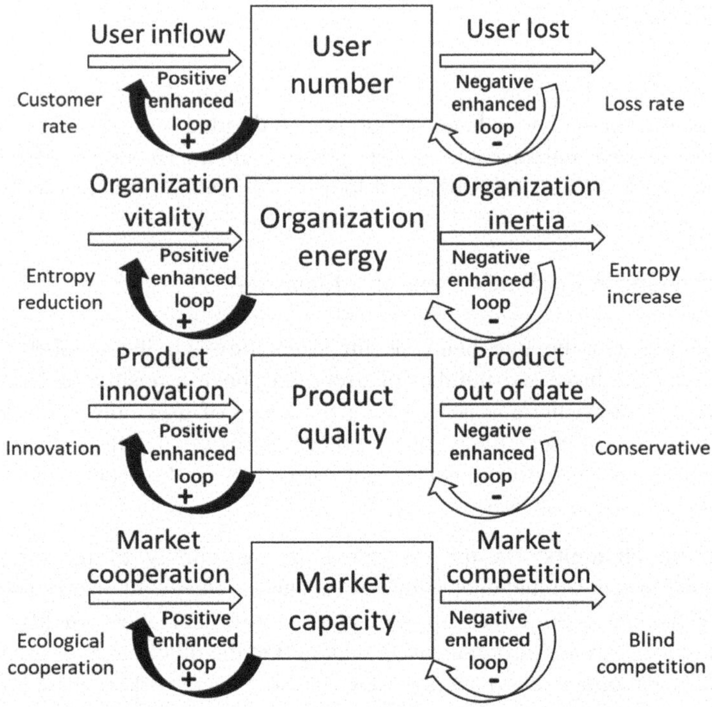

9.1.2 *Mechanisms of Enhanced Feedback Loop for User and Organization Elements*

9.1.2.1 Enhanced Feedback Mechanism for Organization Elements

① Organization goal, points the way for organizational development. When an organization has a clear organizational goal, the organization's energy will increase, and it will also attract more employees with a sense of purpose and mission to join the organization, forming a positive enhanced loop. When an organization loses its clear organizational goals, organizational energy is weakened, and employees with a sense of purpose and mission may leave the organization and form a negative enhanced loop.

② Organization culture, is the value concept that team employees hold in their business activities. The organization implements organizational goals into daily business activities through organizational culture. A good organizational culture can enhance employees' sense of mission, belonging, and responsibility, forming a positive enhanced loop. At the same time, if an organization develops serious organizational inertia with development, it will spread through the organization culture atmosphere and form a negative enhanced loop.

③ Organization growth, is a direct expression of the organization's correct goals and good culture. Team employees need to experience the growth of the organization and benefit from it. A growing organization can motivate the team's employees to form a positive enhanced loop of organizational energy. Conversely, the accumulation of organization inertia can hinder tissue growth, weaken tissue energy, and create a negative enhanced loop.

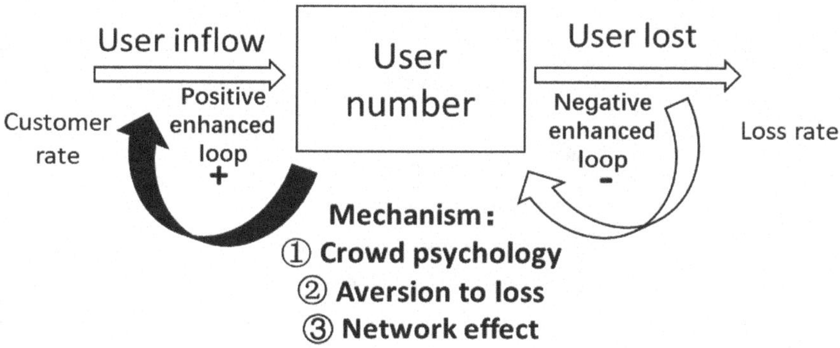

9.1.2.2 Enhanced Feedback Mechanism for User Elements

① Crowd psychology, means that individuals are affected by the behavior of outsiders, and they show their own behavior, judgment, and understanding in line with public opinion or the behavior of the majority. Because users generally have a crowd psychology, the greater the number of users, the greater the attraction to those who do not join, thus achieving a positive loop. Similarly, when user churn reaches a certain level, more and more users will choose to leave, thus forming a negative loop.

② Aversion to loss, means that when a person owns an item, his evaluation of the value of the item will be greatly increased before it is owned. Due to the impact of aversion to loss, the evaluation of the goods or services owned by the stock users may deviate from the objective situation. If the users' evaluation is positive, a positive enhanced loop will be formed, and if the users' evaluation is biased negative, a negative enhanced loop will be formed.

③ Network effect, means that as the number of users increases, users may get more value from other users, that is, the value of a product to one user depends on the number of other users who use the product. Network externalities are divided into positive network externalities and negative network externalities. Forward network externalities means that as users in the same network increase, the value gained by other users also increases. Negative network externalities are the opposite.

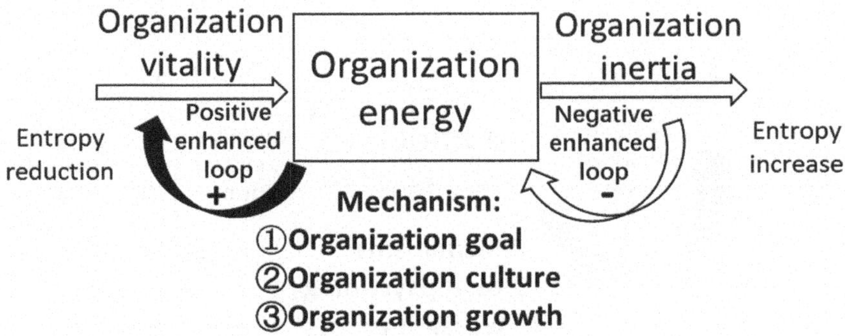

9.1.3 *Mechanisms of Enhanced Feedback Loop for Product and Market Elements*

9.1.3.1 Enhanced Feedback Mechanism for Market Elements

① Path dependence, means that the evolution of technology has inertia, and once it enters a certain path, it may depend on such a path. If the technology path chosen by a company is on the rise, the increased market capacity will further expand the market capacity through mechanisms such as market cooperation, thus forming a positive enhanced loop. However, if the technology path chosen by a company is in a recession, the reduced market capacity will form a negative enhanced loop through limited market capacity such as market competition.

② Risk avoidance, means resource and capital providers usually hope to reduce the risks of the resources and capital they provide. The better the firm develops, the more willing they are to provide the resources and capital. The more difficult for the firm to develop, the less willing it is to provide resources and capital.

③ Ecological effect, refers to the division of labor and cooperation between firms to give play to their respective advantages and form an ecological system of coordinated development, which has the effect of mutual benefit. When the capacity of a market is large enough, firms tend to be more inclined to work together to further promote the development of the market and form a positive reinforcement loop. When a market space is limited, it is easier for firms to emphasize competition among themselves, which further leads to the compression of market space and the formation of a negative enhanced loop.

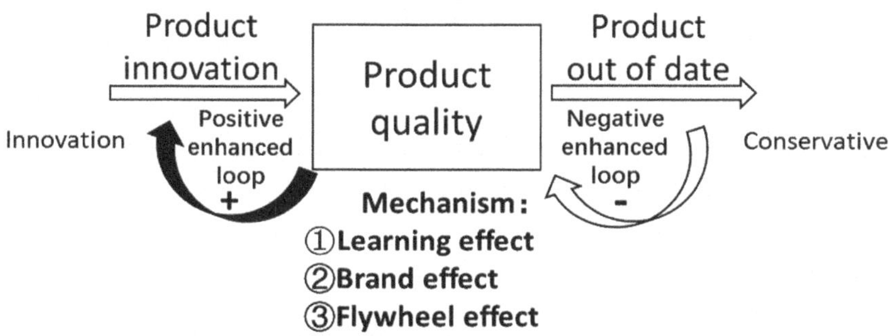

9.1.3.2 Enhanced Feedback Mechanism for Product Elements

① Learning effect, means in the long-term production process, employees of the firm increase the efficiency of product development and production by accumulating product production and technical design experience. The firm creates a positive enhanced loop by motivating team employees to learn to promote product innovation. On the contrary, if the firm product is outdated, the team staff will lose the learning opportunity and cannot improve the product quality through the accumulation of learning effects, thus forming a negative enhanced loop.

② Brand effect, means the use of a unified brand to enhance the user's awareness and recognition of the firm's products or services. By strengthening the brand effect of the products, the firm maintains the awareness and recognition of the products in the minds of users, enhances the market competitiveness of the products, and forms a positive enhanced loop. On the contrary, if the firm product is outdated, it will hurt the unified brand of the product used by the firm, damage the awareness and recognition of the product in the users' mind, and form a negative enhanced loop.

③ Flywheel effect, refers to the organic promotion of each business module of a company, like the gears drive each other. In the beginning, it takes a lot of effort to move from rest to rotation, but once it turns, the gear will turn faster and faster.

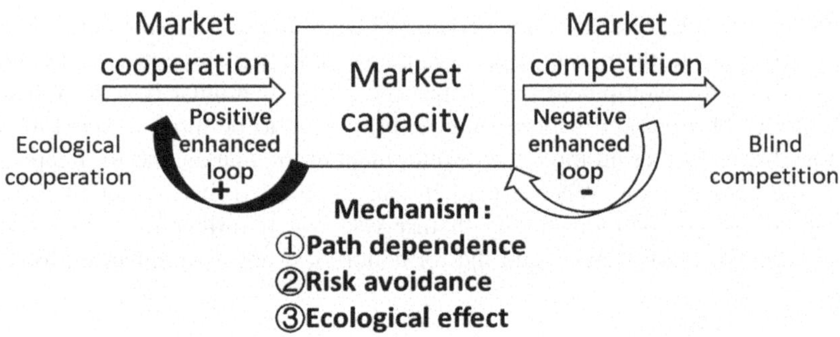

9.1.4 *Feedback Loop System for User Elements in Different Stages of Development*

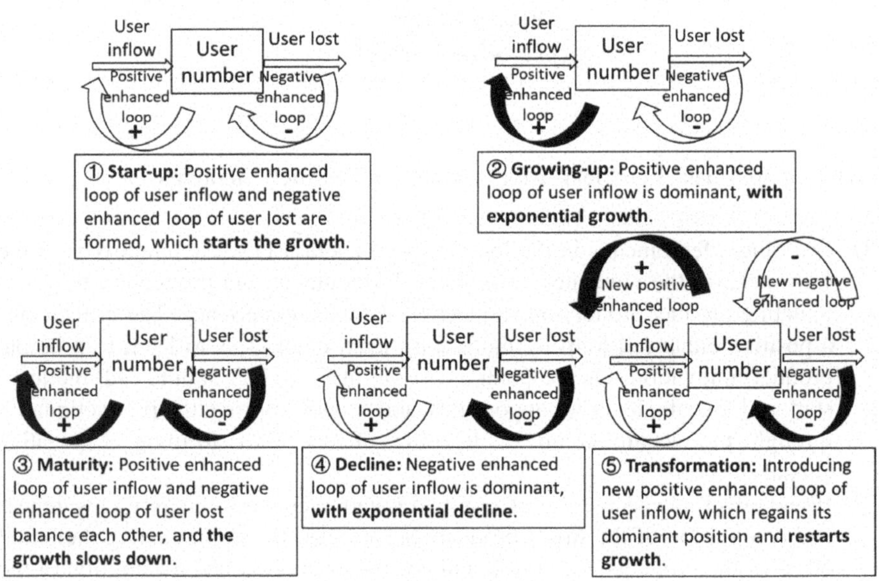

① During the start-up stage, user inflows and outflow levels are low. Correspondingly, the positive enhanced loop and the negative enhanced loop of the user elements feedback are both low.

② During the growing-up stage, as the firm can meet the needs of more users, the user positive enhanced loop is becoming dominant, while the strength of the negative enhanced loop is relatively weak, and the number of users begins to grow rapidly, even in the form of exponential growth.

③ During the expansion stage, the positive enhanced loop of user element feedback will gradually weaken after a period of time. Correspondingly, the negative enhanced loop of user element feedback is gradually enhanced. When the positive boost loop and the negative boost loop power of the user element feedback approach the balance, the number of users tends to stagnate.

④ During the decline stage, as the negative enhanced loop of user element feedback is strengthened, user loss is accelerated, and the firm has a net loss of users.

⑤ During the transformation stage, the firm need to establish new positive enhanced loop in order to restart user growth. Over time, the new loop of user element feedback will increase the net user growth for the firm and restart growth.

9.1.5 *Feedback Loop System for Organization Elements in Different Stages of Development*

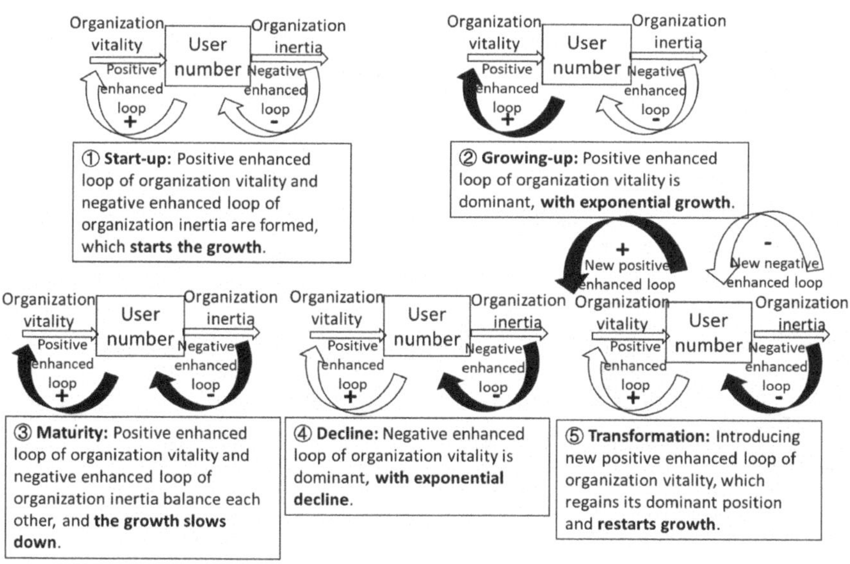

① During the start-up stage, both the positive enhanced loop and the negative enhanced loop strength of the organization element feedback are low.

② During the growing-up stage, as the power of the positive enhanced loop becomes dominant, the power of the negative enhanced loop becomes relatively weak, and the energy of the firm organization starts to grow rapidly, even exponentially.

③ During the expansion stage, after the positive enhanced loop of the feedback of organizational elements reaches a certain level, it will gradually weaken and the organization vitality speed will decrease. Correspondingly, the negative enhanced loop of the feedback of organizational elements is gradually enhanced, and the organizational inertia is rising.

④ During the decline stage, as the negative enhanced loop of organization element feedback increases, organizational inertia increases. In the feedback of the original organization elements of the firm, once the negative enhanced loop dominates, it is difficult to reverse.

⑤ During the transformation stage, to restart organizational growth, the firm needs to establish new positive enhanced loops. Over time, the new organization elements feedback loop will increase the organization's vitality and restart growth.

9.1.6 Feedback Loop System for Product Elements in Different Stages of Development

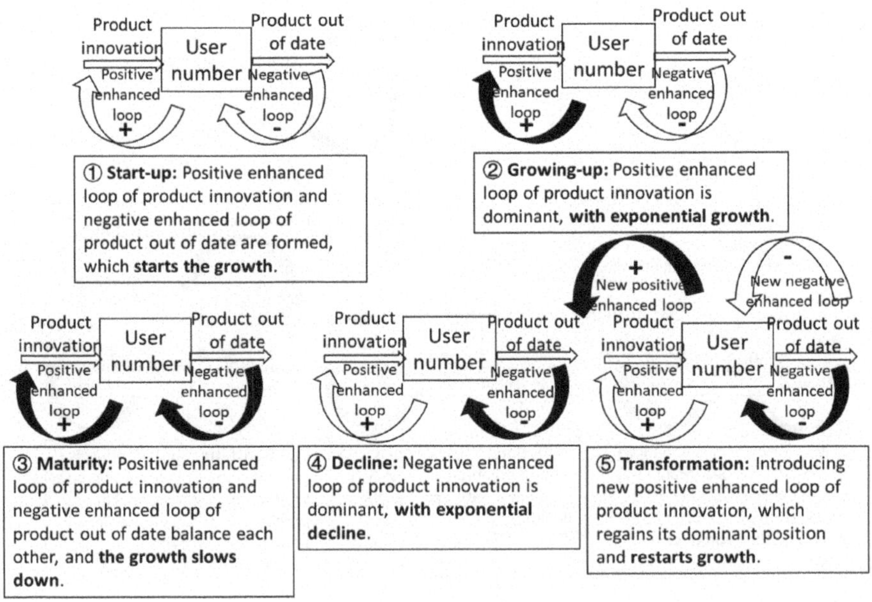

① During the start-up stage, product innovation levels and product obsolescence are low. Correspondingly, the strength of positive and negative enhanced loop of the product elements feedback is low.

② During the growing-up stage, as the power of product positive enhanced loop is becoming dominant, the strength of the negative enhanced loop is relatively weak, and the product quality of the firm begins to increase rapidly, even in the form of exponential growth.

③ During the expansion stage, after the positive enhanced loop of the product element feedback reaches a certain level, it will gradually weaken. Correspondingly, the negative enhanced loop of the product element feedback is gradually enhanced, and the outdated speed of the product increases. Product quality growth tends to stagnate as the positive and negative enhanced loop power of product elements feedback approach equilibrium.

④ During the decline stage, with the strengthening of the negative enhanced loop of product element feedback, the product obsolescence is accelerating and the firm has a net loss of users.

⑤ During the transformation stage, in order to restart growth, a new positive enhanced loop needs to be established. The positive enhanced loop regains its dominant position, and the firm's new product element feedback loop will bring the increase of product quality to the firm.

9.1.7 Feedback Loop System for Market Elements in Different Stages of Development

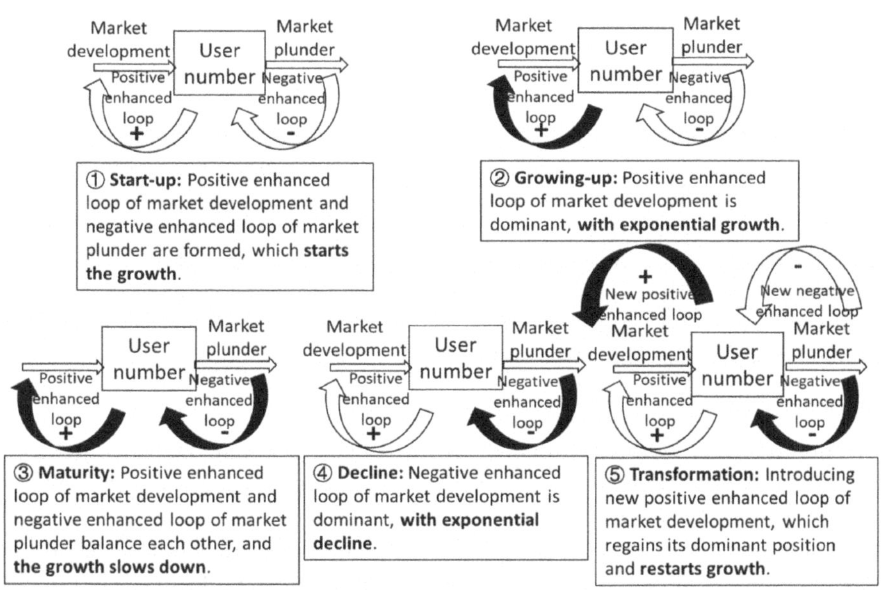

① During the start-up stage, the level of market development and market plundering are both low in the start-up stage, and the strength of positive and negative enhanced loop of market element feedback is low.
② During the growing-up stage, as the power of market positive enhanced loop is becoming dominant, the strength of the negative enhanced loop is relatively weak, and the market capacity of the firm begins to increase rapidly, even in the form of exponential growth.
③ During the expansion stage, after the positive enhanced loop of the market element feedback reaches a certain level, it will gradually weaken. Correspondingly, the negative enhanced loop of the market element feedback is gradually enhanced. Market capacity growth tends to stagnate as the positive and negative enhanced loop power of product elements feedback approach equilibrium.
④ During the decline stage, with the strengthening of the negative enhanced loop of market element feedback, the market plundering is accelerating and the firm enters a decline stage.
⑤ During the transformation stage, in order to restart growth, a new positive enhanced loop needs to be established. The positive enhanced loop regains its dominant position, and the firm's new market element feedback loop will bring the increase of market capacity to the firm.

9.1.8 Four Paths of Evolutions

9.1.8.1 Path of User Evolution

In the four stages of development that firms experience, user elements are constantly evolving. The strategic points of user elements range from angel user, key demand and existing competitor in the start-up period, to mainstream users, common demands and crossing the chasm in the growing-up period, accumulated users, various demands and complementary demands in the expansion period, and redefining users, potential demands and upgrading/downgrading of demand in the transformation period. During the entire evolution process, both the enhanced loop and the regulative loop are working.

Enhanced loop

Start-up firms start with a small number of users and determine the angel users by understanding user characteristics, user needs, and user choices. With deep contact with users, firms begin to understand the similarities and differences between angel users and other user groups. The similarities constitute the basis for firms to understand the mainstream users in the growing-up stage. Firms entering the growing-up stage serve mainstream users which are different from angel users. Due to the enhanced loop, the number of accumulated users is increasing. As the increase of users slows down, firms enter maturity stage, and accumulated users reach a certain number. The aggregated user groups may generate new user characteristics, user needs and user choice patterns, creating a chance for firms to redefine users and enter the transformation stage.

Regulative loop

Start-up firms start with a small number of users. As the number of users increases, different types of users begin to appear, and user needs begin to diversify. These diverse needs have some similarities, and the most similar one is the common demands that firms should give priority to. The emergence of common demand plays a role in regulating the user elements in the start-up stage. That is to say, when common demand arises, the enterprise should not simply meet the key demands of users. Only when the common needs are met, can the enhanced loop which users chose be triggered again, and help the firms cross the demand chasm. Similarly, as the number of users grows slower, firms should be wary of whether they are about to enter the expansion stage. If so, the regulative loop of the user elements will begin to function, and the firms cannot simply and repeatedly satisfy the basic common needs of the users, but should pay attention to the various demands of the users.

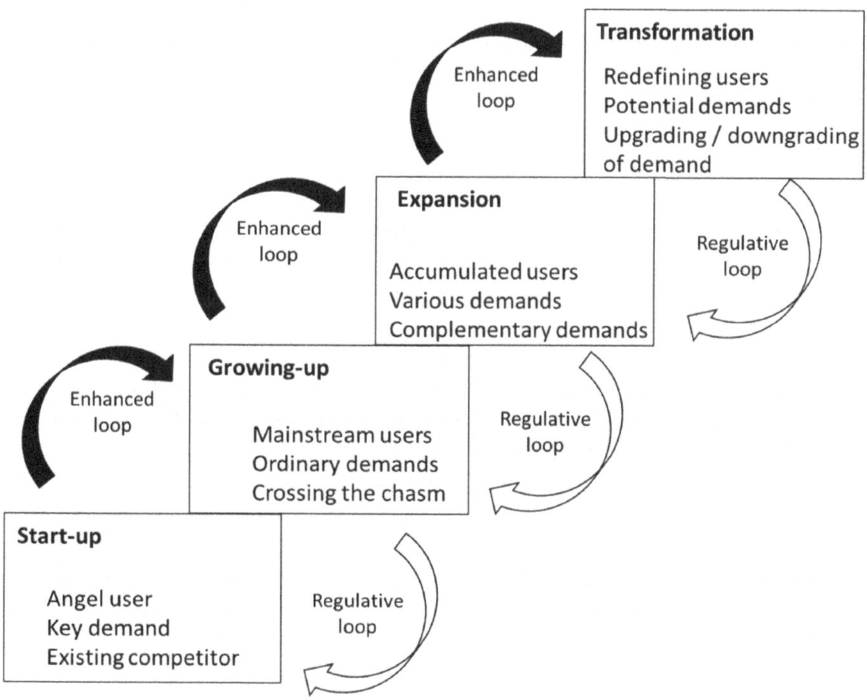

9.1.8.2 Path of Organization Evolution

The strategic points of organization elements range from founder, founding team and flat organization in the start-up period, to founder growth, team specialization and pyramid organization in the growing-up period, founder maturity, team professionalism and divisional organization in the expansion period, and regaining founder spirit, rebuilding entrepreneurial team and reactivating organization in the transformation period. During the entire evolution process, both the enhanced loop and the regulative loop are working.

Enhanced loop

Firms enter the start-up stage from the founders' entrepreneurship. The founders' entrepreneurship relies on past experience, current resources and optimistic expectations for the future. With the acquisition of experience, the accumulation of resources and the deep understanding of the future, the founders continue to growing up. In the process of growing up, the founder will experience a lot of bumps, and mature with the maturity of the firm. When the firm enters the decline/transformation stage, the founders need to regain founder spirit and once again lead the firm to embark on a new journey. Similarly, when an entrepreneurial team joins a firm at the beginning of its business, it also needs to continuously strengthen its professional quality through an enhanced loop, and experience the processes of specialization, professionalism, and entrepreneurship to meet the requirements of firm development.

Regulative loop

Firms in the start-up stage began to develop from a flat organization structure. As the number of people increases beyond the effective management scope, flat organizations are difficult to adapt to the development of the organization, and pyramid organizations began to emerge. However, the emergence of pyramid organizations will bring a certain degree of damage to the efficiency of firm decision-making. Therefore, in the formation process of pyramid organization, the regulation loop will continue to play a role, so that the decision-making efficiency of the flat organization and the decision-making preciseness of the pyramid organization are balanced. For example, companies entering maturity stage usually adopt divisional system or a matrix organization structure. If these formal organizational structures continue to run for a long time, it will lead to an increase in organization inertia. Therefore, even if the firm is still in the maturity stage, in order to improve the organizational efficiency, the regulative role of the organization elements in the transformation stage will begin to play a role, and the firm will begin to introduce the reactivating organization.

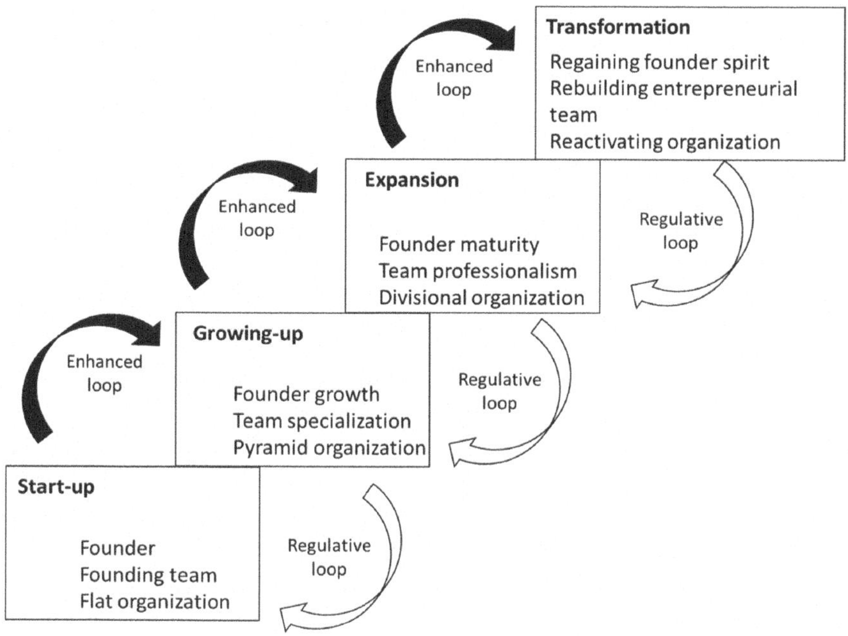

9.1.8.3 Path of Product Strategic Evolution

The strategic points of product elements range from MVP development, word-of-mouth marketing and single breakthrough in the start-up period, to best seller, advertising marketing and economies of scale in the growing-up period, related products, related marketing and economies of scope in the expansion period, and categorical innovation, categorical marketing and ecological model in the transformation period. During the entire evolution process, both the enhanced loop and the regulative loop are working.

Enhanced loop

Firms use MVP development during the start-up period to find products that can meet user needs and market environment with lower cost and faster speed, and form best sellers through word-of-mouth marketing and single breakthrough mode. Firms entering the growing-up stage will expand their scale and enjoy the benefits of economies of scale with best sellers and advertising marketing. After entering the maturity stage, the growth of the original best sellers begins to decline, and the firm will build related products based on the accumulated experience of these products to form economies of scope. On the basis of related products, the firm will further develop. If it can innovate product categories, it will have the opportunity to form an enhanced loop of "point, line, surface and body" from the beginning of the start-up.

Regulative loop

When the firm forms a single breakthrough product in the start-up stage, it needs to consider the market potential of the product. If the product cannot form economies of scale, it needs to adjust the product direction through the regulative loop. In the same way, if the firm can't build related products around major products and form economies of scope, it also need to adjust its product direction in the growing-up stage. Before entering the transformation stage, the firm should also review the products and services it provided, and analyze which products or services can be used for categorical innovation to form an ecological advantage.

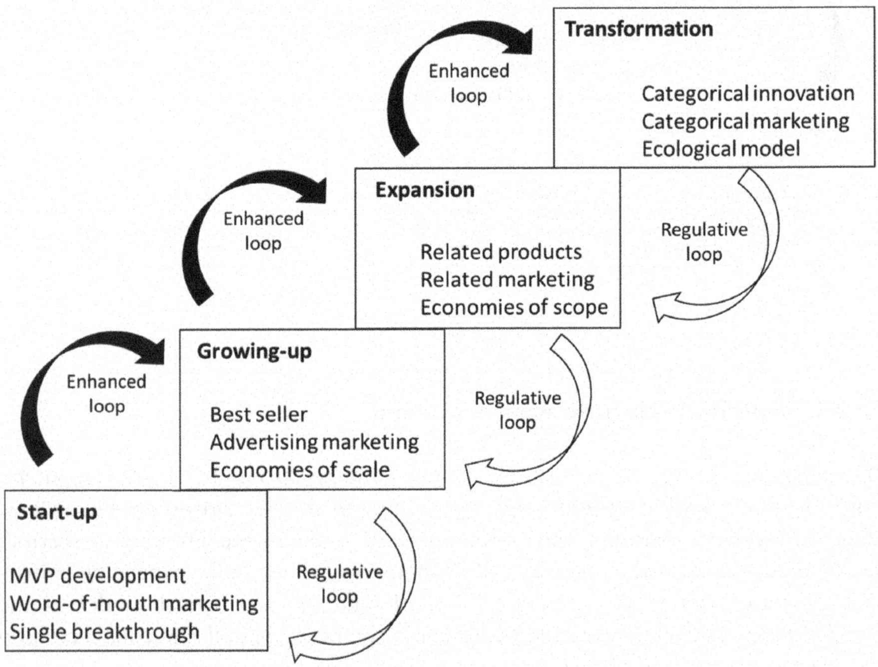

9.1.8.4 Path of Market Strategic Evolution

The strategic points of market elements range from innovative technology, initial capital and chaotic market in the start-up period, to growing technology, lean fundraising and blue ocean market in the growing-up period, dominant design, capital operation and red ocean market in the expansion period, and paradigm change, corporate venture capital and blue-ice market in the transformation period. During the entire evolution process, both the enhanced loop and the regulative loop are working.

Enhanced loop

In the process of development, firms will continue to select specific technical directions according to technology trends, from selecting innovative technologies to focusing on technology growth and standardization, and then achieving firm transformation and greater development by paradigm change which following or even leading the technology. Similarly, the firm develop from simply relying on initial capital in start-up stage, to being recognized by the market, and being able to obtain fundraising from the market. Later, it can expand the scale of the firm through capital operation until it can use ways like corporate venture capital to capture new opportunities. From technology follow-up to technology leadership, from capital acquisition to capital utilization, market enhancement loop plays a key role.

Regulative loop

Whether the market environment faced by the firm is chaotic market, blue ocean market, or the red sea market and blue-ice market depends on the market environment in the next stage. For firms in the start-up stage, if the current market becomes a blue ocean market is far away, the firm needs to consider whether to fight in the current chaotic market, or directly to find a blue ocean market. For firms in the growing-up stage, if the current market is going to become the red sea market soon, the firm need to consider how to find the next blue ocean. In short, in the process of firm development, it is very important to have regulative loop thinking: see the end before you break it.

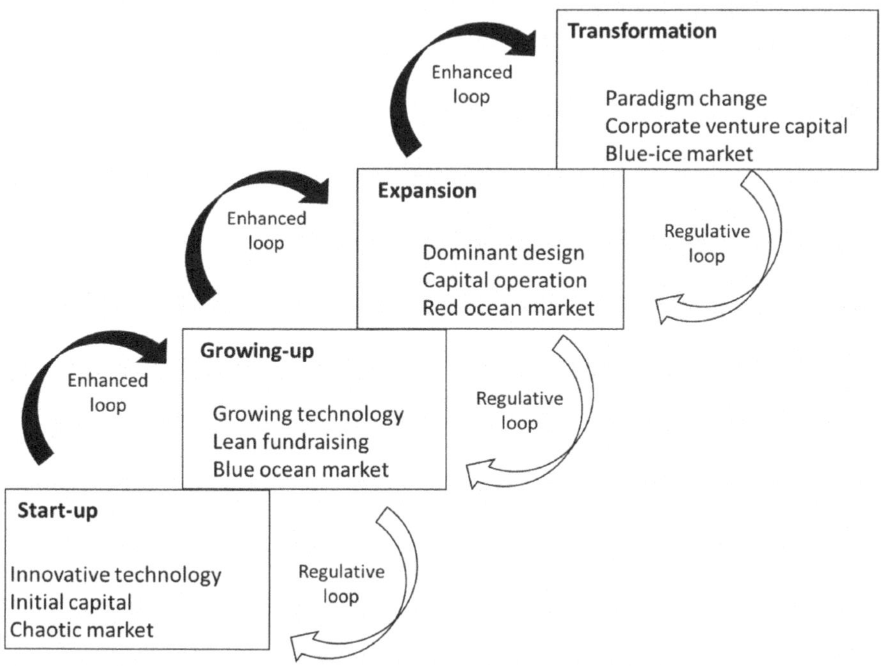

9.2 16-Word Formula of Co-evolution Strategy

Throughout the four stages of the co-evolution strategy, the four elements of users, organization, product and market can be summarized in one word, collectively referred to as "the 16-word formula of co-evolution strategy."

4-word formula of user elements: Precise, numerous, existing and negation
4-word formula of organization elements: Light, fast, strong and rising
4-word formula of product elements: Grinding, specialized, correlation and new
4-word formula of market elements: Accurate, rapid, increase and creation.

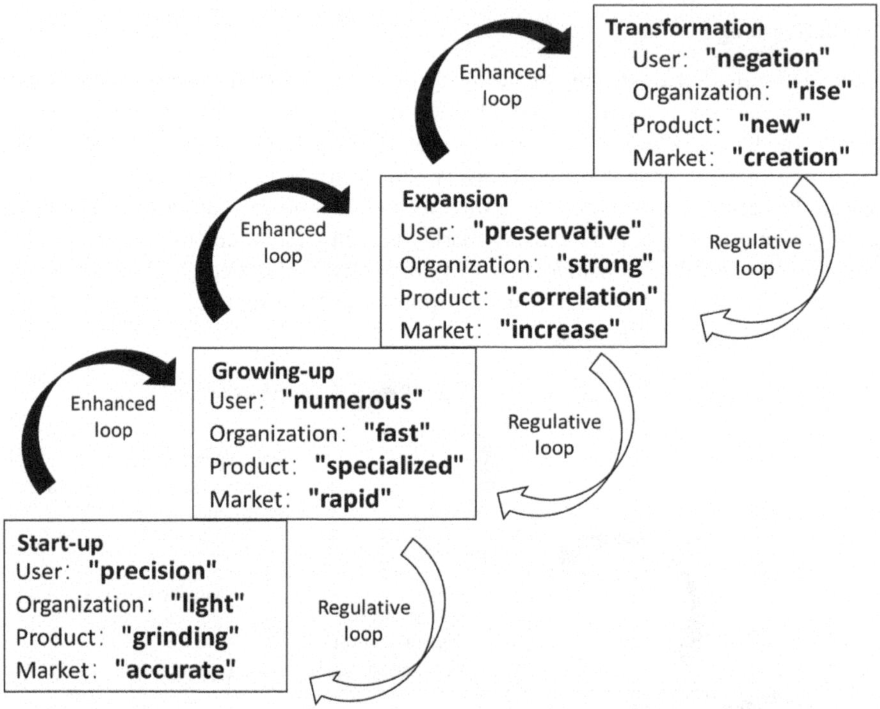

The dynamics of co-evolution strategic elements can be more detailed in the "canvas for strategic element evolution path"

9.3 Canvas and Examples

9.3.1 Canvas for User Evolution Path

Start-up	**Growing-up**	**Maturity**	**Transformation**
Angel user ➡	Mainstream users ➡	Accumulated users ➡	Redefining users
Key demand ➡	Ordinary demands ➡	Various demands ➡	Potential demands
Existing competitor ➡	Crossing the Chasm ➡	Complementary demands ➡	Upgrading/downgrading of demand

Canvas for user evolution path (Example: Tencent)

Start-up	Growing-up	Maturity	Transformation
Angel user	Mainstream users	Accumulated users	Redefining users
• In 1999, after the launch of OICQ, the first batch of users from PCICQ quickly formed a reputation • In 1999, National Day closed the network for 7 days, ICQ users transferred • In 1999, users designed the logo • At the end of 2000, in cooperation with Monternet, early users were young mainstream users in the middle-end and low-end market	• From young, middle-end and low-end users to more popular mass • QQers grow, post-85s, QQ number, virtual expression, multifaceted life	• The number of users such as QQ zone and QQ games has increased rapidly. • QQ portal is comparable to NetEase in major news reports • On March 5, 2010, QQ reached 100 million simultaneous users	• 60% of QQ users are post-90s, and QQ tends to be entertaining • WeChat users have a large span and a wide range

(continued)

(continued)

Start-up	Growing-up	Maturity	Transformation
Key demand	Ordinary demands	Various demands	Potential demands
• Chatting on the Internet cafe computer in time, you can save your friends list and chat history on the server. • Suitable for Chinese people's implicit emotional communication (pager, SMS are the same) • Have a unique image in the virtual world	• Higher-end business needs • More generally, one-stop service under the same entrance • More profound social needs	• Tencent-style operations: lock in a "real appeal point", strive to achieve the ultimate in the user experience—grab the consumer base from a huge user base—launch advanced paid commercial services after forming a certain number of basic users—continuously optimize and try to extend the life cycle of your product—find new appeal points	• Mobile communication changes life • QQ: recreational social contact, scene communication • WeChat: social recreation, scene consumption
Existing competitor	Crossing the Chasm	Complementary demands	Upgrading/ downgrading of demand
• SP: Other partners of Monternet • QQ: Imitators of ICQ, PCICQ, etc.	• NetEase launched Netease Bubble in November 2002 • Competing with Microsoft's MSN • Relying on large file transfer and other functions to cross the chasm	• "Virtual Carrier" Dreams disillusioned • Launched mobile QQ, complementary to PC QQ • Social needs, life needs and entertainment needs are complementary	• Mobile-based QQ mobile game, QQ reading, interest tribe, QQ wallet, QQ red envelope, "parent album" in QQ zone

9.3.2 *Canvas for Organization Evolution Path*

Start-up	**Growing-up**	**Maturity**	**Transformation**
Founder ➡	Founder growth ➡	Founder maturity ➡	Regaining founder spirit
Founding team ➡	Team specialization ➡	Team professionalism ➡	Rebuilding entrepreneurial team
Flat organization ➡	Pyramid organization ➡	Divisional organization ➡	Reactivating organization

Canvas for organization evolution path (Example: Tencent)

Start-up	Growing-up	Maturity	Transformation
Founder	Founder growth	Founder maturity	Regaining founder spirit
• Webmaster Pony likes astronomy • Admitted to Shenzhen University in 1989 • Internship at dawn computer, stock analysis system sold 50,000 yuan • After graduating in 1993, he entered Runxun and engaged in paging business. • Established Pony Station of Huiduo.com in 1995	• Huateng Ma's speech: from "technology-driven" to "application-driven" to "service and user-driven": application entertainment, community, personal information processing, wireless interconnection, security and localized applications	• Deep reflection after the 3Q war, stressing not only to think about what is right, but also to think about what is recognized • "Open the door to the future" mail • Gradually appearing in the public eye	• The 12th Anniversary of "Open the door to the future" email promised "open" • In December 2010, "8 Outlines on the future of the Internet": out of the Three Gorges era, the rise of upstream values, monopoly is the arbitrary crime, occupying the source, experiencing the economy, scarcity, liberation, and great companies

(continued)

(continued)

Start-up	Growing-up	Maturity	Transformation
Founding team	Team specialization	Team professionalism	Rebuilding entrepreneurial team
• His high school classmates Chenxi Xu, Zhidong Zhang and Yidan Chen were admitted to Shenzhen University in the same year; Liqing Zeng graduated from Xidian University in the same year and worked in Shenzhen Telecom Bureau	• At the end of 2004, Chiping Liu joined Tencent from Goldman Sachs • Product manager system	• Recruiting professional talents at home and abroad • In February 2006, Chiping Liu was appointed as the president of Tencent, responsible for strategy, investment and investor relationship, and formulated a "5-year business plan" • In November 2006, Liqing Zeng retired and became a Tencent Lifelong Consultant	• 2011, "Ten Fairs" • Two abilities: capital, flow • Huateng Ma, 2012, "Seven Dimensions of Gray Rule": User (demand); Organization (redundancy, evolution); Product (speed, innovation); Market (open collaboration, flexibility) • In 2014, Dawei Wang, CXO
Flat organization	Pyramid organization	Divisional organization	Reactivating organization
• In 1999, three-year plan, 18 people, sitting in a 100-square-foot office	• In July 2004, the company moved to the FIYTA Building with 760 employees • The first organizational restructuring in 2001: the company is divided into M line, R line and functional departments • General meeting system, "who is in charge, who proposes, who is responsible"	• The second organizational restructuring in 2005 • 8 sequences: 5 business units and 3 functional departments • Formation of divisional organization system • All business foundations are derived from flow, forming a model of "big powers mastered, small powers scattered"	• On May 8, 2012, Tencent announced that it upgraded its original business system to a business group system • In May 2014, Tencent carried out the fourth organizational restructuring, and the business group was reorganized into 7

9.3.3 Canvas for Product Evolution Path

Start-up	Growing-up	Maturity	Transformation
MVP development	Best seller	Related products	Categorical innovation
Word-of-mouth marketing	Advertising Marketing	Related Marketing	Categorical Marketing
Single breakthrough	Economies of scale	Economies of scope	Ecological model

Canvas for product evolution path (Example: Tencent)

Start-up	Growing-up	Maturity	Transformation
MVP development	Best seller	Related products	Categorical innovation
• "Wireless Network Paging System", a bad product, total revenue of 1 million yuan in 1998-1999 • OICQ conducted product micro-innovation according to the habits of Chinese users • OICQ iterated three versions in the first week • Form a product manager system that blends with the culture of engineers	• QQ Show: An acquaintance social circle (Avatar plan). Half a year on the line, 5 million people bought, 5 yuan per capita • QQ.Com: Youth News Portal	• In 2006, mobile phone QQ and Super QQ were launched to create a mobile portal matrix • QQ space, happy farm, QQ church, QQ pet; starting from the casual game, the birth of "king of the game"	• QQ and WeChat • Social products and entertainment game products • Propose a new idea of "connecting everything" and "internet+" • WeChat, red envelope and other new features • Acquisition of Shanda Literature, a new platform to promote entertainment and socialization • Create Tencent Cloud
Word-of-mouth marketing	Advertising marketing	Related marketing	Categorical marketing
• Because of the ease of downloading and use, OICQ quickly became a reputation in the early days and stayed ahead of its competitors • 2 months on the line, users increased 4 times	• Importing on an inflow basis • Create customized marketing with big data • QQ platform provides more interactive elements for games and entertainment, forming word-of-mouth marketing	• "Guangdiantong" started the effect of advertising first, multi-terminal cross-screen platform, 12 years, advertising revenue exceeded Sina	• Sudoku marketing of WeChat platform • More customized ad push • QQ to WeChat flow import • Flow import for Tencent applications and third-party applications on the sudoku of WeChat wallet

(continued)

(continued)

Start-up	Growing-up	Maturity	Transformation
Single breakthrough	Economies of scale	Economies of scope	Ecological model
• In February 1999, OICQ (QQ), software volume innovation, 220KB, 5 minutes to download • Personalized avatars, strangers and friends; buddy lists moved to the server (users often change their Internet locations)	• Import flow from the portal • Imitation and rapid improvement of excellent products on the market, and beyond; "public enemies"	• ICEC (Information, Communication, Entertainment, Commerce) online life platform • Focusing on "one-stop online life" to expand business scope • "Going out to grab the ground and coordinate with the internals"	• In June 2011, the first partner conference: "Please witness the strategic transformation of Tencent" • "Internet+": communication, entertainment, information, shopping, social contact

9.3.4 *Canvas for Market Evolution Path*

Start-up	Growing-up	Maturity	Transformation
Innovative technology	Growing technology	Dominant design	Paradigm change
Initial capital	Lean fundraising	Capital operation	Corporate venture capital
Chaotic market	Blue ocean market	Red ocean market	Blue-ice market

Canvas for market evolution path (Example: Tencent)

Start-up	Growing-up	Maturity	Transformation
Innovative technology	Growing technology	Dominant design	Paradigm change
• Micro-innovation in OICQ technology (1) User content and lists are stored on the server instead of the client (2) The software is only 220K in size, which is much smaller than other products' 3M and 5M. It is easy to download	• Q currency payment system • Hierarchical membership service system	• In 2008, Tencent Games first year. Acting "Crossing the FireWire", "Dungeon and Warriors", developing a series of QQ games • Participation in 2008, the acquisition of Riot in 2011, "League of Legends"	• WeChat launched in January 2011; 100 million users in March 2012; April, moments; August, public number; January 2014, red envelope • A series of services based on technologies such as cloud computing

(continued)

(continued)

Start-up	Growing-up	Maturity	Transformation
(3) Using UDP technology to save server costs		• The game exceeded the grand game in 2009	
Initial capital	Lean fundraising	Capital operation	Corporate venture capital
• In 1998, the founding team invested 500,000 and in 1999 it increased to 1 million. • "Not okay, but I don't want your stock." • In 1999, Shenzhen Telecom invested 600,000 and provided servers and broadband (jointly established, unoccupied shares) • In April 2000, IDG and Yingke invested 2.2 million US dollars, accounting for 40%	• In 2001, MIH accounted for 32.8% • In 2004, Hong Kong went public. Before the IPO, the MIH and founding teams each accounted for 50%	• "Will Tencent do this project?" "If Tencent does, how do you guarantee not to be killed?"	• In January 2011, the industry win-win fund was established; in 2013, it invested in Sogou; in 2014, 20% of the shares of the public comment; 15% of the equity of Jingdong; and 19.9% of the shares of the same city
Chaotic market	Blue ocean market	Red ocean market	Blue-ice market
• Starting from the mobile Monternet business, the market was regulated by the government • A number of Internet companies emerged in 1998-1999. With portals as the mainstream, instant messaging software had not become mainstream, and market imitation and competition were serious	• From the Internet portal, extending to all aspects of user life • Red diamond, yellow diamond, green diamond • Game and entertainment market	• In 2005, the acquisition of Foxmail, versus Hotmail; proposed redefining instant messaging, versus MSN; 2006, Pat Network versus Taobao; QQ Zone versus MSNspace versus 51.com; 2007, QQ Music versus iTunes • 2010 3Q war	• Supported by cloud computing, "connect everything" • "Internet+" new proposition • "Guangdong, Hong Kong and Macau Bay Area"

Appendix

- "Magic numbers" in co-evolution strategy
- Implications of co-evolution strategy from animals

A.1 "Magic Numbers" in Co-evolution Strategy: 1, 2, 4, 6, 12, 48

1 environment characteristic: complexity = uncertainty x discontinuity
2 strategic dimensions: people and issues, internal and external
4 strategic elements: users, organization, product, market

> 4 strategic phases: start-up, growing-up, expansion, transformation/decline
> 4 strategic paths: user strategy, organization strategy, product strategy, market strategy

6 strategic question: Why, Who, What, Where, When, How
12 strategic points:

- user characteristics, user demand, user choice.
- leader, team member, organizational management.
- product development, marketing promotion, business model.
- Technology trend, capital resources, market coopetition.

48 strategic evolution: the evolution of 12 strategic points over 4 phases.

J. Y. Lu, *Co-evolution Strategy Canvas*,
https://doi.org/10.1007/978-981-15-5988-4

A.2 Implications of Co-evolution Strategy from Animals

Facing complexity, to be alert to  and 

For lean start-up, to learn from  and 

For focused growing-up, to become  or 

For amplifying expansion, to choose  or

Facing decline, to avoid  and 

For upgrading transformation, to become  or 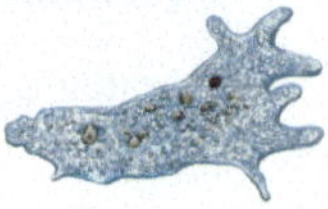

A.2.1 Learn Strategy From Animals

A.2.1.1 Complexity = The Butterfly Effect X The Black Swan Effect

The Butterfly Effect represents "uncertainty".
The butterfly effect means that in a complex dynamic system, small changes under initial conditions can drive a long-term, huge chain reaction of the entire system. This is a chaotic phenomenon. There are fixed and variable parts in the development of things. Although the development of things usually follows a regular track, it still involves unpredictable "variables", which can be counterproductive. A small change can affect the development of things, which means everything's development is complex.

The most common explanation for the butterfly effect is: "When a butterfly in the tropical rainforest of the Amazon River in South America occasionally flaps wings, it can cause a tornado in Texas in two weeks." The reason is that the butterfly's flaps of wings causes the air system around it to change and produces a weak airflow, and the weak airflow causes a corresponding change in the surrounding air or other systems, thereby causing a chain reaction that eventually leads huge changes of other systems.

The black swan effect is very unpredictable and can result in from unusual events. In general, the "black swan" event satisfies three characteristics: it is accidental; it has a major impact; although it is accidental, the nature of human induces us to make reasons for its occurrence afterwards and think more or less that it is interpretable and predictable.

The black swan effect is known for Nassim Taleb's book *Black Swan*. The book describes a turkey which has received food from the owner every morning for the past 1000 days, so it believes that the owner would bring food to it on the morning of the 1001st day, but did not expect that it will be put on the table as the food this day.

The black swan event was accidental because people used to learn about the world in inductive ways. Before people saw the first black swan, they believed that swans all over the world were white. When the first black swan appeared, the cognition about "the swan is white" collapsed, or to say, people's cognition faces discontinuity.

The Black Swan Effect Represents "discontinuity".

Complexity = The Butterfly Effect x The Black Swan Effect. In the face of a complex world, people must always be alert to butterflies flying in the sky and black swan from time to time. A butterfly can lead to a tornado, and butterflies all over the sky will bring greater uncertainty in the future direction. A black swan may bring an unexpected crisis, and the emergence of black swans in groups will make the future development path more discontinuous.

To better understand the butterfly effect and the black swan effect, to deal with uncertainty and discontinuity, and to survive in a complex environment, human beings have been on the road to building knowledge systems.

A.2.1.2 Start-up: Cheetah Versus Wolf

Cheetah speed represents accuracy and relentless.

The cheetah is the fastest animal on land and can reach the speed of up to 115 km per hour. If the human champion of the world and the cheetah join a 100-meter race, the cheetah can let the human champion to run 60 meters first, and finally the cheetah will reach the end first.

Although the cheetah runs fast, it can only run at full speed for up to 3 min, and then it must be slowed down, otherwise it will die due to overheating. Therefore, when the cheetah is preying, it will try to move closer to the prey as much as possible, and try not to let the prey find it. When it is close enough, it will suddenly jump out and pounce on the prey.

In nature, cheetahs are often beaten by some of the larger cats, such as lions, or may be eaten by lions. The survival rate of young leopards is very low. Two-thirds of young leopards are killed by lions and dogs before they are one year old or starved to death due to lack of food.

There is a saying in the startup community goes that "there's nothing can not be destroyed except for the speed".

But even as the fastest animals on the land, cheetahs must take advantage of each of their hunting opportunities. As an entrepreneur, there are not many opportunities for failure. Taking advantage of every opportunity increases your chances of success.

Wolf spirit represents unity and gritty.

There are three wolves in the Disney animation “The Lion King”, Shenzi, Banzai and Ed. The hyenas are an animal on the African grassland that is strong enough to compete with the lion. The advantage of the wolf is not its individual strength, but its group’ collective strength.

Wolves live in groups of about 80, and they can prey on large and medium-sized herbivores such as zebras, wildebeests and gorals. Wolves are good at digesting and can swallow 15 kilograms of prey at a time. They also run very fast, speeding up to 40-50 km per hour.

Many startups encourage the “wolf culture”. For example, in 1997, Zhengfei Ren proposed that “Huawei must have a spirit of wolf, a keen sense of smell, a strong sense of competition, teamwork and sacrifice.” Wolves have a strong desire for success, are persistent when facing setbacks, have the ability to adapt and survive in a changing environment, and have the spirit of unity in collective activities.

There is another saying in the startup community goes that “the person who travels alone goes fast, but who travels in company goes far”.

Many entrepreneurs compare themselves to wolves who are not picky prayers, and never give up. In order to survive, entrepreneurs must unite all the power that can be united, sticking together and being gritty.

A.2.1.3 Grow-up: Pig Versus Unicorn

Pig on the tuyere means those who follow the trend passively.

Pigs are omnivorous mammals. They are fat, with short limbs and long nose. They are tame, have strong adaptability and can reproduce fast.

In 2006, Haier's CEO Ruimin Zhang made a metaphor in his sharing, "There is a saying that 'when the typhoon is coming, even pigs can fly'. Haier is the 'flying pig'. Without the good market environment resulted from the national reform and opening up policy, Haier is also very difficult to have today's achievements."

Later, Lei Jun, a middle-aged entrepreneur, made the phrase "standing on the tuyere, pigs can fly" became a buzzword. The reason why Lei Jun said this sentence is to explain the essence of entrepreneurial success is to find a tuyere and take advantage of the trend. Therefore, he founded a VC firm and named it "Shunwei Capital".

However, Lei Jun clarified for several times that the real meaning of the "flying pig" theory is that anyone who succeeds in any field needs 10,000 h of hard work. Those who have no skills but talk about flying pigs are opportunists.

If companies in the growth stage do not have the ability to fly but rely on the tuyere, they may be able to fly to the sky in the short term, but will eventually fall.

Unicorn represents innovation.

The unicorn is a fictional creature in mythology and legend. It is shaped like a white horse, with a spiral angle in front of the forehead, which means noble, proud and pure.

In the field of management, unicorns refer to those companies that are able to quickly form an advantage in the market segment and are recognized by the capital market during their growth phase.

In 2013, Aileen Lee, a well-known American investor, called the startups with PE and open market valuations of more than $1 billion as "unicorn companies." Generally speaking, it refers to unlisted companies that have achieved high valuations in a relatively short period of time.

In the growth stage, it is necessary for a firm to "make a needle and break the sky". Just as Chairman Mao described in his three poems of Sixteen Characters.

Mountains! I whip my swift horse, glued to my saddle.
I turn my head startled; the sky is three foot three above me.
Mountains! Like great waves surging in a crashing sea,
Like a thousand stallions, in full gallop in the heat of battle.
Mountains! Piercing the blue of heaven, your barbs unblended!
The skies would fall, but for your strength supporting.

Expansion: Octopus Versus Spider

The octopus is a type of marine mollusc with short oval, saclike, finless; the head and body are not clearly defined. The octopus has large compound eyes and 8 contractile wrists on the head.

Octopus expansion.

According to some scientists, the octopus is one of the most different creatures on earth from human beings. The octopus has very developed eyes, which is the only similarity between it and human beings. It differs a lot in other ways: the octopus has three hearts, two memory systems (one is the brain memory system, and the other memory system is directly connected to the suction cup). There are 500 million neurons in the octopus brain, and some of them are still in the body, with very sensitive chemical and tactile receptors. This unique neural structure gives it better thinking ability than common animals.

The octopus is very clever, and an octopus called Paul can even predict the outcome of the football World Cup. But many times, cleverness is wrong. There is a term describing the corporate strategy of the expansion phase named "the octopus expansion", which is actually irrelevant diversification. In the past few years, many Chinese companies have expanded under the rapid economic development, resulting in overcapacity and unreasonable structure.

The word "ecology" was very hot in the past two years, so some companies used octopus expansion as an ecological strategy, which led to failure. The difference between ecological strategy and octopus expansion is that there is a direct link between the sub-ecologies that make up the ecosystem, unlike the octopus expansion, in which businesses are isolated from each other.

Spider strategy.

Spiders are one of the most widely distributed species in terrestrial ecosystems. Except for Antarctica, it is spread all over the world. Most spiders use a small amount of silk to woven into a large net. The net is like an air filter, trapping insects that are flying but not visible. Although the net is complicated, it can be woven in one hour.

The term "spider strategy" comes from the best-selling book "Spider Strategy" by Amit Mukherjee. The author draws on the survival rules of spiders, emphasizing the need for companies to strengthen their cognitive responsiveness, promote cooperation with partners, strengthen organizational learning capabilities, and put key technical capabilities into practice.

Most of today's firms are embedded in a collaborative network. The competition among firms becomes increasingly manifested as competition between different collaborative networks, which makes it impossible for firms to focus solely on the planning and execution of their own strategies. Instead, they have to be able to respond appropriately to situations inside and outside the collaborative network. Firms in the expansion stage can learn from the experience of spider net, building and maintaining a value network centered around themselves.

A.2.1.5 Decline: Ostrich Versus Grey Rhinoceros

The ostrich is the largest bird in the world. They cannot fly, but the hind legs of them are strong and suitable for running.

Ostrich mentality.

Early zoologists found that ostriches often plunged their heads into the ground, thought that they were avoiding danger. However, it is a misunderstanding. The ostrich is actually checking their eggs that are buried in the sand.

Despite that, people still created a word, "ostrich mentality." The word was originally found in a British journal in 1891, and then became a universally used metaphor to describe the mentality of self-righteousness, escaping from reality, turning a blind eye, shirking responsibility, and deceiving people when encountering difficulties.

Some firms that enter the decline stage or are in danger of decline may have a mentality, becoming unwilling to face the reality and dare not take the approach of dealing with danger and solving problems. Such firms are also known as "ostrich firms."

In the book The Innovator's Dilemma, Christensen pointed out that incumbent firms often make "five cannot" mistakes because of vested interests, that are, they cannot see users, cannot respect user demands, cannot understand business models, cannot learn to organize, and cannot keep up with the market. The primary cause of the "innovator's dilemma" is actually the ostrich mentality.

Grey rhinoceros.

The grey rhinoceros are the second largest terrestrial animals with short legs and awkward body. The rhinoceros have a slower wit and a poor vision, but a keen sense of smell and hearing. They prefer night activity. The rhinoceros avoid human beings in most of the time, but during the mating season, or when they stay with female rhinoceros with little rhinoceros, a little stimulation will cause attacks.

Grey rhino risk.

The "grey rhino risk" is known for the book "Grey Rhinoceros: How to Deal with High Probability Crisis", which is used to describe a potential crisis with a high probability and a huge impact. These crises have some signals before the outbreak, but people tend to be biased and often ignore these signals.

Firm decline is a typical grey rhino risk, which comes sooner or later. Faced with the high probability of grey rhino risk, the correct choice is to act proactively, whereas the wrong choice is to evade. The risk of grey rhinoceros is different from that of black swan. The risk of black swan is difficult to predict. The challenge is the imagination and predictive power of the firms. The risk of grey rhinoceros is easy to predict, but requires firms to adapt to the changing environment and act quickly.

A.2.1.6 Transformation: Elephant Versus Amoeba

Elephant.

Elephants are the largest terrestrial mammals in the world. The head of them is large, the ear is as big as a fan, the limbs are as thick as a cylinder to support a huge body, and the knee joint cannot flex freely.

Elephant dancing.

Management often uses the elephant as a metaphor of large-scale and mature firms, and use "elephant dancing" to describe the transformation of large firms. This statement originally came from the best-selling book Who Said that Elephants Can't Dance of CEO Gerstner, who led IBM's successful transformation. It is not easy for an elephant to turn around, let alone dance. Most people who watch elephants' dance think that the action is very simple, but for the trainer (entrepreneur), it is a life or death experience.

Just likes an elephant that requires the coordination of the whole body to dance, successful transformation of a firm requires the transformation of user, the transformation of organization, the transformation of product, and the transformation of market. The transformation of each strategic element should be as orderly and coordinated as possible, otherwise it will cause confusion in the internal management of the firm and endanger the survival and development of it.

Amoeba.

The amoeba has no tough surface, but only a thin layer of plasma membrane. The membrane is a relatively transparent cytoplasm that can flow in any direction around the cell, causing the surface to produce amorphous protrusions.

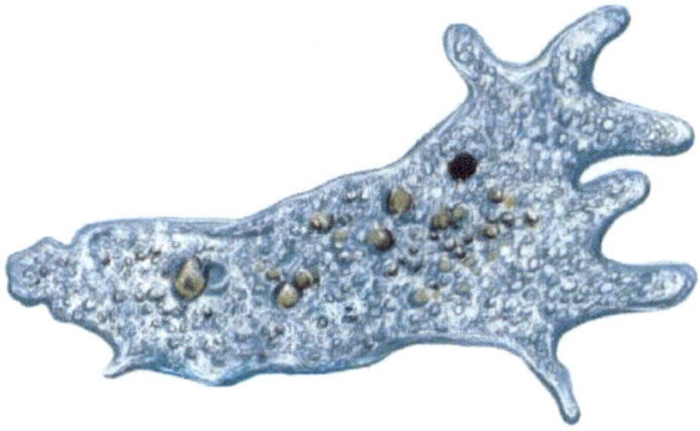

Amoeba (Amoeba organization).

Amoeba is one of the lowest primitive organisms. It is a single-celled animal with strong adaptability. It exists on the earth for billions of years and is the oldest, most vital and continuous organism on earth.

The reason why the amoeba is so strong is that the various metabolic bacteria systems that carry out metabolism and maintain life activities are completely exist in one cell, and the cell itself is an independent living entity.

Mr. Kazuo Inamori, the god of management in Japan, learnt from the amoeba when founding and managing firms such as Kyocera. He learnt to constantly adapting itself to the characteristics of the living environment, as what amoeba do to adapt to the external environment. The amoeba organization, with the leadership of each amoeba as its core, develops its own plans and relies on the wisdom and efforts of all members to achieve its goals. In the process of transformation, many large firms have borrowed the Amoeba management method, narrowed down the accounting units, and implemented a gradual transformation.

The manufacturer's authorised representative in the EU is Springer Nature Customer Service Centre GmbH, Europaplatz 3, 69115 Heidelberg, Germany. If you have any concerns regarding our products, please contact ProductSafety@springernature.com

Printed and bound by CPI Group (UK) Ltd, Croydon, CR0 4YY
06/10/2026
02225252-0005